D0029348

Praise for *Poetic License*

"*Poetic License* is a powerful memoir and a great read. At its core, it covers Cherington's decades-long search for truth and the shaping of her authentic self. Sometimes funny, sometimes sad, but always clear, empathetic, and entertaining, Cherington writes about coming to terms with trauma brought on by a celebrity father with deep flaws. This, with intimate glimpses into the psyches of celebrated poets, including T.S. Eliot, Allen Ginsberg, Dylan Thomas, Donald Hall, Robert Lowell, and Anne Sexton. Readers will be enraptured."

—**ERNEST HEBERT**, author of the Darby Chronicles series and the award-winning *The Old American*

"*Poetic License* is a great achievement that will move powerfully into the world. A compelling memoir that uses elegant prose, vivid scenes, and dialogue to describe coming of age in a poetry-infused household. This is a riveting portrait of a once adoring daughter able to reflect as a mature woman on how she searched for her own truth and freed herself from her father's dominating presence."

—**ELIZABETH GARBER**, poet, memoirist, and author of *Implosion: A Memoir of an Architect's Daughter*

"Pulitzer Prize–winning poet Richard Eberhart was a close friend and beloved colleague. I loved his genial personality and admired his unique poetic gift. He was a generous man but, as his daughter shows, a difficult and complex person as well. This is a vivid memoir, flaws and all. Cherington has crafted a narrative worth reading closely."

—**JAY PARINI**, poet, novelist, critic, and international best-selling author of *The Last Station: A Novel of Tolstoy's Last Year*, made into an Academy award-nominated film starring Helen Mirren

"I feel personally grateful to Gretchen Cherington for her compelling and courageous account of growing up as the daughter of a charismatic celebrity. She describes in her father the narcissistic self-preoccupation and work obsession that are hallmarks of genius in every field. Her story offers a much-needed correction of the popular belief that a public image is an accurate reflection of what a person is like in his or her most intimate relationships. Her account of personal survival will touch all who read it."

—SUE ERIKSON BLOLAND, psychotherapist, and author of *In the Shadow of Fame: A Memoir by the Daughter of Erik H. Erikson*

"*Poetic License* is a courageous and enlightened memoir of the life-long impact of sexual molestation. Cherington dives deep into the murky legacy of her father's life to understand what love between a father and daughter should be, how that ideal can be spoiled, and what she lost. This well-articulated journey gives us the tools we need to take command of our own lives and move into the person we want to become."

—LAURA WATERMAN, author of *Losing the Garden: The Story of a Marriage*

"Gretchen Cherington confronts brutal truths about love, family, and betrayal in this lyrical, moving, and ultimately uplifting memoir. With a backdrop of seemingly idyllic summers on the Maine coast and a parade of literary-giant houseguests including Robert Frost, Anne Sexton, and Allen Ginsburg, Cherington deftly explores the trauma of being sexually assaulted by her charismatic, Pulitzer Prize–winning father—and the hard-won triumph of coming to terms with it."

—MEG LUKENS NOONAN, author of *The Coat Route*

Poetic License

A MEMOIR

GRETCHEN CHERINGTON

She Writes Press

Published 2020
Printed in the United States of America
ISBN: 978-1-63152-711-1
ISBN: 978-1-63152-712-8
Library of Congress Control Number: 2020905666

For information, address:
She Writes Press
1569 Solano Ave #546
Berkeley, CA 94707

Interior design by Tabitha Lahr

She Writes Press is a division of SparkPoint Studio, LLC.

"Opulence" by Richard Eberhart was used with permission of *Oxford University Press* and the Richard Eberhart Literary Estate.

All company and/or product names may be trade names, logos, trademarks, and/or registered trademarks and are the property of their respective owners.

Names and identifying characteristics have been changed to protect the privacy of certain individuals.

For Michael
And for Molly and Ben

And if there's one thing I know it's that writing comes out of tension, tension between what's inside and what's outside.

—RACHEL CUSK, from Outline

Contents

Author's Note

Memory is fallible. I have consulted secondary sources when possible, including people, family documents, and personal journals, along with my father's literary archives at Dartmouth College. With a few exceptions, narration in italics and without quotations is taken directly from his letters, from my mother's letters and journals, and from my own. Some of these have been lightly edited for readability. All people named are real and not composites. A few details of client locations have been changed to protect their privacy.

I am indebted to the staff at Rauner Special Collections Library, and especially to former librarian Philip Cronenwett, former staff member Sarah Hartwell, and current librarian, Jay Satterfield, as well as to the Richard Eberhart Literary Estate for permission to use its source materials. The book *Richard Eberhart: The Progress of an American Poet*, by Joel Roache, was an additional helpful source, as was my mother's article "They Called Dad the 'Polish King,'" published in *Yankee* magazine in 1955.

Portions of this book have been published in other forms: "Breath, Body, and Belief" (2013) in *Crack the Spine* literary magazine; "Cartwheels and Smoke Rings" (2011) and "Maine Roustabout" (2012) in *Bloodroot Literary Magazine*; "Reflections on my Father" (2004) in the *Stonefence Review*; and "Return to Undercliff" (1999) in *Yankee* magazine.

Chapter 1:

No Regrets

I stood in the wings of a large lecture hall in Chicago in 1958. I was seven years old. My breath quickened against the cinched sash of the smocked dress Gram had bought me for the occasion. I watched my father at the podium. He stood tall and had a broad smile across his face. He turned quickly to find me and I noticed his tie was askew. Earlier, in our hotel room, he'd asked me to straighten it. "You do it, Gretch," he'd said. Now, I thought, I must have jostled it off-center when he leaned over to kiss my cheek before taking the stage.

In the spotlight, his oxford shirt was nearly blinding. He smiled out at a thousand fans and gave a wave with his right hand, taking in the admiration. When the applause quieted, he called me out to introduce me. I ran across the wide stage, knowing I wouldn't slip in my shiny black shoes because Mom had scratched their soles on the sidewalk that morning.

My father was good on any stage—in a big city hall; in a university auditorium; in our living room in Hanover, New Hampshire; or on a rocky beach on Penobscot Bay, Maine, where we summered. He read his poems slowly and well, he told funny and prophetic poem-stories, and he shared his family with his audience.

Now, at his side, I stood straight like him, shoulders back, and beamed in the light of his praise, taking in the feel of fame, thinking it was real, and that it might even have something to do with me.

— ∽ —

In 1991, I was forty years old, recently divorced, with two children—seventeen and twelve—and running a young executive consulting and coaching company just starting to show promise. I stared out the window above my desk at a double row of tall pine trees, the same species that circled my childhood home across town. They were my focus when I lifted my strained eyes from looking into one of 147 boxes of letters, books, and other documents that made up my father's literary archives at Dartmouth College, in Hanover. It was a sunny Monday morning, and the collection was being held in a nondescript steel storage building a few miles south of campus.

Friends were surprised I was spending my Monday mornings in a structure we'd all driven by a hundred times and never noticed. With a large overhead door facing a side street for loading and unloading, the warehouse had only a few windows, one of which I could look out of on the woods. The boxes were in storage while the college built its new Rauner Special Collections Library, my father having made this donation to his alma mater several years prior when he and my mother moved into a retirement facility north of town.

Phillip Cronenwett, then librarian for the college, enthused about the gift and his high interest was infectious. He described a treasure trove that included letters to and from nearly every notable writer of the twentieth century. Dad hadn't been surprised when I'd told him I was interested in reading through his letters; he assumed everyone would be.

My father's literary career spanned eight decades. He wrote his first poem in 1919, in Austin, Minnesota, when he was fifteen years old, and scribbled out his last around 2000, when he was

ninety-six. As poet-in-residence at Dartmouth, he taught generations of creative writing students through four decades. He won
the Pulitzer Prize in 1966 and the National Book Award in 1997.
He was inducted into the inner circle of the American Academy
of Arts and Letters in 1982. He served as New Hampshire poet
laureate for five years and as U.S. poet laureate at the Library of
Congress under Presidents Eisenhower and Kennedy.

What was unusual about this collection of more than fifty-
five thousand letters, Phil told me, was that, unlike most writers
who keep correspondence they've received, my father had kept
carbon copies of every letter he'd written to the authors as well.
Contained within the boxes were decades-long epistolary conversations between famous writers as they celebrated and bemoaned
their literary lives. With permission from my older brother,
Dikkon, executor of our father's literary estate, Phil offered me a
desk under a window and an opportunity to peruse the boxes in
any way I chose.

My father, never known for tidiness, had organized the boxes
well. Each was labeled by year and stuffed with folders arranged
alphabetically, by author. I could pluck a handful of letters to and
from Robert Lowell, say, in August 1962, after he, his wife Elizabeth
Hardwick, Dad, and I had spent an afternoon on Dad's boat, *Rêve*.
Or I could pull my father's correspondence with Anne Sexton in
1967, the year she won her Pulitzer and I met her at our house
in Hanover.

The boxes spoke to who Dad was as a literary person; he
corresponded with dozens—perhaps hundreds—of writers, friends,
editors, critics, and publishers, as they did with him. Through that
correspondence, he served as glue between large swaths of writers.
As a little curly-headed girl, I'd watched him write some of those
letters, his shoulders muscled forward as he typed on his Smith
Corona in his study while I knelt on his desk, peering into its guts. I
loved the sound of black ink smacking white vellum and the synco-
pation of the little hammers as his fingers flew across his keyboard,

ending each line with a solid *thwap* of the return bar. I noticed how he lined up his left margins and where he typed addresses on his #10 envelopes, addresses marked to important editors, since the letters were headed to New York and London. I marveled at how he could grip one of his teeth-grooved pipe stems between his canines while simultaneously telling me who was coming for dinner that night. Sometimes I'd get antsy and stand on the desk in my bare feet to gain stature, before bending over and practically falling into the typewriter, blood rushing to my head, making me feel giddy. "Okay, Gretch," Dad would then chuckle, "I can't very well finish this letter with your head in my way."

Now, I was looking at his letters with the eyes of a woman, a woman who had both adored her father and been betrayed by him. My back tensed, my neck strained, and my brow complained as hours flew by. Furrowed with concentration, I blew dust off old pages and removed rusty paper clips from the original letters of Robert Frost, W. H. Auden, Archibald MacLeish, and Wallace Stevens. I'd spent my early life inhabiting the poetic periphery of these men, tugging at their pant legs for attention. I had no idea how many days or months I'd have to be in the world of Dad's letters, as I had no plan, just a lot to learn. On my first day in the storage facility, I'd set aside eight hours and got through three cartons. With 144 to go, I couldn't see out to a finish line.

— ∞ —

The 1990s had opened with too much death—the death of my nineteen-year marriage; the death of my beloved, 101-year-old grandmother; the death of my mother-in-law, with whom I shared respect and admiration; and the death of my extraordinary mother. It continued with the death of my daughter's Alaskan husky pup, given to her to balance the losses she and her older brother had already endured. The death of that puppy was unimaginable. It broke our hearts when our hearts had already been broken too many times.

Sitting at the desk, I had only questions. Questions about the stories my parents told, some of which hadn't squared with my own lived experience. Questions about my father's self-centeredness and his affairs with women outside his marriage. Questions about his tribe of writers, the wonderful—and wacky—men, mostly, who inhabited our living rooms, claiming airspace I would have liked for myself and who, despite their progressive politics, through the 1960s and '70s, when I was coming of age, had already assumed my older brother would be the next-generation Eberhart writer. My father was eighty-seven the year I got started on his letters, and my relationship with him was guarded. I saw him regularly, as he lived only thirty minutes from my home, but I kept my distance emotionally, as I had for decades.

— ∽∝∽ —

We all must square the gifts and harms from our original families—better done, I wager, before leaving home, not in our forties. I hoped I'd find in my father's letters bits of family history I hadn't known, strands of evidence that might support a coherent story of him. Confused by the outward symbols of our privilege—our homes, travel, my father's friends, life on elite college campuses—alongside my inner loneliness from his inattention, his neglect, I didn't know what would surface.

I came from a family of storytellers, of mythmakers, a family perhaps a little too in love with itself. Both parents were superb entertainers; they regaled their visitors with righteous descriptions of their friends, their original families, their children, their hired help, their connections to kings and presidents, a chance encounter with a drunk cousin on Main Street or a store clerk in Boston who happened to read Yeats. I loved their stories. Everyone did. Repeated regularly, a story drawn out by Mom or Dad, or the two together, was funny or poignant and sure to pack a punch. Over cocktail parties in living rooms and on island beaches in Maine, stoked with bourbon and gin, tossed and tumbled, their tales calcified into myth—myths of improbable beginnings in Minnesota and Boston, of wealth created and sometimes lost, of ten-day blizzards and first-row tickets to the theater, of the highest levels of literary achievement and the bastard critics who didn't understand. These accounts seemed special, and I felt special in their reflection. Joining their legion of admirers, I subscribed fully.

Dikkon, five years older than I, inherited their skills. He could spin an adventure as tight as a new ball of string—epic, swashbuckling inventions of pirates and maidens on the high seas, of musketeers and flagons. He could carry on for an hour, even as a teenager, spellbinding my cousins Kate and Susan Butcher and me as we rolled ourselves in moth-eaten blankets under the stars by a fire on the beach in Maine. "Go on!" we implored, and he did. I envied all three members of my family their talents, their way of tossing reality to the wind in favor of wild imagination. My family of origin held in high esteem anyone with those skills. By the age of ten, I could recite my father's CV, I'd heard it so many times, but by my late thirties, I'd begun to question some of the accounts. All I ever wanted to know was what was real.

By the year I started looking through Dad's letters, a dissonance about who my father was had lodged between my ears and eyes, a dissonance too jarring to ignore. One warm, blue-sky fall day in 1995, the fourth year of reading in the collection, I took my notes outside and spread them out on a picnic table, along with my lunch. The air that afternoon smelled different, with the aroma of pine pitch. While tourists mob New England for its maples and oaks dressed in royal ruby and gold, I've long loved the smell of pitch hardening on the trunk of an evergreen, pausing its growth as it gathers itself for winter. My mother had died the year before, at eighty, after living forty years with epilepsy. My father, at ninety-one, was hale and still writing. Hesitantly, I'd begun putting my own thoughts on paper, mostly about Dad, but about Mom, too. I still felt no right to question my father, to poke at the edifice that had grown up between him and me. I finished my sandwich and thought it was time to remind him of what I was up to. It was a quick trip to where he lived, and a beautiful afternoon for a drive through Hanover.

— ⌇ —

"To what do I owe the pleasure of your visit?" Dad asked. Seated in his green wingback chair, he pointed for me to take a seat next to him. He leaned toward me—a lean I'd seen many times when he tipped his weight and attention toward a famous writer and got pulled into literary conversation. I turned away from him and looked out the window at the fading afternoon sun.

"I'm trying to figure things out, Dad," I said, my mouth dry. "I'm trying to figure *you* out. So I'm writing about you." His wide eyes encouraged me. "I'd like to read you a piece."

I'd never shared anything I'd written with him, not even as a kid; he'd just never seemed interested. That day, he looked riveted, which shouldn't have surprised me, since he always was his own favorite subject.

"Speak slowly, Gretch. I want to hear you," Dad said, propping his hands on his knees to listen, while leaning closer to me. I'd written a piece about his childhood years in Austin, Minnesota, an innocent enough starting place. I read slowly, enunciating and emphasizing words, emulating his reading style as best I could.

"What's it like to have me write about you?" I asked, after finishing.

"Why, marvelous!"

"I'll never get through all the boxes, Dad. You kept so much!"

My father smiled, unabashed at being called out as the pack-rat of our family.

"Will I find any surprises?" I asked.

Dad paused for several seconds. "Well, if you do, won't that be interesting?"

He raised his bushy eyebrows, eyebrows a friend of his had once called ferocious because his thick tufts went every which way. As a teenager, his raised eyebrows seemed flirtatious to me.

"When you look back at your long life, Dad, do you have any regrets?"

My father took his time considering my question. Time enough, I thought, to scan nine decades. Time enough for me to scan a line of white birch trees outside his room, their yellow leaves fluttering in the breeze. I thought of Frost's poem about birches and of Frost himself sitting in the green leather chair in our living room in Hanover with his thick thatch of white hair. A chickadee hopped from branch to branch, creating quite a poem itself.

"No," he said finally.

Really? I thought. I had so many regrets.

"Is there anything you don't want me to say?" I asked.

"No," my father said. "Your only job as a writer is to tell the truth."

Chapter 2:

Poetic Space

When I was a little girl, I sat cross-legged on the hardwood floor in the living room of our house in Hanover, back pressed against my mother's bare legs, listening to Dad read his poems. His words wafted on the slip of his pipe smoke and crowned his bald head. Sometimes I imagined his words escaping through the open window behind his chair where a spring breeze blew them through the trees and across the Connecticut River to other states of mind.

Our living room was full of people, always full of people. Visiting writers and literary critics, neighbors who lived on our short street, handpicked college seniors from my father's popular poetry seminar, Mom's friends from her downtown pottery class. And Gram, my only living grandparent, if she was visiting from Cambridge. The long, rectangular room in Hanover could seat twenty, thirty in a pinch. Students, and Mom and I, sat on the floor. My parents collected friends in bunches the way I gathered Queen Anne's lace from the meadow near our summer place in Maine. Their friends came to hear Dad's latest poems or to request their favorites, occupying our living room like he was their guru. All our eyes were on him. It was his voice that mattered. Even our dachshund, Star, circled her tail three times and quieted on the floor beside me.

"If I could only live at the pitch that is near madness," my father would read, his well-worn book in his outstretched hand, his eyes closed, "When everything is as it was in my childhood / Violent, vivid, and of infinite possibility."

Madness? Violent childhood? Possibility? I didn't know what the words meant, but I felt their importance in the sadness I heard in his voice, or, later, in his sudden delight at their brilliant beauty. I absorbed the rhythm and cadence of his lines, leaning toward him on the uplift of a phrase I especially liked and back against my mother's legs when he finished. It didn't matter if I understood or not—his words were like friends I could count on. They were ever-present, my constant, repeated over and over, when asked for and even when not. Poetry was the daily music of my childhood.

If my father cocked his eyebrow at me, I felt like I was the only one in the room. When he stared off into the slippery ether, it was as if he'd handed me a slice of poetic space, space in which I could think and feel. Surely, he was telling me, time given over to the reciting of words strung out on a page was the only sustenance we really needed.

Sometimes I'd squirm my bottom and try to indent the cool hardwood floor. Or I'd grab Mom by her ankles to straighten myself. She'd wrap her arms around me and whisper, "Sit still, Gretch."

No one else's father held court in this way. It wouldn't have occurred to me to make a fuss or a demand. He enjoyed telling us where and when he'd written a poem, and why. He confided in us about his personal anxieties. He was in conversation with us, only he was doing all the talking.

At Undercliff, our summer cottage in Maine, my father sat on the small lawn giving way to the big sea and tried out stanzas on his writer friends. Down East Maine has long attracted artists and writers to its rocky shores. Philip Booth and Robert Lowell—who we called Cal—summered across the bay in Castine. Dan Hoffman was a neighbor on Cape Rosier. My father gathered those three with him as a poetic quartet to test their verses on each other while their wives—Elizabeth, Margaret, Liz, and my mother, Betty—formed their own foursome, walking the beach while commiserating about the wounded souls of their writer husbands. I hung around the poets and watched the ice melt in their jelly glasses of bourbon while passing the cocktail peanuts.

My father's oxford shirt was rolled up past his elbows, frayed from another teaching year, his nose covered in zinc against the August sun. I climbed on his lap as a little girl, and he flexed his biceps, Popeye-style, making me giggle. "See how strong I am," he said, unabashed at doing this in front of his friends. "That's from dragging boats up and down the beach all summer."

Poetry conversations with groups of his peers usually ended with a series of questions Dad posed—about the meaning of life and death, the insanity of the latest war, the politics of our current president, and the weather on Penobscot Bay. He listened to Phil and Cal and Dan, but rarely concluded anything; such decisiveness would have thwarted his enormous curiosity. He preferred rehashing the same questions year after year and keeping his options open.

I doubt it ever occurred to him that one thing a father can do for his daughter is to help her interpret the world in which she must live. Instead, he preferred to live in his own world, the one he told us through his stories, the one enhanced each summer by the sea and wind, his daily cocktails, and his deep inquisitiveness. The world we really lived in, the big world outside our family homes was a great, poetic mystery to Dad. Its interpretation—I'd need to figure that out on my own.

Chapter 3:

Cartwheels and Smoke Rings

In 1956, when I was five years old and Dikkon was ten, we moved into a large white colonial with dark green shutters at the dead end of a short street in Hanover, New Hampshire, named Webster Terrace. From there, my father could ride his bike one mile to the Dartmouth campus, where he'd been hired as its poet-in-residence, following his predecessor, Robert Frost. Mom gave directions to new acquaintances she met on Main Street by telling them our home was the deadest of the dead end. The house was perched on a narrow glacial esker high above the Connecticut River; tall white pines ringed the large backyard. In autumn, when the maples and oaks that dotted the steep riverbank dropped their leaves, we could see across to Vermont. As Frost famously quipped, "The best thing about living in New Hampshire is that you get to look at Vermont." He could have said that when sitting with Dad in our octagonal wooden gazebo, large enough for six more poets and cantilevered over the bank at the edge of our lawn.

The five houses on Webster Terrace comprised a close-knit, 1950s-style neighborhood. Each home had unique features, and I quickly figured out the best use for them. Neighbors, whose back doors faced the short street, welcomed us kids at any time. Every father was a Dartmouth professor, and all the moms stayed home.

The Maslands owned the only TV, so we watched *Bonanza* after school while Mrs. Masland fed us the richest and creamiest tomato soup, which, Mom learned after I'd raved about it, was Campbell's in a can, the same I had at home. It just tasted better at the Maslands'. Mrs. Hennessey, who had become Mom's best friend and lived next door to us, doled out fluffernutters, which I preferred to the apples and raisins my mother gave us. At the Ehrmanns', I learned enough German to understand Gram when she said things like *Danke schön* or *eins, swei, drei, vier*. Mom gave over our front yard for an adult-free zone of kids' play, after helping us tear up the grass so we could convert it into hills and rivers with our trucks and bulldozers, replicating the contours of Vermont and New Hampshire, while she taught us about glacial erratics. Mom didn't care about the mess as long as the Webster Terrace kids felt welcome. Dikkon and I were taken into the gang and our family was thereafter named "The Ebs."

Dad, who fussed over navigating the muddy mess with his visiting writers, reserved the backyard and gazebo for entertaining, while I used the yard to perfect my cartwheels. That yard, reined in by the tall white pines and edged by my mother's flower gardens, formed a perfect cartwheeling gymnasium. As my short legs catapulted me, my arms reached for the ground and my curly hair circled my head like sun rays. I turned cartwheels outside on that lawn, on the hardwood floor of our living room between readings, and all the way down Webster Terrace. The first thrust would ignite my flame. I'd leap and turn, building momentum, over and over, stretching my arms, thrusting my legs, sucking in my belly, holding my breath. I turned cartwheels in my summer pajamas and in my winter mittens and boots. I turned them in the cheap red swimsuit from Rockdale's Clothing Store in Lebanon that dyed my torso a one-piece red. The exact distance from one end of my parents' lawn to the other was six circles. After that, I'd fall into my mother's flowerbed.

"Gretchen Eberhart, don't you trample my geraniums," Mom called to me from the kitchen porch one day when I was six. She was pinning laundry to our clothesline and pulleying it out over the dried-up mountains and valleys in our front yard.

"Okay," I said, and started again.

My father sat in the shade of the pines, tugging on a pipe. Half-watching, he suddenly noticed me and asked, "Can you do more?" I could. I would do them all day long and into the night if they got his attention. Dad's delight fueled me. Back and forth across the lawn I went. Cartwheels made me feel free.

My acrobatics would show up in my father's letters to his friends, like the poet Dudley Fitts. In 1956, shortly after we moved to Webster Terrace, my father wrote to Dudley, *Gretch is full of blond brisk fun.* Sometimes his friends would write me back directly, like the anthologist Oscar Williams did when I was ten. *Gretchen, will you marry me when I grow up?* Dad exaggerated my cartwheels, as he exaggerated everything we did, turning my simple childhood fun into high art.

— ∞ —

Five Webster Terrace was our fifth home in as many years. Every fall, Dad found a new job on a new college campus and my brother would have to join a new school and make new friends while Mom and I tagged along. My first year was split between Cambridge, Massachusetts, and Seattle, where my father took his first college teaching job, at the University of Washington. Our home was a small, single-story, ranch house without shade, in a development full of young professors. As if to compensate for the sterile, bulldozed development, we had a big view of Mt. Rainier out our back door. The next year we moved into faculty housing at Wheaton College in Norton, Massachusetts, where my father was Wheaton's first-ever visiting professor. That spring he received a citation from the National Institute of Arts and Letters and the Harriet Monroe Poetry Award, which came with a check for $1,000 (this would be $9,000 today).

We spent my third year in Storrs, Connecticut, where my father taught at UConn and my parents became friends with fellow English department colleague Pete Dean and his wife, Dorothy. In Storrs, we lived in a two-story row house of faculty apartments that shouldered up to huge slabs of rock left over from construction, which gave us the same kind of fun we had running across granite slabs at the edge of the ocean in Maine. Dad edited *New World Writing* that year and came out with a new book, titled *Undercliff*.

My father was at Princeton University for my fourth year, where he was hired as guest lecturer and I was enrolled in the fanciest school I would ever attend, Miss Mason's Nursery School. For Halloween that year, Miss Mason wrote to my mother, "We want the children to dress up, of course, and the mothers, too. It makes it so much more fun that way." Mom loved dress-up parties. She rummaged in our closets and found a worn-out bathrobe of Dad's, a moth-eaten fox fur of Dikkon's that he'd received on a visit to our New Mexico cousins, a Tom Sawyer straw hat she wore on hot days, and dirty rubber boots from the porch. I never heard what my costume was, but she and I headed off to Miss Mason's, only to find every other mother in a mink coat and alligator pumps. "Oh, *that* kind of dressing up," Mom whispered to me, not the least bit fazed, while the other moms looked horrified. As my mother used to tell the story, they'd probably already assumed a visiting poet might be odd, but now they knew, for sure, his wife was, too.

After Princeton, Mom put her foot down, appealing to Dad: "The children need a home, a place where they can stay put and make real friends." Luck arrived quickly for us when Dartmouth inquired about Dad's availability for the fall of 1956. Through correspondence, my father asserted he would move only if the college provided some form of employment security. At fifty-two, with two children then ages ten and five, my father was made poet-in-residence, succeeding Frost, and would teach undergrads creative writing and modern poetry. Along with a tenure-track position, he was offered the purchase of our big white colonial at the end of Webster Terrace. Any doubt Dad had had about embracing academia or eschewing it through his twenty lean years in the 1920s and '30s was dashed the moment Dartmouth offered him the job. He was home. Over the next forty years at the college he'd attended as an undergraduate, he would publish sixteen books and arrange for dozens of poetry readings for himself and his writer tribe. We moved to Hanover in August so Dikkon could start fifth grade, and my parents enrolled me in kindergarten.

— ∞ —

My father was equally as powerful a physical man as he was a pondering intellectual. He'd hunted, fished, and camped growing up in his native Minnesota, had starred as quarterback on his high school football team, played football for Dartmouth, enjoyed hiking in the mountains of New Hampshire, and had flown enormous kites through his Navy years. At five foot ten, he had a stocky, rugged build and enjoyed being out of doors in the "elements," as he used to say.

Dad loved our big, snowy winters in Hanover, as he relished shoveling it into piles from which Dikkon and I could carve out caves. He'd wrestle with my brother on an old mattress Mom wedged between the potbellied oil burner and her potter's wheel in our cellar. Those basement brawls—usually taking place while Mom fixed supper and I played with my dolls—were audible through the open kitchen door to the cellar. My brother and my father would grunt and tussle and appear for dinner smelling musky, after proving their manhood. Sometimes Mom would say to me, "Boys will be boys," but it struck me as odd right from the beginning, their pinning and pushing of body against body, their competitions forming a backdrop for our early years in Hanover, while I watched from the sidelines. Measuring up and winning was important to Dad. Dikkon and I were measured for height, book held on top of our heads, magic marker dates detailing our growth on the kitchen door frame. Taller was better, so I learned to stand straight, shoulders back, head tipped a smidge to add to my frame.

— ෴ —

"I'll show you a trick, Gretch," Dad said one day when we were in the living room and I'd been jealous of his wrestling time with Dikkon. He bent over at the waist and took my small hands in his large ones, bracing one foot behind the other, and with lightning speed, flipped me through his legs to stick the landing.

"Marvelous, Gretch," he said. "Do it again." We did five more, perfecting them as we went.

"More!" I pleaded.

"No, that's enough for now," Dad said, and walked me over to the leather chair, sat me on his lap, and lit up a pipe. He pulled damp strands of tobacco from his tartan plaid pouch, tobacco we'd purchased together on our recent trip to Boston at his favorite Irish smoke shop, on Boylston Street. He tamped down the tobacco with his silver plunger, lit the bowl with a paper match, and sucked air through the teeth-worn stem. He backhanded the spent paper match, missing the ashtray he aimed for, while I trailed its arc until it landed on the floor.

"You can't just throw matches on the floor." I giggled at Dad. "What if you burn down the house?"

Dad winked as he gave the match on the floor a glance, before circling his arm around me. With a nice burn going, he rolled the smoke around in his mouth and blew big, cheeky puffs into perfect circles above my head as we snuggled in a silky aroma of fruit and wood.

"Go ahead, Gretch," he encouraged, and I poked my finger through the circles like he'd taught me. Busting apart the wheeling threads, we smiled in our smoky little heaven.

Later that day, I pushed out the back door to practice my cartwheels before supper. Dad was sitting on a bench under the pines, smoking another pipe, stringing out fragile lines of poetry on the back of an envelope. He didn't notice I was there. I knew he wasn't to be disturbed. He was in trance. He was in poem. Cartwheeling and supper could wait.

Chapter 4:

One Morning in Maine

On July 1, following Dad's first year at Dartmouth, and every summer thereafter, he packed his briefcase with writing materials and heaved his Smith Corona into the family station wagon. Mom filled the car with our toaster, dishes, books, and clothes, wedging them into every space she could, saving a spot for Dikkon in the backseat and making me a bed in the way back, squeezed between her suitcase and her modeling clay, with Star nuzzled against me. We had an eight-hour drive to the coast of Maine and over the next dozen years, as *Stuart Little* and *Charlotte's Web* gave way to *Johnny Tremain* and Nancy Drew, this daylong journey from Hanover to Harborside became a rhythmic pattern in our academically oriented year.

Carried into other fictional worlds, I read and napped in the way back, as Dad drove us up and over the hills of New Hampshire and across the potato fields of western Maine. Two stops were tradition: first, to see the sorry tourist bear, chained to a post in the White Mountains, that could pull up a can of peanuts for food; second, for Dad to buy us pieces of pie at Mrs. McGillicuddy's pie shop in Augusta. When the windows were open, I could tell where we were by the smells—from the flowering lilac of Hanover to the smelly paper mills in Rumford and Skowhegan to the salty scent of Cape Rosier. Star woke up with the first whiff of that ocean air.

Our destination was a small saltwater cottage, its white clap-boards torn off for new shingles that would later go through many shades of red paint as my tiny mother directed the summer kids who vacationed in the four cottages around our cove, along with visiting writers, to work for their dinners. That way, she got one wall newly painted each summer, each a different shade of red, before we started the process again.

Set high on a mound of hay, seventy-five feet from the rocky beach, the cottage was backed by a hundred-foot granite cliff and, from its top, a full view of East Penobscot Bay. This was a place of big sky and some of the best sailing in the world. That summer, we arrived late and were put to bed after a supper of Campbell's tomato soup and grilled cheese sandwiches cooked in the diminutive and dingy kitchen.

— ∞ —

"There, Betty," my father said to Mom one morning. "There's your fire." He'd been crumpling pages of the *New York Times Book Review* and throwing them in the fireplace. He pulled a paper matchbook from his frayed khakis, struck a match, and threw it on the pile. Much later, I would wonder, if the *Times* had contained a negative review of his latest book, would he have especially enjoyed the conflagration? But that wasn't really Dad. He'd rather have stowed the review in his files for eternity and assailed the reviewer over cocktails before dinner. "What do any of them understand about poetry anyway?"

As with every morning in Maine, the damp night air had seeped through our leaky walls and settled around us. A daily fire was required, even in the middle of summer.

Dad cut two pieces of bread from a loaf he'd bought at Condon's store in South Brooksville, the store made famous in *One Morning in Maine*, by Robert McCloskey, who lived on Scott Island, just out of our view. Dad stuck the bread in our toaster, popped it up barely warmed, because he couldn't wait, and lathered it with

Fleischmann's margarine. A concession to his doctor, who was trying to get him to lose some weight. He heaped on blueberry jelly made by the farm lady in a cotton apron with an open shelf of jams in her garage, on the road to Deer Isle. A few minutes later, when I toasted my own bread, I found strands of margarine in the jar and knew he'd been there before me. He poured himself a half cup of leftover black coffee, cold was fine, and glugged orange juice directly from a container, all the while standing at the tacky kitchen counter, in a rush to get on with his day.

Dikkon, then ten, was old enough to be sleeping in. Mom was the earliest riser and had already downed two cups of coffee. She sat in the living room at our picnic table, with her back to Dad and me in the kitchen. Stacked on a plate next to her were six pieces of toast, each spread with real butter. With her thick brown hair clipped in a tomboy style, she was wearing a wool sweater against the chilly cottage and would string out those pieces of toast over two hours if she was reading a good book. Years later, when I was in high school and she was perennially on a diet, she'd cut back on her toast to four. Unlike Dad, Mom wasn't eager to get on with anything but the next chapter of her latest James Michener.

"Where shall we go on *Rêve* this afternoon?" Dad asked Mom from the kitchen, to her back. He liked nailing down a plan even if the plan was usually the same: If it was fair weather, he'd collect whoever was interested in an afternoon ride on his thirty-six-foot cruising boat, which the sailors called a stinkpot. With dozens of islands laid out before us, we had our pick, back then, of any of them for a swim and a hike. Occasionally, he'd take us to Buck's Harbor for ice and gas for the boat and ice cream cones for the humans. If the tide was right, he'd motor partway up Horseshoe Cove to anchor and then pile us into his outboard, all the way to the shallow end, just before the tide changed and we could run out the rapids. In Dad's archives, I'd find his first letter announcing his new boat, written to his brother: *She is 36 feet long, 10' 10" wide, with a galley amidships, sleeps four fore of that, has a head and also can get*

10, 15 aboard (especially if a lot of kids) with ease. That last point was the reason for buying her. She was big enough for cruising, like a trip we took in 1957, with Marie Rexroth, Kenneth Rexroth's wife, who'd flown in from San Francisco for a three-day excursion to Northeast and Southwest Harbors on Mount Desert Island. We anchored up Somes Sound for the night, then stopped in Blue Hill Bay for a picnic with Andrew Wanning, the seventeenth-century scholar and Bard College professor. Phil and Margaret Booth had joined us there.

"Can't you see I'm reading, Richie?" Mom said from the table in the living room. It wasn't a question, even if she'd phrased it that way.

I floated between them, trying not to disturb Mom's reading while wanting Dad to hurry up and finish his money work so we could go to Lib Leach's store. He spent that morning catching up on correspondence on his Smith Corona while I uncreased his carbon papers, before licking the smudged ink off my fingers.

"All right, Gretch, we can go now."

Dad handed me his finished letters, and I put stamps on them.

"Why do they go there?" I asked, pointing to the upper-right corner.

"That's just the way it's done." Dad laughed. "Finish up, and maybe we'll stop at Lib's." As far as I was concerned, there wasn't any maybe about Lib's. I'd been going there with Dad nearly every day of summer since I could walk. Lib's was the point of my waiting around all morning.

With envelopes addressed, stamped, and placed—cool feeling—between my palm and fingers, Dad took my free hand and walked me out to our station wagon. *Click*, he opened and shut his door. *Click*, I opened and shut mine. We rolled down the windows and passed the long inlet of Weir Cove, turned right at the Grange, then left down the lane in Harborside. At each turn, the road became narrower and we didn't pass a single car. The air warmed as we moved inland from the sea, and I pulled off my sweatshirt and sat on my knees so I could see better out the window. Star squeezed against me and stuck out her tongue to suck up bugs in the hot breeze.

— ⌾ —

The Harborside post office was just a hole in the wall of a room in Dot's house. She made no notice of the addresses on Dad's letters, even though they were miraculously flying out her door to New York and London.

"I had a poem in the *New Yorker*," Dad said to Dot.

"Well, I'll be," Dot said to Dad.

"Okay, Gretch, now we can stop at Lib's."

Lib's tiny store took up the front room of her small farmhouse, a house set back only eight feet from the road. Dark and dank, it had sagging floors that made my eyes wobble, but it was the closest place to buy groceries unless we drove to Condon's or Eddie Nestle's in South Brooksville. Dust blanketed Lib's canned goods, but her eggs came fresh from the henhouse behind her store, and sometimes she'd have peas or green beans from her garden.

Dad picked up a dozen eggs and placed them on her counter. "What else did Mom want?" he asked me, having not listened the way I had.

"Deviled ham and tomato soup, she said. Three of each." Mom figured Lib's canned goods were safe enough, dust and all, and you never knew who might stop by for supper, but someone always did.

"And bread for the seagulls," I added. Dad picked up a loaf of Wonder Bread, which we'd never eat ourselves but was good enough for the gulls we liked to feed while Dad steered *Rêve* around in circles out behind Spectacle Island.

Lib was rail thin, her face the color of a warm hen's egg, her skin hardened by outdoor labor and long winters. Behind the thick wooden counter, arms folded across her chest, adorned in her cotton dress and a faded apron, she held her ground, as still as a tree. Mom called her a tough beauty, while Dad considered her slim frame regal. Her sharp facial features were stern yet warm. When I was older, I'd liken Lib to the rockbound coast of Maine itself—sturdy, resolute, and not going anywhere. She was as smart and real as Mom.

"Dikkon wants to build a fort in the woods behind the house," Dad offered. Lib nodded.

"We're having a reading at the Robinsons' farmhouse in August. Perhaps you'll come," Dad added. Lib nodded again. I'd learn that was unlikely; his readings were attended mostly by the summer people, though on occasion a year-rounder showed up— like Hal Vaughan, who owned the boatyard where *Rêve* was stored each winter.

"There's a storm coming," Lib offered, "a sou'wester, they say."

"When will she be here?" Dad asked.

"Don't suppose I know, but trust we'll find out in time."

I was starting to think Dad had forgotten me, which wasn't unusual, since he frequently misplaced things, including his children. Just then, he told me to reach in his pocket. I pulled out pennies and stepped on my tippy toes to fetch candy from Lib's glass jars. A root beer barrel; a fireball; a piece of bubble gum with comics; a Mary Jane; and two Tootsie Rolls, one for me and one for my best summer friend, Sarah, who spent every August in a cottage on our cove, too. I counted out my pennies for Lib, struggling to corral them from my fist, while Dad pulled four Hershey bars off the shelf and separated them from the pile he would give to Mom. He'd hide the bars in the glove compartment of the station wagon so Mom wouldn't find them. They'd melt in the afternoon sun and congeal overnight. If Dad found an old one at the end of the summer, back behind maps and pipe tobacco, it'd be covered with dried-out white film, but he didn't care and neither did I. We both loved chocolate.

Lib punched out our purchases with the reedy notes of her heavy black register.

"How's Betty?" she asked before we left.

"She's halfway through *Return to Paradise*," Dad said. "I'm not sure I'll get her out on the boat." He stuck our bag of groceries under his arm, and we headed out into the blazing sun, where Star sidled up to me for a scratch between her ears.

— ∞ —

Each year, the outdoor chairs at Undercliff filled with writers and artists, local people who took care of the cottage and our boats, and summer families who ringed the cove. Gram had her own cottage down the road. Mom and Dad doled out invitations to friends, most of whom said yes, coming from as far as San Francisco and Florida or as near as New Hampshire and Vermont. Our Eberhart cousins from Chicago and New Mexico made regular trips east. Our Butcher cousins (Mom's side) came up from Cambridge. We were out on the water by 1:00 p.m., and back for cocktails at 6:00 p.m. sharp. We bought our vegetables from Scott and Helen Nearing and, later, from Eliot and Sue Coleman, whose homesteads were on the backside of the cape. Milk and fish were delivered to our door. We picked up lobsters from Paul Venno and dug for clams and mussels on the beach at low tide. Mom and I fished from the rowboat for mackerel when they were running in the cove. When we had all that beautiful food in abundance, it's a wonder we ate canned peas, deviled ham, and Spam from Lib's, but we did. "Spam's a great American product," I can hear Mom say. "It fed our soldiers during the war." I knew it was invented by the company my father's father helped build, now Hormel Foods, in Austin, Minnesota. "It's just like us Americans," Mom would continue, "a conglomeration of things that are better off when united." Mom liked serving up civics lessons with lunch. She fed people for years on end, but it was never about the food; it was about the conversation and laughter that Mom and Dad stirred up. What mattered to my parents were the people around them, especially if they were interesting, and the long summer conversations, as they retold their stories to the rhythm of the sea.

Undercliff was a child's idyll. I roamed the fields, forests, and beaches with no barriers, no fences or signs between one lot of land and another. I hardened my bare feet on the rocky beach; caught fireflies in the meadow at dusk; sailed my tiny sailboat, *Ozzie*; and read books in the hammock under the spruce trees. I loved the forest behind the house, which shot up the cliff, with its rich aroma of balsam needles for pillows and its carpet of thick moss. Sarah and I met up after Lib's and could spend hours in that forest, perched on the rocky precipice high above the cove. With our Barbie dolls laid out on moss-covered rocks, we stretched their little plastic shoes over their feet while keeping an eye on the cottages, the beach, and the boats below. Across the water, we could hear every conversation as Dad made his walking rounds inviting everyone for an afternoon on the water. "Ahoy, Perry and Anne!" he yelled to Sarah's parents that day. "*Rêve* sets sail at two p.m." Sarah and I ran down from the cliff to find our life jackets, to be on the beach on time.

In August, Dad organized his annual poetry reading at the Robinsons' farmhouse up the lane. Mary McCarthy, Cal Lowell, and Phil Booth were there from Castine, Dan Hoffman from around the cape, and E. B. White from Brooklin. Whatever writers or artists were within an hour were invited—in later years, Donald Hall and Walker Evans, Buckminster Fuller and Maxine Kumin would be at those summer readings. That evening, I strung my short legs through the balusters of the stair railing and listened to the poets string together words like pearls, offered up as testimony to a summer day. The sound was intoxicating, like the gentle rocking of *Rêve* on its mooring. Soon I was drowsy and slid down the stairs on my bottom to sidle up next to Dad. Lying on the floor under Mrs. Robinson's piano, I drifted into poetic dreams while

Dad read the lines I loved: *The seals at play off Western Isle / In the loose flowing of the summer tide.*

After it was over, Dad carried me in his arms down the tiny path to Undercliff, jostling me awake a few times as he stumbled on a rock, and chatted with Mom, who held a flashlight to illuminate our way. Upstairs, under the steep eaves, Dad laid me down on my bed and flashed his signature eyelash kiss—Eskimo-style—across my cheek. I turned over on my stomach as he pulled heavy wool blankets around my shoulders against the damp air he knew would seep in overnight.

As he settled me back to sleep, his wide hands soothing my back, I took for granted I was safe. I expected the idyll would last. I assumed I'd trust my father for as long as I lived.

Chapter 5:

Fairy Napkins

I never liked Percy Gray, even if he was Lib's cousin.

"He's as smart as a tack," Dad said to Gram and Cal Lowell, who were sitting with my father in the outdoor chairs at Undercliff. I was seven that summer, and had been cartwheeling around the grown-ups, listening in on them.

"Tacks can't be smart!" I yelled. "They hurt!"

Percy Gray was mean when sober and downright scary when drunk, which was often. Gram, embroidering a pillow cover while sipping her glass of sherry, had a basket of colored floss at her feet.

"You must call him *Mister* Gray," she said.

"I can't see any reason for that," I answered. "He stinks!"

"Mind your manners," Gram said, looking at me sternly while eyeing her needle with one closed and the other squinting. I knew she'd love me whether I minded my manners or not. Gram's love was never in question.

— ∞ —

Percy turned on our water line every June and turned it off in September. He fixed our little cottage problems and ignored the big ones. He almost never got our house painted, which is why Mom enlisted the poets and us kids. He mowed a narrow swath of hay outside our door for cocktail hour and doled out advice to Dad on how to fix the boats. My father's friendship with Percy confused me, but it resumed each summer, stoked through winter, I would see much later in Dad's letters, via regular correspondence. Percy's letters detailed everything from the spring storms we were lucky to have missed to cottage recommendations for my father, and they were full of surprises. Like that he shot ducks out near Gray Ledge, the ducks I liked watching every summer through Dad's binoculars. *Swell eating,* Percy concluded. *You should try them sometime.* During the 1970s, Percy sprinkled his letters with political barbs about Nixon and Carter and jibed over Watergate: *Just what does Watergate mean anyway? Is it a gate near a boiling spring or the name of an Indian chief?* He signed each of his letters with *See y'all in the cabbage patch next season. Say hi to the tribe.*

Despite being on opposite sides of the political spectrum, Percy and my father shared a strange male bond. Maybe it was Dad's envy of Percy's considerable experience on the sea and Percy's enjoyment of being taken seriously by an Ivy League professor. Still, I didn't like him.

— ⚓ —

A few days after Dad told us how smart Percy was, we stopped at his house after picking up Wonder Bread at Lib's. Dikkon was away at camp that summer. I knew where Percy lived because we passed his house every time we drove to Gram's. Dad called it a shack because it had only one room and sat far back from the summer people's waterfront views. To me, his house looked like an oversize playhouse, something Sarah and I would have liked to use with our Barbies.

Dad pulled into Percy's yard. I wanted to go inside, but he told me to stay put.

"Why?"

"It's no place for a girl. It's only big enough for Percy and his dog."

"You mean his *mean* dog," I said, pointing to the barking mutt pulling on its chain in the dirt yard.

Dad knocked on the door and waited on the stoop. In time, Percy emerged, towering over my father, hard muscled and red faced, without a hint of his cousin Lib's quiet steadiness. He looked wild and angry, like we'd woken him up even though it was past noon. His heavy pants and wool shirt contrasted with Dad's baggy khaki shorts, which hung low below his belly, and his untied sneakers, the backs flattened by his heels, which he wore as slip-ons. We'd come from our sunny cove and were about to head out on the water. Percy's house was in the cool, dark woods.

Percy and Dad stepped down to the gravel and conducted their business while I leaned out the window of the car, one knee pinned against the steering wheel, aiming my ears to listen. Dad told Percy our toilet was leaking and that he needed to fix it. He said if Percy didn't get our rowboat caulked and painted, we'd never get it in the water that summer at all. At the moment, we were borrowing one from the Cliffords. Percy scuffed the ground with his boot and changed the subject, flicking his cigarette in the direction of the hippies, as he called them, the homesteaders who'd built their houses over near Scott and Helen Nearing. "They're taking over. The long-hairs," Percy said. I couldn't see what the friendly, hardworking people who grew the sweetest carrots I'd ever eaten had to do with our toilet.

— ∞ —

Next morning, I was practicing my cartwheels outside and waiting for Dad to finish his work so we could go to Lib's. I cartwheeled down the mown alley to the beach and back up again. It was high tide, and seawater lapped the grass, giving me a water tempo to keep, in time with my wheels. The sun hadn't quite lifted over the cliff, so the spruce trees made the morning air feel cool. Dewy spiderwebs—Gram and I called them fairy napkins—clung to the damp grass. The spiderwebs fascinated me. Every morning they appeared, and as soon as the sun came out, I couldn't find them. I could sit on the damp grass for a long time and stare into them, though, silky worlds of magic, dotted with dew. The fairy napkins got me thinking of Charlotte, the spider over in Mr. White's barn. I liked swinging on the long swing in his big barn and thought calling Mr. White *Mister* made sense. He was a nice man who had promised us a puppy from his dog's next litter.

As I wheeled by the open kitchen window, Mom was washing dishes at the sink, keeping half an eye on me. An expert at saving water, since our shallow well usually ran dry by August, my mother dripped water on our plates and shut off the faucet between each one. Sometimes she barely rinsed our cups at all.

"It's easier going *down!*" I called to her after my third run, figuring out an early lesson in physics. Suddenly, out of nowhere, Percy thundered at me, his booted stride shaking the ground. Grabbing me by my ears, he lifted me off the ground and jerked me back and forth, cackling. His face was grizzled, his eyes huge, his stubble only a few inches from mine.

"Mom!" I screamed, feet flopping.

"Percy Gray!" Mom yelled as she stormed out the door, soap suds flying from her hands. "Put her down! Now!"

Percy dropped me to the ground, right on top of a fairy napkin. "Aw, Betty, can'tcha take a joke?" He swilled up a wad of spit and let it fly through his brown teeth. I knew Mom's yelling at Percy wouldn't do any good. He didn't listen to women or girls. My ears burned and my head hurt, but I didn't dare move.

Mom pulled me into her arms. "Go away," she told Percy.

Percy lifted his cap and scratched his scalp. "Where's Dick?"

— ∽∾∽ —

A week later, Percy appeared again. This time, still drunk, he grabbed me by the skin under my arms and shook me back and forth. His breath stank, and he heaved me to the ground like a piece of split firewood he'd thrown from the back of his truck.

"Mom!" I wailed.

"Get *out* of here!" Mom screamed, waving her dish towel at Percy again, as she might a drunken fly in late August.

Upstairs in my room, Mom peeled off my shirt and we watched red welts rise on my skin, the size of Percy's hands.

"He's just a mean man," Mom said, shaking her head, trying to console me. I knew that already. What I didn't know was why he kept coming around.

— ∞ —

Late that afternoon, I was playing in the kitchen, arranging blocks into a castle on the floor while Mom made supper. I'd made it so tall I was having a hard time balancing my wooden elephant on top.

"It'll be August soon," Mom said. "The Deans and Williamses will be here next week."

"Oh boy—Betsy and Sarah! I can't wait!"

The sun was going down, painting the sky crimson, which got me thinking about the next day and whether we'd feed the seagulls out at Spectacle.

"Look, Mom," I said. "'Pink sky at night, sailor's delight!'"

"That's right, Gretch. Now, go outside and tell your father supper's ready."

I pushed the screen door open and stopped short. Percy and Dad were sitting outside together, smoking their pipes. My skin still burned from Percy's hands. As he and my father raised their jelly glasses of bourbon to toast the sunset, I felt, in the pit of my stomach, there'd be no convincing Dad to get rid of Percy. I watched the two through the screen door, their drinks going down like the sun, and left them to finish whatever it was that men talked about when they were friends.

My father frequently warned me about dangers on the sea, but he never warned me about dangers in my own home.

— ∞ —

In the early 1980s, Dad wrote a poem about Percy, titled "A Maine Roustabout," which aptly described the man, including his meanness toward children. Dad anguished through several summers about whether to tell Percy about it. The dilemma heated up when the verse was included in Dad's *Collected Poems: 1930-1986*, published by Oxford University Press in 1987, and appeared again, in 1989, in *Maine Poems*, also by Oxford. If Dad told Percy, what would Percy think? If he didn't tell him, might Percy find out about the poem and be angry he hadn't known? Would Dad's description of him hurt Percy's feelings? This was the kind of morally ambiguous dilemma that could stump my father over drinks with family and friends.

What I never saw until I was an adult and had gone through Percy's correspondence with Dad and had reread the poem, was my father's clear concern for Percy's feelings and absence of consideration for mine. Percy's hurtfulness and my intense fear of him hadn't made it into the family stories. What mattered was the unanswerable dilemma Dad chewed on about his responsibility to his friend. I don't think he ever told Percy about the poem, but the following three summers after Percy abused me, my mother sent me to Aloha Camp in Vermont—perhaps her way of protecting me while Percy remained my parents' caretaker in Maine.

Chapter 6:

Summer Thespians

The shade under the fir trees cooled our bare feet as Sarah and I practiced our lines in Mom's skit. It would be the final extravaganza for the end-of-summer beach party that marked my parents' anniversary. Our dads were on the beach lining an enormous pit with rocks for the clambake. Soon they'd build a fire in the hole, then wait for its embers to burn down, before covering it with a foot of fresh seaweed. They'd lay in clams and lobsters first, then potatoes and corn on the cob, then more seaweed, and, finally, a layer of hot dogs, covered with more seaweed. Sarah and I knew a clambake would take most of the day to build and that, following our rehearsal of Mom's skit, she and I would help peel away the layers to uncover tasty summer treats from the land and the sea.

It was a sultry day at the end of August 1960, and I was sad about heading back to Hanover. I'd gotten only one week with Sarah, since I'd been at camp most of the summer. I never liked leaving my summer friends—Sarah, Lisa, Pinkey, Betsy, and Jenny—for another school year. I'd been complaining to Mom about it all week.

My mother dealt with my emotions mostly through distraction. If I grew bored of playing mosquito-infested games of capture the flag after dark, or humiliated at not catching a crab with bacon tied to a string, or too competitive with Dikkon when we skipped rocks at low tide, Mom would pull out Dad's old Navy trunk, full of musty castoffs we called costumes, and produce a skit out of thin air. Her small stature belied a fierce and industrious personality; she was as visionary and creative a person as I've known. The summer Percy threw me to the ground, she produced a fund-raiser for the volunteer fire department, complete with real firemen throwing dolls out my second-story window to grown-ups below holding four corners of a double-bed sheet. The year I studied the American Revolution in school and learned about the Boston Tea Party, Mom staged a replica on *Rêve*, for which we kids collected buckets full of pine needles from the forest, rowed them out to the boat, and, at the revolutionary moment, tossed our "tea" overboard. She organized flotillas of canoes and rowboats, festooning them with flowers and ferns for waterborne parades. One July Fourth, she borrowed the Robinsons' horse to pull off a moonlit ride of Paul Revere. In 1955, Dad wrote to his brother Dryden, *Betty is commanding a small regiment of kids for the party this afternoon for persons on the Cape.* "Persons on the Cape" might mean the half dozen families summering on Weir Cove or four times that if he invited everyone he knew within a reasonable drive. Mom's biggest annual production took place every August 24, when we portrayed her courtship with Dad and brought down the curtain on another summer.

"Richie was so handsome," Mom told Sarah and me while we practiced our lines in the woods the summer we were nine. It was my parents' nineteenth anniversary and the black-and-white photographs she showed us of my father as a young man in his Navy whites proved her point. Back in 1940, my father was trim, had perfect posture, thick blond curls, and a winning smile. From my earliest years, I heard that my parents' marriage was filled with both passion and conflict.

— ∞ —

My mother and father met when Dad was thirty-six. Mom was ten years younger. Dad was teaching English at St. Mark's School, a private boys' academy in Southborough, Massachusetts. It was at St. Mark's that he became known for collecting poets to join him where he taught—that year, he invited W. H. Auden for a three-week residency. My father's most famous student at St. Mark's was a young Robert Lowell, whose face would be on the cover of *Time* in 1967, the year I turned seventeen. Another of Dad's students at St. Mark's was Ben Bradlee, who would become editor of the *Washington Post* and would cover the Watergate years. At St. Mark's, Dad was given two nicknames, both of which Mom appropriated, calling him Richie when she felt affectionate toward him and Dreamy Dick when she thought his head was too far up in the clouds.

My father befriended a fellow teacher at St. Mark's, a young man named Charlie Butcher, in the math department. Future heir to the Butcher Polish Company in Cambridge, Massachusetts, Charlie thought Dad might be a good match for his energetic older sister, Betty, who, at twenty-six, had yet to land a husband.

Betty Butcher had thick, straight, brown hair with blond highlights, straight-across-her-forehead bangs and didn't quite reach five feet. "I'm four feet eleven and a half," Mom would say, "and don't forget the half!" I think of her the way I do the small spruce trees in Maine that sprout at the edge of our yard at Undercliff. Their roots barely grip the earth while their tops reach impatiently for the sky. Mom had two speeds—buried in a book or fast on the go.

My mother had graduated with a degree in sociology from Smith College in 1936 and received a second degree, from Simmons College, in 1937. She'd spent two summers working for the Frontier Nursing Service in Kentucky, where she'd assisted in delivering babies of poor, rural women. In 1938, she'd moved home to her parents' house in Cambridge and was teaching fourth grade at Buckingham School. Mom was unfiltered, a bundle of fun, and ever so sure of herself.

"Mother and Daddy were worried I'd end up a spinster," she told Sarah and me while we practiced our lines in the shade. "They thought I was taking too long to make up my mind on a husband." I doubt Mom worried much about her matrimonial fate, since she'd enjoyed a succession of beaux, most of them promising young men attending the Harvard Business School. To evaluate their potential, Mom had perfected an approach. She'd tour a prospective suitor through her father's wax factory, then located in a small barn behind the family home. If the young man was intrigued by how her father produced so much wax in such a space, he'd get a second date. If he recoiled at seeing the antiquated equipment and disorganized factory, Mom would let him go. By 1940, my guess is, she just hadn't found any of the business types interesting enough.

I'd never met a real live poet before, my mother wrote in her journal from that year, so *I was boning up on the Romantic poets. I wanted to make a good impression on Dick.*

Charlie arranged for my father to dine with the Butcher family in Cambridge before an evening of theater in Boston. Descending the wide central staircase of her parents' home to meet her date, Mom passed etchings of her stern-faced German ancestors and the grandfather clock that took up half the stair landing. I suspect she nearly bounced on the pads of her feet with excitement. On the bottom step, Mom stopped, catching sight of my father lunging at Gram with a cane, showing off his bayonet drills and jabbing at her as if she were an imaginary German. Gram was German by birth but pragmatic and pacifist by conviction. My father's aggression, along with his naiveté, piqued her as she leaned back in her chair and cried, "But, Richie, that will never defeat Hitler!" *I took one look at Dick lunging at Mother*, Mom wrote to her friends, *and it was love at first sight.*

Any line about defeating Hitler was a hit in our beach skits in Maine. That morning, we'd fashioned a bayonet out of sticks and string for Dikkon to use when he acted out my father's lunges. Gram came over to play herself. I played Mom, dragging down the beach the hem of an old nightie repurposed as an evening gown. I made a right turn around the stick in the clay that served as the grandfather clock, while Sarah and the rest of the summer kids held

pictures of stern-faced Germans we'd drawn on shirt cardboards
with magic markers.

—⦿—

By the time my parents met, my father had graduated from Dartmouth College in 1926, and had worked for a year at Marshall
Field's in Chicago, selling men's hats and writing ad copy. Quickly
restless and unsure what to do next, he quit his job and applied for
a year of study at Cambridge University. He wanted to learn from
the Cambridge dons and study the great British poets of the past.
Looking to occupy his time while he waited to hear if he'd gotten
in, he boarded a bus to San Francisco and looked for work that
might get him to the Far East, about as distant as an imaginative
young man could travel in 1927. Eventually, he landed a position
as a deckhand on the SS *Faralong*, bound for Manila. *I left Chicago
with two suitcases and the spirit of odyssey*, my father wrote in his
journal that year. *Man must move.*

After seventy-two days at sea, he finally spotted land, and it
was Japan. Over the next two weeks, he sailed up the Yangtze River
into Hong Kong Harbor and on to Shanghai. He was struck by the
poverty in China: men carrying yokes on their shoulders to trans-
port goods, women with bound feet. He wrote of opium and houses
of "ill repute." From Manila, he hopped a German freighter to cross
the Indian ocean to Subang, where he caught the SS *Rajputana* for
Europe, arriving just in time to accept an offer from Cambridge
University to study at St. John's College.

Before he met Mom eleven years later, my father had published two volumes of poetry: *A Bravery of Earth* (Jonathan Cape,
1930) and *Reading the Spirit* (Oxford University Press, 1937). He
pursued but didn't complete a master's degree at Harvard, where he
lived at Eliot House. It was at Harvard that he first met T. S. Eliot,
who, my father noted in letters to his friends, had *a Renoir on his
wall and a cold sore on his lip.*

After Harvard, Dad spent several years tutoring the offspring of wealthy parents, the most significant of whom were the twin sons of King Prajadhipok of Siam. When I was a kid, Dad would tell Dikkon and me these stories of far-off lands, of working his way around the world, of knowing kings. He also rolled out the events and years in conversations with visitors, or I'd hear them spoken of in introductory remarks before his poetry readings. If small-minded friends taunted me about how old my father was in comparison with theirs—which he was—I thought his accomplishments more than explained how busy he'd been before settling down with a wife and children.

Like Mom, my father was no stranger to love. He'd enjoyed a string of lady friends through his college years, as well as acquaintances in eastern ports of call. His most serious love interest was Louise Hawkes, daughter of a wealthy linoleum executive whose father later became a US senator from New Jersey. Lou was introduced to my father by a mutual friend, who forwarded to her a sheaf of his early poems. The two struck up a heady correspondence that started while Dad was in college at Dartmouth and would continue through decades. Lou's was a household name, though I never met her and didn't really understand who she was to him. Later, when I landed on his lengthy correspondence with Lou in his letters—long, flowing, youthful professions of desire—they were another surprise.

Their letters nearly sparkle with effervescence, as if the two popped champagne corks into their respective bathtubs, poured themselves glasses of bubbly, and wrote to each other, basking in fizz. As they got to know each other via correspondence, their fantasies grew to the point of blurring all lines of reality. My father became fashioned as Lou's Italian lover, "Ricco," while Lou became my father's imagined goddess, "Maia."

During the spring of 1929, while my father was studying at Cambridge, Lou planned a research trip to Italy for her graduate thesis at Scripps. The two consummated their epistolary affair over several passionate weeks on the island of Sicily and in Florence. To locate where my father should meet her in Taormina, Lou drew out a map for him and marked the spot with an X. She would be sitting on that rock, she wrote, in a green frock, gazing at Mt. Aetna. Preparing Dad for their denouement, Lou offered, *Dear haloed saints yawning with boredom in Heaven, have mercy on us sinners now and at the hour of death—and think how far you'd sail your gold-plated halos out into the blue Mediterranean for a chance to climb to the red rock marked X with us tomorrow.*

In Taormina, the young lovers stayed in bed for days, reading aloud from Blake and Shelley. On his reluctant return to England, my father wrote to Lou, *Don't you know yet the insatiability of my soul? When we crossed the Arno in Florence? We glided down the river of Love. O my beloved, I clasp you lest I drown! Let me kiss you a thousand times before you die.* From Avila, Lou replied, *Sicily and Springtime, Ricco and Maia. They should have a story—because they are a story, a tragic-comic-romantic modeling of Destiny.*

A few weeks later, Lou foreshadowed what would come. *Ricco mio!* she wrote. *Four weeks ago today, you were sitting on the bed in my dingy little thirty-lira room at the Villa Regina, the view of the gray sea from the terrace before the temple of Juno, and I sat watching you in delight, and prayed to the still-loved Queen of Gods to make me more your Maia and less the girl who is Louise.*

In 1929, upon completing his year at Cambridge, my father rented a room at 159 Boulevard du Montparnasse in Paris, where he finished his first manuscript, *A Bravery of Earth*. In 1931, he returned to New York at the beginning of the Great Depression, painfully low on cash, and took a small room on West Forty-Fifth Street. He tried for weeks to find work. Small writing assignments came and went. Editing positions that looked promising evaporated. Eventually, he had to rely on his father, a meatpacking executive from Austin, Minnesota, for contacts on the "killing floors" in New York. The job didn't last. The city's meatpacking district was a rough place for a Cambridge-educated poet, and he left after only a few weeks. Still, he captured the gruesome scenes in long, detailed letters back to his family in Austin. *Rising at 4:30, he wrote, to appear upon the killing floors at 5:00, impaled upon the spikes of a harsh reality all day; at least there are blood and bowels in this business; a certain exhilaration comes at the mere awareness of acute odors, sights, and sounds. One can do worse than to live neck to neck with men as big as Amazons who cleave hogs through the spine with one blow.*

Lou and my father rendezvoused in New York and New Jersey to evaluate their potential for the long term, but the affair was losing steam. Despite their mutual reverie, Lou's parents asked their daughter whether she might not just as easily fall for a wealthy businessman, as she had for a poor poet. Soon, Lou agreed that Dad's poetic vision was unlikely to pay the bills. She and my father began to acquire other companions, and my father was endlessly jealous of hers. Lou assured my father of her role in his life, a promise she would keep. *Your unique responsibility to me,* she wrote, *is to believe in your Dream as much as, if not more than, Maia believes in it.*

Lou married a wealthy businessman, which broke my father's heart. To his Dartmouth friend Andy Foster, he confided, *After the awful summer of 1930, I began the painful process of outgrowing her. The mere difference between our stations in life almost precludes anything but blind devotion to the abstract ideal. Would that I knew what I wanted in life and then could cough up the guts to get it.*

I'd long wondered about Lou, since I'd heard about her through my first two decades. Her letters portrayed a woman far different from my mother. Betty Butcher was not classically glamorous, but was born with her two feet planted solidly on the ground. She loved dressing up for the theater and going to debutante balls, but her heart was in the great outdoors. She skied in the Laurentians, hiked the trails of Mount Chocorua in New Hampshire, swam off the coast of Nova Scotia. She liked wild places that set her heart and mind free. She admired my father's looks, his clear ambition and talent, his charm, his wide and fascinating circle of friends, and the excitement of a life she could imagine with him. She knew she'd never be bored, and one thing none of the women in my family likes is being bored by their mates.

Mom was petite, whip smart, precocious, fun, and funny—all things Dad probably found balancing for his melancholic poetic soul. Drawn to Betty as my father was, he still sought consolation from friends and family on her shortcomings, mostly in the beauty department. His letters describing Mom infuriated me. To Andy Foster, he wrote, *Betty Butcher is 27, blond and blue-eyed, a graduate of Smith, not beautiful, but would make a good wife. She is not a great student or anything of that sort.* To his father and stepmother, he wrote, *I am thinking of marrying Betty. Suppose I ought to do it now if ever, but one never quite knows what is best. She would make a good wife, but is no Phi Beta, nor too beautiful, but has a good spirit, enjoys life, and is in no way temperamental or neurotic.*

Really, Dad? I thought, flushing at his words.

My father was hopelessly indecisive in matters of the heart, and he worried that marriage would derail his literary momentum. To Foster, he wrote, *I made a deep wager I would never give up my creative gift.* To his younger sister, Elizabeth, he penned, *I question how I could further my career as a married man. . . . Maybe marriage will kill off the poetry?*

Eventually, my father invited Mom to Chicago to meet his family, who loved her. Still, no proposal from Dad. Mom's impatience grew, and she threatened my father that she'd return east on her own. To placate her, Dad suggested a drive along the shore of Lake Michigan. Mom sobbed over his indecision, and the two got into a fight. As the story goes, Mom threw herself out the door of his slow-moving car. Dad searched high and low, and when he finally found her hiding behind a bush, my mother said she saw real terror on his face. "How romantic!" Mom laughed. "You're imagining me throwing myself into the lake, and all for you!" Then it was my father's turn to be angry at Mom toying with his emotions, something I'd watch her do through the middle years of their marriage.

When, in my early teens, she talked to me about sex and warned me about getting too involved with someone too soon, I asked if she'd slept with Dad before they married. "No," she said, "but I wasn't being puritanical; I just didn't want to be another of his affairs." She would be prescient on that score. Still, I took from her message that true love was a high-stakes game, one in which you had to strategize and manipulate to win.

In Chicago, the two made up, and fifty cents bought them a speedboat ride out to the middle of Lake Michigan. My father slipped his mother's pearl ring on Mom's finger and kissed her, though he never did ask her to marry him. Still, the passengers were elated by the surprise engagement and, the way I look at it, probably served as the first swirl of people my parents drew around them to bolster their marriage.

On August 24, 1942, six hundred guests attended my parents' wedding at Christ Church in Cambridge, including the entire Eberhart family from Chicago. The newlyweds honeymooned on Cranberry Island, in Maine, for *two blissful weeks*, as Dad wrote home, where they drank champagne, skinny-dipped off granite ledges, napped in the hot sun, and commenced their lifelong love of the Maine coast.

Despite the passage of time, my father never said goodbye to Louise Hawkes, nor would he give up the illusion of Maia and Ricco. Lou prompted in him an outpouring of thirty sonnets, published in 1967 by Eakins Press—a beautifully crafted, boxed edition, which arrived twenty-five years into his marriage with Mom and the year I turned sixteen. Dad's old anger at losing Lou remains unedited from the page: *and while this soft-nosed male shall call you true / I lust still after the great dream of you.*

My father and Lou corresponded regularly through their lives, usually on publication of Dad's latest book and especially in April, his birth month and the month they'd spent together in Italy. Lou would praise his latest and confide in him about the shortcomings in her marriage.

— ◄◙► —

To reenact the Lake Michigan speedboat ride on our beach in Maine, my father pulled a dinghy up onto the rocks and Mom filled it with cottage thespians. Sarah's older brother, Dave, donned his father's cleric collar to pronounce Dikkon and me newlyweds while the grown-ups raised their glasses to cap off another perfect summer and one more year of my parents' marriage.

— ◄◙► —

It was 1998 by the time I came across the letters between Lou and Dad. Renovations for the new Rauner Library at Dartmouth were complete, and my father's archives had been moved there. I quickly got to know Sarah Hartwell, whose job it was to catalog Dad's collection of letters. She and I often talked before I left for the day. One day, we wondered together why my father had pre-served his correspondence with Lou. Did the letters illuminate, perhaps, some artistic evolution? Did any item with his name on it simply deserve library space? Did he ever think about whether either of his children might read them? We came to no conclusion. I reached out to my friend Ellen, a psychologist and consultant, texting her on my BlackBerry, "Wait till you hear what I've just read! Meet me later?"

Ellen is the kind of friend who shows up in your life through a chance encounter and becomes the long-lost sister you didn't know you had. As I chiseled my way into Dad's archives, it was Sarah and Ellen, especially, who saw me through.

Ellen and I sat at a small window table at the Canoe Club, then a popular restaurant in Hanover, named after my father's poem, "Canoe Club," about the Yale University boathouse. In the late 1940s, Dad met fellow businessman-poet Wallace Stevens, then vice president of the Hartford Accident & Indemnity Company in

Hartford, Connecticut, where my father tried to sell the company on using Butcher's Wax on its floors. Stevens took Dad to lunch at the Canoe Club, where, he pointed out, there were no canoes and he hadn't seen one pass for thirty years, but where, he insisted, they served the best martinis. So began a long friendship over many lunchtime cocktails. A lithograph of Dad's poem hung on the wall not far from the table where Ellen and I sat. Ahead of the dinner crowd, the restaurant was quiet that afternoon. We looked out on Main Street as I filled Ellen in on my father and Lou and the skits Mom produced on our beach in Maine.

"Don't you think it's weird that you acted out your parents' courtship?" Ellen asked, cutting to the chase, as she would.

"You mean you didn't do the same?"

I'd acted out that scene so many times, it hadn't seemed weird to me as a kid. In my forties, I was only just figuring out which parts of my upbringing were typical, and which weren't.

"Are you kidding? A little too much about them?"

"Narcissistic, you mean? That's the word I've been toying with lately."

"And keeping those letters from Lou. What did your mother think about that?"

"I don't know. I don't know if she knew he kept them. I don't remember her in his study or having much to do with his correspondence. I know Dad didn't edit his poems much; maybe he didn't edit his life, either. He was hard pressed to toss anything."

"It must be hard to read all this stuff."

I raised my glass of wine to salute the sentiment. "It is. At least some of the time. I just thought I'd find some missing pieces to the puzzle of who he was and how he affected me. I didn't really think about the emotional consequences for me of what I'd find. There's real stuff to process."

Ellen flagged our waitress for refills.

"Sometimes I wonder if Mom's acceptance of the other women in his life," I continued, "was the only way she knew how to hold on to him. Maybe the skit was her way of reminding us and Dad that she'd been the one who got him, not Lou."

Ellen paused, noticing and waving at a friend walking by outside. "Different generation, right? Women stayed with all kinds of men because they loved them. Still, to keep another woman on display like that, that's rough."

"He didn't shed his lovers easily," I said. "As Mom got older, I think she found that more challenging, or at least it looked that way to me."

I stared out the window at college students jaywalking across Main Street and thought back on my mother's last decade, through her seventies, and how she had seemed to lose some of her interest in Dad. I thought of the way she disregarded him and seemed more hurt by things he did. I finished my wine and reached for Ellen's hand.

"Right now, I just feel sad for my mom," I said.

Chapter 7:

10 Hilliard Place

Naval officer life during World War II suited my parents well and carried them through their first four years of marriage. My father was commissioned as a lieutenant in the Naval Reserve, but color blindness kept him out of direct combat. Instead, he put to use his talent for teaching by instructing young recruits in aerial gunnery.

My parents, naturally patriotic, enjoyed the pageantry of naval events, and the officer parties, at which they made fast friends for life. Mom gave up what had been a beloved teaching career to be a full-time housewife and would follow Dad through three tours of service in Hollywood, Florida; Dam Neck, Virginia; and Alameda, California. In Hollywood, Dad wrote to a friend about his *long hard hours, from 6:00 a.m. to 4:00 p.m., at a most interesting new teaching experience. We have bananas, oranges, grapefruit, and papayas in the garden. I plucked a grapefruit right off the tree for breakfast this morning.* Meanwhile, Mom depicted their domestic life in whimsical watercolors, including one of my father napping with their two cats, Shelley and Keats, which she captioned *In service to his country.*

Living in the Jim Crow South offended Mom's view of how the world should be. Having hired a woman to press my father's Navy whites, Mom was incensed that her new friend had to finish up before 5:00 p.m. in order to catch the only Negro taxi in Hollywood. She heard from a neighbor, "If they ride in our taxis, the next thing you know, they'll want to be president," about which Mom wrote to her parents, *There is little or nothing you can say to a person who is as afraid as whites seem to be*, and, presciently, *There is very little likelihood that we will have a colored president for some time to come, if we ever do, but when we do, he's as likely to be as good as any other man who is elected by the people.*

Alcohol flowed freely at officer parties and gave Mom a clear view of her husband's drinking—*prodigious* was her word—though, as she wrote home, he could handle it well. She was perhaps more surprised by the role of a wife in the 1940s. My mother came naturally to the notion of equality, because she believed in it, because she was educated at Smith College, and because she'd observed it in her parents' marriage. When I was a junior in high school, she told me, "There wouldn't be a battle of the sexes if men would just let women be equal." Willing to keep the house and entertain new friends in Hollywood, she quickly learned Dad's interests usually eclipsed hers.

A sketch from that time illustrates her point. My father regularly picked up hitchhikers, and Mom didn't usually mind, except, as a newlywed, she sometimes wanted Dad to herself. Her watercolor shows her and Dad in the front seat with a Navy sailor squeezed between them. In the picture, Dad is happily conversing with his new friend while Mom is steaming. *Shall we pick him up?* the caption reads. To which Mom responded, *No. So we picked him up*.

My father's easy assimilation into the Navy was the subject of many letters, such as one to W. H. Auden, writing, *a complete refreshment from the stuffiness of literary people, literary attitudes.* Dad's concern that marriage would interfere with poetry hadn't materialized. Jack Sweeney, a friend from Cambridge University, wrote, *Your letters seem happier and more whole than I've ever known them to be. I suspect that transfiguration is chiefly due to your extraordinary wife, though part of it comes from the new, more outward focus of your eyes.* My mother, who'd worried, too, that marriage might deter Dad's literary momentum, noted in a letter home that *between beer, swimming, entertaining guests, going to parties, and working hard at Dam Neck eight hours a day, Richie has done well along the poetry line.*

In 1944, my father wrote his seminal poem, "The Fury of Aerial Bombardment," said to be the best verse to have come out of World War II. He was predisposed to weighing moral rights and wrongs. Even against Hitler, he had the example of his brother-in-law's decision to serve as a conscientious objector to the war. Dad regularly told people he believed Uncle Charlie had made a higher moral decision than he. He especially bemoaned teaching young men in gunnery and, soon after, finding their names on the Navy's death list.

In the fall of 1945, my parents were transferred to Alameda, and one week later, the war ended. Dad served out his teaching post while scouring the West Coast for artists and writers. He and Mom quickly befriended Kenneth and Marie Rexroth, and the two couples spent long days together, hiking, rock climbing, and exploring the California coastline. With Kenneth and Marie, Dad began to shed his military persona to reclaim his poet's path. He lectured at Mills College, dined with the poet Muriel Rukeyser, spoke to the writer Josephine Miles's class of students at UC Berkeley. As my parents celebrated their fifth anniversary, Mom and Dad fantasized about where they might live next—would it be a farm in Vermont, by the sea in southern France, in a fifth-floor walk-up in Manhattan? Soon, they learned Mom was pregnant and opted instead for an offer from her parents in Cambridge, who would renovate their third floor into an apartment. They moved east, and Dad went to work for his father-in-law at the Butcher Polish Company. On October 30, 1946, they welcomed my older brother, Dikkon.

— ⁓ —

In 1950, after four years in Navy housing and three more under the eaves of the Butchers, Mom and Dad bought their perfect first home, at 10 Hilliard Place, just off Harvard Square, in Cambridge. The tiny, 150-year-old Cape-style house, complete with gray clapboards and a pitched roof, was much to their liking. Dad described it in letters to friends as *quite commodious, upon which we have lavished months of devotion in the way of paint and fixing up.*

Cambridge was an East Coast Mecca for poetry in the 1940s and '50s, more so than New York or other creative hotbeds. Dad's Cambridge University friend Jack Sweeney, who would become a world-renowned scholar and critic, was then curator of Harvard's Woodberry Poetry Room and organized poetry readings at Widener Library. Nearby, Gordon Cairnie's book shop, Grolier Books, on Plympton Street, became the de facto spot for poets to sell their work and meet other writers in Harvard Square. My parents' little cottage was a mere ten-minute walk from Grolier's and quickly became the place for writers and literary-minded people who partook of my parents' warm hospitality and their well-stocked liquor closet.

My mother cared deeply about the poets, not just about their latest work and their ideas, but also about their romances and marriages, their health, their divorces, and their artistic and human vulnerabilities. She supported and challenged them in turn. If one was short on cash or needed a bed or a meal, she'd provide it. If she thought another was procrastinating about a book he'd promised to write, she'd give him a pep talk or a kick in the pants. The tiny living room on Hilliard Place swelled with the famous, the infamous, and the yet to be discovered, who traded their craft, competed over publishing successes, and commiserated over each other's failures. A river of poets flowed through that house and, the way I see it, established our future living rooms as virtual public spaces and our evening meals as communal.

Some, like John Ciardi, came to Hilliard Place for literary gossip. Conrad Aiken, Mom once told me, came just to drink. I never saw my father drunk, but during my high school years, I watched him pour himself a fourth bourbon every night. When I was fifteen and worried about his drinking, Mom changed the subject and suggested an approach I might consider in controlling my own consumption when I would begin to drink. In her instruction, I should thank my host for refilling my glass and then place it next to a heavy drinker, like Aiken.

"But, Mom, you were aiding and abetting him."

"I don't think Conrad really cared," Mom said. She understood Aiken's demons—including that his father, a prominent Savannah physician, had become increasingly violent and murdered Conrad's mother before shooting himself. Aiken was eleven when he found them. "Besides," Mom added, "isn't the difference between being drunk and really, really drunk rather academic?"

Wallace Stevens was a regular, often after attending Harvard football games. While working full-time at Butcher's, Dad was trying to gain momentum as a poet. Sometimes he longed to focus only on his art. To the British writer Stephen Spender, he wrote, that year, *I agree that working in the world is probably better than living in an ivory tower. I always long for contemplation, complete surrender to one's sensibility, the life of the spirit, yet know the supposed damaging lassitude of that. I write when I can, sometimes in long fits of night releases. When [T. S.] Eliot was here I had a short chat with him about this.* This dilemma between succumbing to paid work and allowing one's mind to wander, responsibility-free, snatching new phrases from the celestial ether, was the subject of a letter to Dad's later publisher at New Directions, James Loughlin, whom we called Jay. A year before I was born, Dad wrote to Jay, *You used to chide me that I thought every line of mine good; I was the arrogant, ruthless fool to think so. Now I wonder how poetry is written at all—it seems so highly improbable. I suppose it is time and family and offspring, and necessity of supporting others, which occasions so many compromises with the rampant ego! But time, too, makes one more stubborn in the innermost place. Lives of poets are ridiculous: I spend 9/10 of my time at gainful work, 1/10 writing. I deeply wish it were the other way* *around. But then I would probably make $1,000 a year, which would only keep up our cats and goldfish, with a force of liquor thrown in.*

— ∽ —

At 10 Hilliard Place, a cast of characters came and went, and after each evening, letters flew from my father's typewriter to whomever had been there and to those who'd missed out. To [William Carlos] Bill Williams, he wrote, *The fight is still going on about the nature of poetry and we had some the other night with Ciardi and* [Richard] *Wilbur. Nothing was settled of course but a lot of fur flew.* The modernist poet Marianne Moore visited regularly, thanking Dad for his *beautiful hospitality and your philosophy of benevolence which were an example I needed and shan't forget.* Sir Osbert Sitwell and his sister, the British poet Dame Edith Sitwell, were lecturing at Harvard that year and held court at Hilliard Place. *Edith,* Dad wrote to friends, *was wearing a turban and an enormous pair of Tibetan hand-beaten silver bracelets.* Robert Frost regularly stopped by, as did Donald Hall, then a graduate student at Harvard. So, too, Robert Lowell, then an undergrad at Harvard. Dick Wilbur brought his new wife, Charlee, and became lasting friends with Mom and Dad. As did Archibald MacLeish and Robert Penn Warren. Growing up, I knew them all by their nicknames: Don, Cal, Dick, Archie, and Red.

Ten Hilliard Place gave rise to the Poets' Theatre, which Dad, Ciardi, Wilbur, MacLeish, and Sweeney established in my parents' living room in 1950. My father was installed as its first president. The theater's purpose was to stage performances of debut plays by poets. It scraped together enough money to survive, in one form or another, until 1968 (and was resurrected in 2014), staging plays by Samuel Beckett, Edward Gorey, Alison Lurie, James Merrill, and Dylan Thomas, along with my father's verse play, *Visionary Farms.*

— ∽ —

Dylan Thomas was in Cambridge, from Wales, early in 1950 for a reading at Harvard and stayed at Hilliard Place for four days. Dylan, my father wrote, was a *roly-poly, lovable child, an amorous leopard who likes to shock everybody*, and *an inspired alcoholic who reads masterfully*. On Dylan's second notable visit to Hilliard Place, he made a stir, drinking all my parents' beer, eating nothing but two strips of bacon over three days, and coming on to my mother. He *left a wake of affection, whimsies, great warmth, and jollity*, Dad wrote.

"Dylan was too insecure to be taken seriously," Mom told me when I was in high school and was old enough to better understand the Dylan stories.

"But wasn't he Dad's friend?"

"He was just too drunk to worry about in his fawning, but I didn't think the poets should romanticize him the way they did. They could laud his poetry, but not his drinking."

One night, a fully inebriated Thomas seemed to be missing from the house. The poet John Malcolm Brinnin, whose role it was to drive Dylan from Cambridge to Manhattan the next day, became increasingly agitated.

"Where's Dylan?" Malcolm asked Dad, then deeply occupied in conversation in the stuffed-to-the-gills living room. Dad waved Brinnin off.

"Where's Dylan?" Brinnin asked again, after midnight, still not having seen the bard.

Finally, my father climbed the stairs to look for the Welshman and found him in Dikkon's room, drinking from an open bottle and cooing Gaelic verses through the bars of my brother's crib. That scene would make it into the 1964 production of *Dylan*, headlined on Broadway by Alec Guinness. I learned early that my parents' stories made for sensational entertainment, and if they landed on Broadway, I supposed, they must be worth a lot.

———

In 1950, Dikkon got his first puppy, our dachshund, Star, and eight months later, on May 26, 1951, he got me as his little sister. Dad wrote the same letter to a dozen friends: *Betty is doing nicely and so is Margaret Ghormley Eberhart, who showed a sensible reluctance to enter this world but came with a rush when she decided on our fallen estate.*

Neither Dikkon nor I was given an easy name. Mom wanted to name me Gretchen, after Gram, but Dad insisted on Margaret, a name I'd never use and that few people, unless of German heritage, imagine as having any connection to Gretchen. My brother got Richard Butcher Eberhart, but was called Dikkon, not an easy name as a teenager, even if he could claim it was a fresh spelling of the original diminutive for Richard, in Middle English.

It was Dikkon who Mom worried would be jealous when I was born, after he'd had her full attention for five years, but I was the one born with the jealous streak. From a very young age, I didn't think I belonged in my family. I was sure Dikkon was my parents' real child and that I'd been adopted. I saw proof when I felt unseen in my family.

My need to be noticed reached its first of many zeniths the year I turned four and we lived in Norton, Massachusetts. One morning, I hopped into the kitchen on one leg and announced that my other leg didn't work. Mom and Dad checked me over but saw nothing wrong. After Dad left for campus and Dikkon was at school, Mom spent her day trying to trick me into putting my leg down, but I kept it hitched behind my knee and skipped around on one foot. Uncle Charlie was coming for a visit the next day, and Mom kept it a secret, hoping that when I saw my uncle unexpectedly at the door, I'd run into his arms. I didn't. Finally, after two days of this, Mom took me to see a doctor. He lifted me onto his table, examined every inch of me, wiggled my good leg and inspected my bad, tapped my funny bones with his funny-bone tapper, and, while I played with his stethoscope, asked me serious questions. Some of this I heard about through Mom's stories; some of it I remember. When Mom intervened with answers, the doctor shooed her away. What I remember is the feeling of being carefully listened to, of being of interest. The doctor asked me how I felt and what if he moved my leg this way or that, and when had I first noticed the problem? Was I sleeping all right? Was I worried about something?

After all his attention, he called Mom back into the room, folded his arms across his white coat, and said, "Well, Gretchen, I think you're fine. I think your leg will work now." I nodded, jumped off the table, and walked out of the room. Later, in Mom's story, she'd add that after I'd exited the room, the doctor turned to her and said, "I think you may have just learned something important about your daughter. She'd do well with a little more attention."

With two children at Hilliard Place, Dad needed paying work from poetry to supplement his wan wages and was grateful for whatever he could get. To an editor at Houghton Mifflin, he wrote, *Many thanks for the handy check—milk for Gretchie, gin for Daddy?* Frances Bacon, known to us as Brownie, the longtime editor of the *New York Times Book Review*, regularly asked Dad to review new books of poetry. That year he reviewed his friend Bill Williams's *Collected Poems*, for which Brownie sent him a $40 check.

The year I was born, my father won the Shelley Memorial Award, and in 1952, he joined John Ciardi's poetry workshop, along with May Sarton and Dick Wilbur. Ciardi, an Italian American poet, ten years younger than Dad and then teaching at Harvard, was known for a much-heralded translation of Dante's *Divine Comedy* and would later become poetry editor of the *Saturday Review*, a position from which he'd accept and publish poems of my father's. Ciardi's popular *Mid-Century American Poets* came out in 1950, and its dust jacket is essentially a list of poets who frequented our house at 10 Hilliard Place.

Ciardi's workshop provided time and space for the poets to critique each other's work and talk about their literary challenges. Some writers were dogged in their discipline, rising early, toiling late, and revising a poem for months, to the point of perfection. "I've taken as long as a dozen years to complete one poem," Donald Hall would tell me years later during one of my visits with him as an adult, at his farmhouse in New Hampshire.

Dad's muse offered up thousands of poems, but many of them weren't good. He frustrated editors and friends alike, as well as Mom and me, by refusing critical feedback. In 1951, my father asked Red Warren for a blurb for his next book, and Warren put it this way: *I'll be delighted to express my deep and abiding partiality for* some *of your poems.* In high school, I came home one day to find my father crestfallen for being turned down by the *New Yorker*, which had regularly taken his work. "Dick, that poem really isn't very good," Mom told him directly. "She's right, Dad," I added. "It isn't." Dad shrugged his shoulders and walked out of the room.

— ∿ —

Hilliard Place may have housed us for only two years, but it's nearly as notable in memory as our family homes in Hanover and Maine. Reading through Dad's archives from that period, I'd see how that house set the stage for my parents' energetic and social lifestyle and for the way they would run their future homes. I'd renew my affection through Dad's correspondence with Dick Wilbur and Don Hall in their younger years, two poets who'd treated me like one of their own kids. And in those letters I could imagine Frost, in Cambridge, five years younger than when I first met him, in Hanover. Or reexperience Dame Edith Sitwell, whom I would meet when I was ten, and we lived in Washington, D.C.. Sitwell appeared like an apparition in our backyard, a muse herself, dressed in a bold turban with glass earrings grazing her shoulders.

Reading those letters, I could hear the poets' voices, understand better who they were, and ponder how I felt about them. I also saw in the letters a reason I never felt part of my family and why our homes never really felt like mine. I was on the outside of their literary circle, mostly observing. As a child and early adolescent, I had no real standing with my father. I wasn't his son, nor one of his friends. I was just a girl, useful for showing off with her cartwheels or playing the piano, but never a member of his club.

As I finished up with the Hilliard Place years, I sat with Sarah at Rauner Library and reflected on my impressions. She had read every letter while I thumbed through them, stopping where I wanted and flipping through the rest. Sarah helped provide context and insight. The Hilliard Place period had been especially meaningful to her for its rich depiction of literary life during one of its heydays.

"What a place," Sarah said that afternoon.

"It was almost like a character on our stage," I mused.

"Your parents were tireless in their socializing."

"They were." Hilliard Place was where it all started, but each of our homes felt like a whirlwind, pulling me into its vortex.

I placed the letters back in their folder. A few seconds passed. "There wasn't much room for a kid, at least with Dad. He liked showing me off and tolerated me for short periods of time, but he kept a tight circle of poets and academics around him who sucked up the air. I think that little girl is still sad."

Late-afternoon light filtered through the tall windows of the reading room at Rauner making shadows on the walls. The sky was darkening, and I'd read enough. Students who'd been staffing the information desk were picking up their backpacks and heading out. I was ready to go home.

"The sheer number of visitors they entertained is astounding. And, oh, to have been at some of those parties—goodness me," Sarah mused. "What that must have been like."

"It's true," I said, pausing. "They were legendary. But they took over. I usually put myself to bed."

Chapter 8:

As Certainly as Autumn

Waiting for my cousins to arrive at Gram's house in Cambridge was excruciating. I paced between the living room and library and asked a hundred times, "When will they *be* here?" I'd poured three crystal goblets of ginger ale and had snitched crackers and dip from Gram's tray of hors d'oeuvres. Spirited away in our secret hiding place, we'd have cocktail hour on our own, away from the grownups. It was 1959, and we were eight, six, and four—I the oldest, Kate Butcher the middle, and Susan Butcher pulling up the rear. Spending a weekend at Gram's meant they'd join me from where they lived, across town.

Suddenly, the two sisters burst through Gram's heavy front door like two little hurricanes. We hugged each other so tight, I thought I'd never breathe again and didn't care if I did.

"Come on, Gretch!" Kate yelled, already ahead of me.

"Under the stairs!" Susan squealed. She ripped off her coat, top button flying, and dropped it on the floor.

"Susan, pick up your coat," Aunt Aggie said. Susan ignored her.

"I have our cocktails, dahhhlings, and our hors d'oeuvres," I said, trying to sound fancy.

Our four-foot cube of a nest was in back of Gram's powder room, and it was ours alone—no adults, no second cousins, no boys allowed. It was our own little house in the middle of Gram's big home. To get there, we had to be inside the powder room and push through a rod hung thick with coats. First, we stood on the heat grate and watched our dresses float like butterflies around us. It was steaming hot inside the powder room. On tippy toes, we fake-powdered our noses, crowding our faces to the mirror, conjuring ourselves as very posh ladies, like Gram, going to the Ritz for lunch. "Oh, Susan," I said, "you look luvely, dahling!"

"Oh, posh," she said, never missing a new word she could exploit. Kate and I pushed through the coats, but Susan got stuck and had to crawl under them.

Behind the wool and fur was our nook, with its slanted ceiling too low for our parents to enter. Right under the wide central staircase, the room was barely big enough for the three of us and the dolls Gram brought back from her trips to Japan and China, India and Spain. With cocktails and crackers, plus pillows and blankets, doll beds, and a tea set, we squeezed in, right under the footfalls of grownups coming downstairs for cocktail hour, which sent us into giggles.

Susan, always antsy, crawled back out under the coats and propped open the powder room door an inch so we could listen to Uncle Charlie and Mom talking about the family business, Aunt Aggie and Dad discussing his latest book, and Gram striking matches for a fire in the library. Sometimes we learned things they'd never say in front of us, like which friend or cousin was getting divorced. Dikkon, then thirteen, and his friend Tony, who lived in the carriage house behind Gram's, had just told her they'd be outside but back in for dinner.

Dad visited the bathroom, surely having no clue we were there, and Susan, Kate, and I tried to hide our giggles in our armpits, listening to his pee hit the water in the tank. Throughout our childhoods, we shared everything within those four short walls: the birth of new cousins; crushes we had on Dikkon's friends from Lakeview Avenue; how old my father was compared with their father, Charlie; which of our mothers was nicest—they loved Mom's fun; I loved Aunt Aggie's style—and which of our two German great-aunts had the biggest bosoms.

"Auntie!" Kate squealed, pushing out her chest. "Her bosoms are *sooo big* and *sooo jiggly.*"

"Look at *my* bozzums!" Susan whisper-yelled, flinging up her shirt, showing off her flat chest.

—— ∽∾ ——

The next morning, Mom and Dad were sleeping in after their night at the theater in Boston with Uncle Charlie and Aunt Aggie. Dikkon had stayed over at Tony's. Kate and Susan and I had Gram to ourselves. As soon as we woke, we ran into her bedroom and hopped on her bed to watch her elaborate ritual of fixing her hair.

"I wish *my* hair was as long as yours," Kate said, stroking Gram's waist-length gray tresses and cuddling up to her on the edge of her bed.

"I wish mine was as *straight* as yours," I added, already disappointed that my curls did whatever they wanted, no matter how much I brushed them.

Gram was seventy-one years old and had the longest hair of anyone I knew. She took her silver-backed hairbrush and pulled it through her locks over and over, until it shone.

"Shh," I said. "Let's listen." We cocked our ears and celebrated the sound of a brush going through hair while little sparks of static electricity flew.

"Now, Susan," Gram said—Susan being the wiggliest and needing the most corralling—"you hold my brush while I make my braid." Gram pulled her long hair into three equal parts and carefully plaited them. She pushed her tortoiseshell comb through her brush to extract loose hairs, which she twisted into a string she could use to tie off the end of her braid.

"Why not a rubber band?" I asked.

"We learned to be frugal when we went through the Depression," Gram said.

"Were you depressed?" Susan asked.

"No, Susan." Gram laughed. "It was a period in our history when many people didn't have jobs or enough food and we all had to be careful about spending money."

"Did you and Grandfather Butcher have enough food?" Kate asked.

"Yes, dearies. In fact, we opened our front door and fed others who didn't."

"That's *amazing*," Kate said, as she watched Gram tie the hair-string around the end of her braid. We loved the things Gram knew about that we didn't, and the ways she did things, so different from any of our parents, like saying, "They're so combatable" when she meant "compatible," or "a stitch in time saves nine," when she tried to get us to clean up our messes as we made them instead of later after we'd forgotten.

Gram smiled, cocking her head a little, which I knew meant she loved Kate.

"It's *amazing*!" Susan echoed her sister, wiggling her way between Kate and Gram.

Gram handed Susan eight wavy bobby pins and told me to keep track of them, since I was the oldest and Susan usually dropped them on the floor or lost them in the bedcovers. Then Gram curled her braid on top of her head and pinned it in place, pushing through the bun one pin at a time. I couldn't see how those pins would hold all that heavy hair on top of her head, but they did.

"Now, dearies," Gram said, "let's go down to the kitchen and make our steamed eggs."

"Steamed eggs!" we yelled in unison.

In Gram's sunny kitchen at the back of her house, shaded in summer by an enormous horse chestnut tree my father featured in a poem, a long soapstone sink ran the length of her eastern window wall, while her fridge and stove cornered the other side of the room. In the middle, the heart of her home, was a big, square wooden table where we'd eat breakfast and lunch; where we'd lay out puzzles and board games; and where, as we got older, we'd do our homework, write in our diaries, or share a cup of tea and talk with Gram.

Gram placed her four-egg aluminum pan on the stove and lit a match under it. "I love that smell," Susan said, whiffing the gas. Waiting for the pot to boil took patience. Kate and I pulled up chairs to watch. We dropped hunks of butter in the egg wells, and Gram broke an egg into each one, salting all four but peppering only hers.

"Why can't I do it?" Susan squealed.

"When you're older, deary," Gram said. "You don't want your nightie to get close to the flame."

"But Kate and Gretch's nighties are close to the flame."

"Well, Susan, you'll be just as big as they are very soon."

Gram popped the top onto the steamer, and within a few minutes the eggs were perfectly steamed. She slid out the slippery, salty delicacies on top of heavily buttered toast and placed two strips of bacon on each of our plates.

"These are *sooo* good!" I said. "They're even better than pancakes!"

"I think so, too!" Kate said, nodding her head, her mouth full.

"I think so, three," squealed Susan, our caboose. "And the bacon. I *loooove* bacon." As if in a nod to Dylan Thomas, Susan existed through an entire school year on only chopped up bacon and powder donuts. Except at Gram's when steamed eggs were added.

—⚬⚬⚬—

My maternal great grandfather, Charles Butcher, emigrated to America from England in the early 1870s, by himself, at the age of sixteen. Sailing from Liverpool to New York City, he landed in the new country without a penny in his pocket and took what jobs he could find. Soon, he ventured north to Batavia, New York, where he learned the carpentry trade and married his boss's daughter. With one child in tow, the family made its way to Boston, where my great grandfather laid many of the parquet floors in the best houses on Beacon Hill.

Over many washings with soap and water, his customers complained that their floors grew dry and splintery. Charles knew that wooden floors in London, and at Versailles, were covered in beeswax and "skated" across by young boys in felt boots to make them shine. Charles experimented with turpentine and beeswax in his small carpentry shop behind his house in Cambridge, but the first concoctions proved too sticky. In 1880, Charles was invited to Toledo, Ohio, to lay a parquet floor for a rubber manufacturer and described his challenge to his customer. The businessman gave him a small piece of "wax" from the carnauba palm tree of Brazil, a gum then used in manufacturing rubber. The palm gum fixed my great-grandfather's stickiness problem, and, with a thousand-dollar investment from a group of Providence, Rhode Island, architects, Charles Butcher went on to develop America's first floor polish, naming it Butcher's Paste Wax.

As his small company grew, Charles moved his family to a farm in Cambridge, just across from Fresh Pond, and set up his wax factory in the barn behind the house, naming it the Butcher Polish Company. His two sons, William and Charles Butcher, took over the company, and that Charles married Margarethe Magdalena Theresa Carstensen, or Gram, as her grandchildren called her. Gram, too, was a second-generation German immigrant, whose father, known as Honest Hans, ran the Carstein Coal Company in Cambridge.

Charles and William would turn the small family business into a real company, and they became known through the Northeast and beyond as the Polish Kings. As Butcher's Wax grew, Charles wanted a bigger home for his wife and children and procured property and built a house at 117 Lakeview Avenue, where Kate and Susan, and I, visited Gram.

Gram's house had two large drawing rooms—her words— facing the street. Her living room, with its fireplace and baby grand piano, had a bay window filled with geraniums. Its walls were hung with framed etchings of our German ancestors, looking very stern. Kate and Susan and I had to act like ladies in the living room. Our legs, held together, were supposed to dangle straight over the edge of the squishy sofa, and our socks were to remain pulled up. Showing any underwear in the living room was not allowed—*das ist verboten*," as Gram would say, in German. Gram's library, on the other side of the foyer, had its own fireplace and bay windows but was less formal, a gathering place for the family, where my father enjoyed his pipes, sitting in the corner chair next to Gram's desk and we cousins could jump and wrestle, like heathens, as Dad affectionately called us, even showing off our underpants if we couldn't help it. Gram drank a glass of sherry every evening, while Dad had bourbon.

—⚭—

On Saturday, at 5:00 p.m., Gram built a fire just for Kate and Susan and me, as our parents were going out again. We would have our own cocktail hour together—her sherry and our ginger ale—as we watched her spread butter on a cracker, shake salt on it, take a small bite and chew it well, then spread more butter and more salt and take a second bite, and then repeat the ritual a third time, until the cracker was barely visible under the butter and salt. Even at eight, six, and four, we knew eating that much butter and salt wasn't good for us.

"Gram, you'll *die!*" Kate squealed.

"Well, if I do, I do," Gram said, enjoying her snack.

Gram's heart held out for nearly 102 years, until 1989 when Susan, Kate, and I made sure a pound of butter and her silver salt-shaker joined her inside her wooden coffin when she was buried at Mt. Auburn Cemetery.

—⚭—

If Gram's two front rooms were for entertaining, the back half of the house, shaded by a horse chestnut tree, was for Gram's working kitchen, where we ate breakfasts and lunches; a butler's pantry, looked over by Stanton; and a grand dining room with a fireplace, where we ate our dinners, prepared by Aurelia—Arie, as we called her. Stanton and Arie had been with Gram since my grandfather had died, in 1951, the year I was born. They commanded the back rooms of the house and were tirelessly patient with my cousins and me. Stanton—tall, trim, and orderly—carved Gram's roasts of turkey, ham, or beef, ordered inventory for the pantry, and answered the service bell when Gram rang it from the dining room. Arie—soft and round—had an ample brown bosom in which we frequently sank our teary faces. She cut my cousins and me inaugural slices of ham or turkey at Thanksgiving and Christmas if we just couldn't possibly wait any longer, and she laughed raucously as we ran circles around her at the kitchen table while she prepared our dinner.

It was Gram's order and routine, and her big kitchen table, that made her house feel like home to me and made it my safe harbor amid the swirling spontaneity of my family's noisy dwellings. It was a place where, inside the boundaries of a few clear rules, there was nothing but unconditional love. Mom sometimes called Gram a benevolent dictator, but I didn't see her that way. The fact that she structured our days gave me confidence and made me feel cared for. Her rules made sense because she followed them herself, unlike Mom, who often said, "Do as I say, not as I do," and Dad, who seemed to do anything he wanted. If, in my parents' homes, I felt an observer from the periphery, at Gram's, Kate, Susan, and I knew we were the center, even if hiding in our secret room under her stairs.

My grandfather Charles Butcher died of meningitis in 1951. Gram was sixty years old when he died, and I would know her only as an independent, strong, and single woman. She was made chair of the board of the Butcher Polish Company and spoke to Uncle Charlie and other managers at the factory regularly from her home while presiding over the quarterly board meetings. When I was little, I loved watching her sign important business papers at her desk in the library, dipping her Parker pen into her crystal inkwell, propping its lever out to suck up black liquid, pushing the lever in to seal the ink, then carving her name in careful, steady script. Then she'd pick up the page to blow the ink dry. I couldn't see why any woman wouldn't want to work from a home office and couldn't go all the way to the top.

Of the three of us, Susan was the renegade. She wore her winter coat backward, climbed over the exit bars of Boston subway stations to enter them, and brought home half-dead mice and birds to whisper them back to life. She especially loved dogs, climbing trees, and wrestling with Dikkon. She hated dressing up. "But, Gram, I can't *breathe*," she'd say when Gram bought the three of us matching smocked dresses and cinched our sashes tightly. And she detested shoes. That unfettered freedom Susan craved, along with her way with animals, would lead her to the wilds of Alaska at eighteen, where she would raise her own pack of huskies and win the Iditarod Trail Sled Dog Race four times. I wore her T-shirt with pride: ALASKA: WHERE MEN ARE MEN AND WOMEN WIN THE IDITAROD. When her face appeared on the cover of *Sports Illustrated*, I wasn't surprised, just damn proud of my zany little cousin. I knew no dream was too big, no goal unreachable, when I hung around Susan.

If, as a kid, Susan took everything grown-ups said as either true or stupidly wrong, Kate and I were quicker to see the nuanced underbelly of our extended family. We readily picked up on discord between our parents and speculated about their motives and flaws. We could talk right through a twelve-hour day, digging into our feelings, confiding in each other, testing our ideas, mining for each other's interpretations of what our families were and how we fit inside them. Kate was as creative as Mom but had real artistic talent, and she was devoted to perfection when she took on a project. She would go on to learn the carpentry trade and would hand-build several houses with her husband, customizing them with tiny drawers for stamps, spices, and teas, each with perfectly dovetailed joints and beautifully sealed with Butcher's Wax. As we grew up, I would envy both my cousins for their enormous abilities and I'd forever be grateful they were the heart sisters I'd never had.

— ∞ —

By the end of our weekend together at Gram's, our secret hiding room smelled of little-girl sweat, ground-in potato chips, and spilled ginger ale. For Saturday night supper, Gram worked on our manners, starting with our first course: a cream-of-celery soup.

"Now, girls," Gram said, "we turn our spoons outward, like this."

"It's too hard," Susan complained.

"Try again, Susan," Kate scolded, sometimes frustrated with her little sister's impatience.

"But I'll starve," Susan said, "and it makes my hand hurt."

"Susan, dear," Gram said calmly, "practice will make perfect. It's the way proper young ladies drink their soup."

"Why?" I asked, seeing Susan's point.

"When we do it this way, we are sure not to be burned by the soup and we won't spill it on our dinner clothes," Gram explained, suddenly making perfect sense out of something that had seemed odd.

After dinner, we stripped off our clothes and complained about our aching finger muscles. "Gram is a riot," I said, "but, Susan, you have to try harder to follow her rules."

"I'll never eat soup that way," Susan declared, while sticking out her bare belly and comparing hers with mine and Kate's.

"You could at least *try*," Kate insisted.

A few minutes later, with our nighties and socks on, we were sitting cross-legged on Gram's four-poster bed.

"Now, dearies, I'll hang up my dress to breathe," Gram said, placing her dinner dress in her closet.

"Breathe?" we squealed in unison, giggling at the thought.

Gram slipped into her nightgown and we followed her into the bathroom where she removed her false teeth, first the upper bridge, which sounded like a suction cup letting go, then the lower. We thought it remarkable that you could remove a part of your body and put it right back in the next day. Gram brushed her gums and returned to her bed with a glass full of water and us in tow. She dropped her teeth in the water glass, and then her words started sounding funny. Even Susan knew not to laugh, though, once Gram's teeth were out.

"Now, run along; it's time for bed," Gram said, as well as she could. We showered her with hugs and kisses, and she shooed us away.

"Remember, I love you more than tongue can tell," she said, as we scurried across the well-waxed Butcher floors and slipped around the hall corner in our socks, before jumping under the thick down comforter in the room next to Gram's. Spooning by age, we cuddled together under the quilt and whispered so Gram could go to sleep.

"Who's Tunkintell?" Susan asked.

"Third cousin?" Kate wondered.

"I don't know," I said, "but she loves us more than him!"

Chapter 9:

Electric Storms

I was eight years old in the spring of 1960, when my mother's hand slipped from mine as we crossed Boylston Street in Boston. It was six months after my weekend with Kate and Susan. I'd seen hundreds of her seizures, but not on my own and not in city traffic. Mom's body slumped toward me, like a small tree falling against another when it loses its grip in a steady rain, and then she collapsed in the street. A car honked and swerved.

That morning, we'd been at Best & Company, shopping for a new dress for me. The London Liberty with a blue satin sash spilled from its bag, too pretty to be lying in the road. The dress no longer mattered. Our weekend in Boston no longer mattered. The theater tickets in Mom's pocketbook no longer mattered. All that mattered was to get us off the street before we were hit by a truck.

Instinct took over, my body mimicking what I'd learned by watching Dad, but I was barely strong enough to get Mom's deadweight body off the road. Her stockings tore, and I scraped her legs against the curb. I placed her head on my lap and tipped it back so she wouldn't swallow her tongue. The seizure wouldn't last long—maybe a minute?—but then she'd need a nap.

"Are you all right?"

I looked up at a Saturday shopper, covered in brown fur, like a bear.

"We're fine," I said, a bright sun behind her making my eyes blurry. My first, best lie. I kept my eyes on Mom and didn't look at anyone else.

— ∞ —

My mother's first seizure came in the middle of the night when she was thirty-nine years old and I was in diapers. Dikkon was six and had just started first grade. It was 1952, the year we'd moved across the country from Hilliard Place in Cambridge to Seattle so my father, then forty-nine, could accept his first college teaching position, at the University of Washington. Teaching on a big, public university campus like UW gave him ample opportunity to invite his poet friends to visit and speak with his students. Dick Wilbur ventured west that year from Wellesley. Kenneth Rexroth drove up from San Francisco. For me, Seattle got tagged as the place Mom had her first seizure and I learned that you could swallow your tongue.

One morning, Mom woke with a sore tongue and looked in the mirror to find it morbidly blue. Dad canceled his class. My parents got Dikkon to school and me to a neighbor's house and went to the hospital, where they learned it would have been impossible to bear down hard enough on her tongue to turn it blue unless Mom's brain had seized. She was lucky, the doctors said—she could have suffocated. My parents just hoped the seizure was an unfortunate and single incident. That hope—mixed with a lot of denial—would fuel my family through forty years of epilepsy while Mom suffered thousands of seizures and I buried my fear to take care of my mom.

— ∞ —

If a seizure landed while Mom smoked a cigarette, the cigarette would drop from her fingers and burn a hole in her skirt. If she seized when reaching into the oven for a casserole, she'd fall against the oven rack and blister her hands. From nowhere, her legs might buckle and she'd fall to the floor while Dad and I stood over her like small-town lawmen pondering a dead body. Every seizure hobbled my super-energetic mother while electric currents crisscrossed her brain. Seizures made her lips smack, her legs jerk, her tongue cluck. Sometimes she drooled. Friends of mine were uncomfortable. Early boyfriends were scared away. When Mom's hand slipped from mine on Boylston Street, she'd handed me the parenting baton.

"It's just a damnable disease," she would say, rolling her eyes before getting on with her day. Her resilience never wavered; her life was too fun to be missed.

My father kept copious notes on her seizures, stacks of them scratched out on paper napkins and envelopes noting the date and time; a possible trigger, like a cigarette or a cocktail; whatever had happened just before onset: food eaten, pills ingested, poets visiting. In ninth grade, I thumbed through a stack of his notes in his study in Hanover and declared, "You're being neurotic, Dad. What do any of these change?" My own denial, wishing I could erase his sad commentary on our otherwise privileged life.

Dad used euphemisms for Mom's seizures, rarely calling them by their given name. "Your mother's had a spell," he'd say, or, "Betty's had a fit." I remember when Robert Penn Warren and his wife, Eleanor, were visiting us in Hanover in 1965, when I was fourteen. The grown-ups were in the living room, having drinks, while I floated between them and the kitchen, where Mom was finishing up her company pot roast. Suddenly, she slumped and fell. I ran for Dad, and he and I helped her upstairs for a nap.

"Well, there you have it," Dad said, returning to Red and Eleanor in the living room and lighting his pipe. "She's had another attack. Dinner will be late." My father was patient and gentle with Mom during her seizures but frustrated when his needs were pushed to second place in the family queue.

"It's a seizure, Dad. Why can't you call it what it is?" I asked, glancing at the Warrens for support. As a teenager, I bristled at his using words to sensationalize things. I stormed off to our dining room, where the thick Webster's dictionary stood on its maple pedestal. Flipping back to the start of the book, I thumbed through the *a*'s until I landed on *a-t-t-a-c-k*. I wanted badly to win this quibble with my father, but Webster's definition, I conceded, sounded exactly like what we'd just witnessed, and I returned to the living room, contrite.

An hour later, Mom came down after her nap and Dad said, "Betty's back! Now we can have dinner." It was the surprise in his voice at her return that had registered with me through my first decade. I pin my first anxiety to that tone in his voice and the very real possibility I inferred from it that one day she might not come back.

I feel like I died a thousand times with those seizures, Mom would write to a classmate after her Smith College reunion in 1974. She was sixty years old then and only halfway through her forty-year battle with the disease. I felt like she died a thousand times, too. The weight of each seizure compounded. I didn't understand them when I was little and didn't like them as a teenager. Every one of them could ruin an otherwise very good day. I assumed the role of protector, carefully watching out for impending danger, and educating strangers about epilepsy. Vigilance got imprinted like a tattoo, permanent and with its own pain. I tried to discern a minuscule movement on her face, the slightest tremble in her hands, or the first slur in her speech that might signal the onset of a seizure. If only I could predict a brewing storm, then maybe I could pull an emergency cord on a subway train before it left the station. Maybe I could get her out the exit of a theater before the show started. In Boston and New York, I created maps in my head of museum locations with restrooms, park benches in the shade, marble steps in front of a public library, hotels with sizable lobbies where we might not be noticed during a nap. I don't think it ever occurred to my mother or my father how truly frightened I was. It was never discussed.

— ∞ —

"That's it," Mom said one rainy day in April, a year after we'd been on Boylston Street. She'd been talking on the phone with my godmother, Julie Clayburgh, and had dropped the heavy black handset into its cradle with a thud. She'd been in a dreary mood for two weeks, ever since the Hanover skating pond had thawed out and ski lessons had ended. Dad and I were sitting at the kitchen table—he was catching up with the *Times*; I was doing my homework before supper. "Gretch and I are going to New York!" Mom exclaimed.

"What?" Dad said, caught off-guard by his ever-spontaneous wife. "You can't just pick up and go somewhere whenever you want."

"Why not?" Mom asked, squaring her small frame to his. "Besides, Gretch needs to see her godmother." My godmother, my grandmother, my Butcher cousins in Cambridge, or my Eberhart cousins in Chicago—all were in play when Mom wanted a weekend with me or a break from Dad; it was hard to tell which.

"How will you pay for it?" Dad asked, as if that would deter her.

"We'll use my mad money!"

I shot Mom a glance. She didn't look mad, at least not about going to New York. "What's mad money?" I asked.

"It's money that's mine that I can use whenever I want. Without asking for permission from your faaaather." By the time she'd drawn out that *a*, she'd drawn me into her two-way conspiracy, a triangulation used against Dad since he was hard-pressed to counter a double dose of assertiveness from two strong women, even if one of them was a nine-year-old girl.

"Yippee!" I said, sealing the deal.

That Saturday, Mom and I flew off in a six-seater plane out of Lebanon, New Hampshire, and watched the magic of New York City rise like self-stacking blocks from the flatland around it. She and I crowded the tiny airplane window as she pointed out the Hudson River, the Chrysler Building, the Empire State Building, the Statue of Liberty. If you keep those in your mind, she told me, you'll always know where you are. It's just an island, like the ones in Maine, she added, only with a lot of people on it.

At Julie's, we traveled by private elevator from the first-floor guest room to the fourth-floor dining and living rooms for meals. Julie and her husband, Bill, a textile executive, had become friends with Mom and Dad during their Navy years together. The Clayburghs were the only people I knew who had a private elevator inside their house. Julie was assistant to the Broadway producer David Merrick, which may have explained how Mom got good tickets to Broadway shows. We were going to *My Fair Lady* that afternoon. Julie and Mom were godmothers to each other's daughters. Jill Clayburgh, who would later become an actor, and her brother, Jim, who would become a technical designer, were city-savvy teenagers whom I emulated.

Mom wanted me to know that there was more to New York than the Upper East Side, and that Harlem was her favorite neighborhood. It was where her senses came alive as she breathed in the smells and delighted in the sights and sounds of urban America. Mom was way ahead of her time, wanting me to know the diversity of our country. We took the bus to 125th Street and walked west. Almost immediately, Mom pointed out a group of girls jumping rope. "Go ahead, Gretch—you know how."

I did know how to jump rope, but I didn't know how to jump into the middle of a group of friends who'd never met me. I felt intimidated and sure I was disappointing Mom. She could see I wouldn't budge, so she took my hand and walked me across the street and around the neighborhood, pointing out the people and things she found interesting: the saxophone player twisted into a pretzel, chasing his notes; the multicolored pants, shirts, and socks drying on a rope between two tall buildings; fast-talking mothers who could practically touch each other out their first-floor windows across a narrow alley between their apartment buildings. We stopped to watch three little boys playing jacks on the step of a grocery while an elderly couple, arm in arm, in brown wool suits, stood with us. There was garbage on the sidewalk and run-down cars at the curb, but it was the beauty of the people and how they lived so tightly packed together that Mom wanted me to see, not just the inside of a Broadway theatre.

— ᨊᨆ —

Three times a day, Mom had to swallow a handful of pills. "Argh," she'd say, screwing up her face while tossing them down with a slug of water—strong chemicals masked by cheery pastel yellows, pinks, and greens. Each must have had a purpose, but none individually, nor collectively, stopped her spells. Her seizures were like inconsolable toddlers who can't communicate their problem but let you know they're the only thing that matters. Through four decades, Mom would swallow her way through Dilantin, Tegretol, and valproic acid for seizures; Ativan and Valium for anxiety; phenobarbital and diazepam for sleep; Dexedrine, Benzedrine, and Ritalin for sleeping too much. If she missed a dose by accident or on purpose; "I'm sick of them," she'd say on occasion—her brain rarely let her get away with it. Even with the pills, her brain seized regularly.

I came home from school in Hanover one day in fifth grade to an empty house. Dikkon was at boarding school. From the age of twelve, I was virtually an only child. I looked all over for Mom— downstairs in the basement, where she'd sometimes be throwing pots on her wheel; upstairs in her bedroom, to see if she was taking a nap; outside in her gardens. She was nowhere.

Dad returned from his office on campus at five. "Where's Mom?" I asked.

He looked dejected. "She'll be in the hospital this week."

"The week?" I said, feeling equally dispirited. Why hadn't I been told?

"They're cleaning her out."

"Cleaning her out?"

"They're straightening out her pills," Dad said with a shrug.

"Can I go see her?"

"They say children aren't allowed."

"I'm not a child," I implored. "I'm her daughter."

I knew enough about hospitals to know that if you stayed for a week, it usually meant something serious. I'd overheard Mom and Dad worrying about Cal Lowell when he was admitted to McLean, the psychiatric hospital near Boston. Was Mom that same kind of sick?

— ∞ —

My mother's greatest fear was that she might pass her disease on to Dikkon or me. Regularly, she consulted neurologists at Harvard, Dartmouth, and Columbia, and each said that she was an unfortunate member of a small cohort of adult-onset epileptics whose brains had been scarred at birth by their high-forceps deliveries. The year my mother was born, 1914, cesarean section was available in Boston, but uncommon, and Mom was born at home in Cambridge. As Gram's labor intensified, then stalled, the family doctor clamped my mother's head with forceps and pulled her into the world. That action may have saved Gram's life, but it formed a tiny scar on Mom's brain, detectable in future scans. To me, treatment for her seizure disorder, from the first, in Seattle in 1951, until her death in 1993, never seemed like much more than a wild-eyed dart thrown at a stubborn board. Even with the best doctors and latest medicines, Mom rarely went a week or two without a seizure. Many weeks, she'd have three or four.

— ∞ —

After Harlem, Mom and I took the subway to the Lower West Side. Rumbling along in the dark tunnel, swaying inside the train, Mom asked if I'd liked her tour and if I remembered seeing the Statue of Liberty out the airplane window. I did. "That's what we mean when we say, 'Give me your tired, your poor, / Your huddled masses yearning to breathe free.'" She could make history come alive by linking abstract concepts to people and places I could see and hear.

At the Chelsea Hotel, where Dad stayed when he had poetry business in New York, Mom showed off the lobby—like a free art gallery, she said—and besides, we never knew who we might run into there.

"Isn't Gretch growing up?" Mom asked the clerk. My face reddened.

"She certainly is," he said. "How's Dick?"

"His new book will be out later this year," Mom said with pride.

The hotel clerk seemed like someone to tally on my list of potential helpers if I needed him. The hotel clerk, the older couple in Harlem, the English-speaking flower seller on Twenty-Second Street, the big-bellied cop on Seventh Avenue, and the white-gloved doorman on Fifth—one every couple of blocks seemed about right for my list. My vigilance would persist through decades until it took on a life of its own. I became good in emergencies, practiced at taking charge. I disallowed fear, sadness, or despair. They'd do me no good when a seizure came. It would be decades before I recognized how abandoned I felt, how alone in the world I often was to cope with Mom's illness. I could do it, but not with the emotional resources I needed to balance my instinctive will.

— ✺ —

By the end of our tour of the Big Apple, Mom and I found our way to Washington Square Park. Tulips were blooming in waves of pinks and yellows. Men were shrewdly moving chess pieces across boards. Kids were riding circles around the fountain on their bikes. Babies were out in their strollers with nannies. Mom and I bought ice cream bars from a vendor and found a place to sit on a bench.

"That's a nice little boy you have," Mom said to the man sitting next to us with his son. I noted the *New York Daily News* in his hands, with its headline about President Eisenhower. My parents never read the *Daily News*, but Mom and Julie had remarked on a similar headline in the *Times* over breakfast.

"What do you think of our president?" Mom asked.

"He's a crook, like the rest of 'em. The mayor, too. They're all crooks. Look at this place. They don't even pick up the garbage."

Julie had complained about her garbage not getting picked up on Seventy-Second Street, too, I thought.

"It's your city," Mom said. "Write to Mayor Wagner and tell him. And while you're at it, tell him about the holes in the sidewalk. This is the greatest city in the world, and these things should be fixed."

That night, after dinner with the Clayburghs, Mom and I got ready for bed and she made three wishes for me.

"I wish for you to be happy," she said, pulling my covers around me. "And I wish for you to help fix problems you see in the world."

"Like the potholes?" I asked, wondering what she had in mind.

"Yes"—Mom laughed—"but also the buildings those little children have to live in and the schools they have to go to." Mom wanted equality for all, but fixing such problems felt like a tall order.

"What's the third thing?"

"I wish for you to be brave—and unafraid. You don't need to be afraid, Gretch." I wondered if she was referring to the girls jumping rope.

"That's four, Mom," I said, "all you get," and hugged her good night.

Under my covers, I felt ashamed. Even in the quiet serenity of Julie's guest room, I couldn't tell Mom that I didn't *feel* brave and that I *was* afraid. That I'd already learned I couldn't count on Dad who hadn't protected me from Percy, and that I could only count on Mom when her brain wasn't seizing. I had no language for the feelings in the pit of my stomach. I felt as if I'd failed her a thousand times, and knew I'd fail her a thousand more. My father's response to emotional conflicts was to shrug his shoulders and walk out of the room. My mother's response was to advise me to "keep a stiff upper lip" or to "roll with the punches," but how could those help when we were about to be hit by a bus? Like a flash flood through a western canyon that leaves rubble in its wake, I could feel the underbelly of my family's response to Mom's disease, even without words. After each seizure, we'd go on as if it hadn't happened. I'd learned to think about and feel things through my father's poetry readings but was never asked or taught how to describe them. Only as an adult would it occur to me that those long-buried emotions had manifested into chronic stress.

— ∝ —

Four years after that trip to New York with Mom, she and I were back at Julie's for my February vacation week. It was 1964, and I was thirteen. We'd made it through four full days without a seizure, and on February 7, we were scheduled to fly back to New Hampshire out of JFK.

After breakfast, Julie called a taxi. She'd just told us the Beatles were landing for their first time that day on US soil. Mom and I climbed inside the car, and the cabbie gave us an earful.

"I'll get you as close as I can, but it's going to be a mess," he said, one arm gesticulating wildly in the air. "You may have to walk some."

"This is wonderful, Gretch!" Mom said, squeezing my hand. "It's historic! You'll see the Beatles!"

At the airport, three thousand screaming girls, most of them just like me, filled the sidewalks, runways, and rooftops— full pandemonium.

"You stay here!" Mom shouted once we'd made it through the outdoor mob and were inside the terminal. "I'll stall the plane!"

I watched Mom's short and sturdy legs carry her down the hall while I pressed my nose against the plate-glass window separating me from the tarmac outside. The cacophony of three thousand girls screaming was unlike anything I'd ever heard. I couldn't believe my luck. I didn't know how she would do it, but I knew Mom would charm the pilot into holding the plane. I waited and waited, and waited some more, until finally, out came George,

John, Paul, and, last, Ringo, squeezing through the door of Pan Am flight 101 from Heathrow, right before my eyes.

That's what Mom could pull off any day of the week if an electric storm didn't blow through her brain. I'd go anywhere with her for that magic. The Beatles! For moments, I could forget my vigilance and revel in being a normal girl, out in the wonderful world with my mom.

Chapter 10:

Puppy Love and Swiss Chocolates

It was three years after we moved to Hanover, and about the time my mother probably thought we'd be settled there for the five years Dad had promised, when, in 1959, the Library of Congress invited him to serve as its poet laureate. He'd turned them down the prior year. Now, he would succeed Robert Frost, as he had at Dartmouth, and my parents went forward with another relocation. The opportunity was too good to turn down, as Dad got to serve in the highest poetry post in the land, for a year under President Eisenhower, and for a second year, under President Kennedy. Mom was so excited about moving to our nation's capital, she immediately rode her bike down to Main Street and shopped for new dresses at Campion's Women's Store while sporting an I LIKE IKE button pinned to her jacket.

Georgetown felt like a small town inside a big city. Our block of Thirty-Fourth Street was bookended by two small neighborhood groceries that Mom visited daily, trying to even out her purchases between them. Being in Washington, my parents had the opportunity to invite anyone they wanted to visit, and their parties continued in our narrow living room and minuscule backyard. Marianne Moore came to visit, wearing her tricorn hat and a long black cape.

"She looks like Paul Revere," I whispered to Mom. I was keeping an eye on my mother, since the excitement of parties sometimes triggered a seizure. She was smoking a cigarette while putting a pot roast in the oven.

"I love her hat!" Mom said, not whispering.

"It makes her look like a boy."

"She can wear anything she likes. She can wear what the men wear. She certainly works as hard as they do."

Dame Edith Sitwell visited, too, with her own signature bird's nest hat and long glass earrings reflecting the sunlight of our yard as they touched her regal shoulders. She arrived with a floor-length cape over her shoulders and my father took her hand and kissed it.

"Why does she look so sad?" I asked Dad while he was fixing drinks.

"Sad?" he said, pausing before responding. "Why, isn't everyone at least a little bit sad?"

My older cousin Bill Eberhart was visiting us that week, and was made bartender for the party, which led to his passing glasses of beer to my fifteen-year-old brother. I watched from the outside steps as Dikkon swigged one after another and got so tipsy that Bill had to lead him upstairs to bed.

Dad's office at the Library of Congress was spacious, with secretaries and librarians at his beck and call. In his position, my father now had access to more people than he'd known before. He quickly organized poetry seminars for students and faculty in Washington-area universities and helped receive the king and queen of Nepal, chatting up the king, who himself dabbled in poetry. In the spring of that first year, he organized a Frost week in the auditorium at the State Department and hosted a more intimate gathering for Frost at the Library. Dikkon and I went to that one, where we met Chief Justice Warren and Senator Udall. The daughter of Eleanor Roosevelt was there—lithe at seventy years old—and told Mom that she was raised on poetry. As my father wrote to Donald Hall after the event, Roosevelt said, *Papa* roared *it. We all roared poetry as we walked through the country.* To which my father added in his note to Don, *How glad I am there is one roarer left in America!* Mom and Dad loved the glamour of Washington.

One of my father's greatest contributions to the library was a substantial expansion of its collection of recordings by contemporary poets reading their own work. Over his two years, he added more than ninety new poets to the collection, drawing from his wide network of friends, as well as recruiting those he wanted to meet.

On arrival in D.C., the librarian had discouraged my father from accepting too many invitations, which he was sure to get, but that went against Dad's grain. Instead, he said yes to all of them. Doing so put him on more than sixty stages across the country. Not only did he read from his own works, he lectured on the importance of arts in modern society, and the events led to increased book sales and greater renown. As Mom used to say, he was a small-*d* democratic poet and didn't mind reading to a women's club or in a church basement, on a university stage or in a small-town library. By making himself accessible, he built a sizable and loyal fan base. He was away so much that I felt more and more in charge of watching after Mom.

Through the fall of 1960, John F. Kennedy was running for president. He, Jackie, Caroline, and John-John lived just a few blocks from us; their house was on my walking route to piano lessons. Sometimes, after my lesson, Mom and I would stop at the park where John-John and Caroline played under the supervision of two nannies and Secret Service men. I'd seen them several times, and we'd paid no attention to each other, but one day, feeling cheeky, I got up my nerve to say something to Caroline, who was four years old at the time.

"What's your name?" I asked.

"You know my name," Caroline said, immediately putting me in my place and teaching me that fame, like everything else, is relative.

Mom bought our first TV in Washington so Dikkon and I wouldn't miss Robert Frost reading his poem at Kennedy's inauguration. Mom and Dad took a phalanx of poets with them to the balls and dinners, including Allen Tate, Cal Lowell, Katherine Anne Porter, and W. H. Auden. In a letter to J. H. McCallum, editor at Harcourt Brace, Dad wrote of that week, *We had lunch for Robert here last Thursday. I stood in front of the Capitol on cold Inauguration Day to hear him read his poem, and last night at a party in Georgetown he was in fine fettle, having seen the President yesterday noon at the White House. I asked him what Mr. Kennedy had to say. His reply was characteristic: "I did most of the talking."*

Kennedy's election signaled new enthusiasm for the arts, which emboldened my parents' final six months in Washington. Despite criticism from library personnel, my father hosted three Russian authors in the middle of the Cold War. A planned visit to the nation's capital by Nikita Khrushchev afforded a spot for the novelist Mikhail Sholokhov, author of *And Quiet Flows the Don*, the most widely read work in Soviet fiction at the time, which would win Sholokhov the Nobel Prize four years later.

Yevgeny Yevtushenko visited our house that May. In letters I found in Dad's archives, my father described Yevtushenko as *tall, handsome, open in manner and with his short-cropped blond hair and grey flannel suit, he could have passed very easily for an Ivy League college student or graduate, except for one unmistakably Russian touch: fireman red bow tie and matching bright red socks.* A ceremonial book exchange occurred, with Yevtushenko preening about the sacred place of literature in Soviet life, noting to my father that his book had sold more than 1.5 million copies. Yevtushenko was accompanied by Andrei Voznesensky, whom Cal Lowell would describe as one of the greatest living poets in any language. Dad admired the virility, the passion, and the poetry of all three Russians.

—〜〜—

I liked Fillmore, a public school on Thirty-Fifth Street, where I'd made friends with sisters, Catherine and Ioana Razi. Each classroom held two grades, so I shared third grade with fourth-grader Catherine and fourth grade with third-grader Ioana. Of Greek and Romanian descent and fluent in multiple languages, they took me under their wings, and dazzled me as they switched from one dialect to another. I spent many after-school hours enjoying their mother, Eggie's, snack of melted Belgian chocolate inside warm baguettes. Our parents became fast friends.

Despite my new chums, I felt lonely in D.C. By Christmas time, in part because Mom joked repeatedly that I was likely to get coal in my stocking that year, I'd saved up most of my allowance and walked over to Wisconsin Avenue to a shop that a friend of Eggie's owned. I bought several gifts for myself, wrapped them up, and put them under our tree. When Mom found them, she was aghast.

"But, Gretch, you didn't think I really meant it, did you?"

I had. And I was proud of taking my situation into my own hands and protecting myself from the shame of coal on Christmas morning.

— ∞ —

When the cherry trees were in full bloom, Mom invited Eggie, Ioana, and Catherine to join us for a trip to the Smithsonian. I was learning French in school and could pick out a few words of what the Razis were saying. Catherine and Ioana and I were lined up in the backseat of the car, while Eggie was in the front. Suddenly, Eggie screamed, "Betty, stop!"

Through the windshield, I watched helplessly as we drifted across the middle line. I braced my feet against the front seat for impact. I'll never know how Mom's brain engaged enough, with Eggie yelling at her, to get her foot on the brake just in time to avert a serious crash.

Later that day, back at home, I listened and watched as Mom and Dad went about their chores, trying to discern whether Dad knew. He didn't appear to. What would happen if I told him? What would happen if I didn't? What should I do? At ten years old, I felt like I was tattling on my best friend, but I didn't think I had a choice. This time, she'd endangered not just me but the Razis as well.

After dinner, Mom appeared in the living room in tears and ripped up her driver's license in front of Dad and me.

"I will *not* hurt anyone else with this dastardly disease," she said.

It was too late, I thought to myself. We'd already been hurt. We just couldn't bring ourselves to admit it.

— ⦿ —

After two years in Washington, we returned to Hanover, where I entered fifth grade and my brother went off to boarding school for the next four years. In 1962, my father was awarded the Bollingen Prize, for "many true poems and thirty years of vigorous imagination." Established in 1948 by Paul Mellon, it is awarded every other year for the best volume of poetry over that period. It was the prize that meant the most to Dad, as his peers, Malcolm Cowley, Louise Bogan, Allen Tate, Robert Lowell, and Donald Hall decided it. My father, buoyed by his Bollingen and two productive years at the Library of Congress, was in peak demand. If he'd received a couple hundred dollars per reading in the past, now he was pulling in a thousand or more. Where his audiences had mostly been less than a hundred before D.C., they now started at a thousand and stretched to ten or fifteen thousand. My mother found Hanover dull and missed the excitement of living in Washington. And with both her son and husband frequently away, I believed I was entirely in charge of watching out for her seizures.

I missed taking French, so Mom found me a private tutor to continue my conversational learning through eighth grade. By then I wanted more, and Hanover High School couldn't provide it.

"I want to be fluent," I insisted to Mom and Dad over a rare dinner on our own. "I want to be able to roll my *r*'s."

"Maybe you should study abroad," Mom mused.

"Really?" I asked.

"Well, that way you'd become fluent," Mom said.

"Betty, this is too much," Dad said. "You can't just send her halfway around the world."

Amid Dad's resistance, related to geography and cost, Mom enlisted Gram, who helped support my year of boarding school. Meanwhile, Hanover High put up its own fight. As Mom would repeatedly tell the story, my guidance counselor spoke to her as if the only rightful education was in Hanover. "You must remember, Mrs. Eberhart," he said, "Gretchen will apply to college next year. It is important that she have all the required coursework on her transcript. They surely won't equal our math or science."

"But she'll be fluent in French," Mom insisted.

"We're only looking out for your daughter," the counselor returned. "You must think of the consequences of your decision. She might not be accepted by the best colleges."

"Consequences?" Mom responded, annoyed with such small-mindedness. "I'm trying to educate her, not get her into a club."

Mom chose Château Brillantmont, a small international school for girls in Lausanne, and, at fifteen, I said goodbye to my cute, blond boyfriend and prepared to go abroad, while my father received a doctor of letters degree from Skidmore College and enjoyed good sales from his book, *Shifts of Being*. Mom was right on this one. That year would turn out to be one of the best decisions she made on my behalf, and a hopeful sign that she'd support my future goals, too. After the summer of 1966 at Undercliff, I joined my summer Barbie doll friend, Sarah, and her family on the SS *Constitution* to cross the Atlantic. Sarah's father, Perry, was taking the post of rector at Emmanuel Episcopal Church in Geneva, and the family would serve as my home away from home if I needed one.

— ◊◊◊ —

Of the seventy girls in grades nine through twelve at Château Brillantmont (now called Brillantmont International School), only a
handful were Americans. Most of their fathers were corporate
executives with Dupont or Arco, stationed in Paris or Athens. I
was immediately awakened to the reality that not all kids' fathers
were poets or novelists but were diamond mine owners and kings
in Africa. Most notable, perhaps, was Haifa Faisel, the tall, shy
princess of Saudi Arabia. At sixteen, she was already betrothed to
a young man she'd met once. We felt sorry for her as she tearfully
confided her plight.

I shared a small, third-floor walk-up room with a Swiss girl
from Zürich who spoke five languages. In that small space painted
white, we had twin beds with iron frames, a washbasin hung on
the wall, and a long-range view of the Swiss Alps out our narrow
window.

I took well to the structure and rules of boarding school,
which reminded me of Gram's house. Our days were orderly, and
meals were scheduled predictably. In Lausanne, our mornings were
devoted to reading, writing, and conversing only in French—no
English allowed through our midday meal. In the afternoon, I tried
to make good on geometry and chemistry for my Hanover transcript. Monsieur Masroff taught us geometry. My new best friend,
Lucy, from London, and I called him Maz-rot for the armpit stains
that showed on his enormous wool suit coats; coats that hung down
to his knees. At three hundred pounds, we guessed, and speaking
Swiss French with a German accent, I suspected he wouldn't have
impressed my guidance counselor.

He's disgusting, I wrote home to Mom. *His stomach hangs out
about four feet! He hasn't cleaned his jacket in years!* When Masroff
walked by my desk, I'd recoil and then burst into giggles with Lucy.
But within a few months, my feelings about him shifted, as he
turned into the kindest math teacher I'd ever had. I loved watching
him sharpen his chalk to a pencil point with his pocketknife and
then draw beautiful pastel triangles on the chalkboard. He'd label

them "*angle droit*" and "*triangle isocèle*," making simple lines sound sexy and sophisticated. As chalk dust fell below the board, his precise script and simple shapes, along with his patience, gradually made me feel less stupid in math. Besides, he seemed to like me.

"Can you believe it?" I whispered to Lucy from my desk next to hers, pointing at his elegant penmanship at the top of my page. "I got another ten!"

"You have him wrapped around your bloody little finger," Lucy hissed. "I only got a seven!"

I took Chem Lab at Lycée Jaccard, the boys' school across town, where the subject was supposedly taught to US standards. Our instructor, a short, slim Turkish chemist who wore a white lab coat and held a cigarette between his fingers, was erotic as hell. He swiveled his hips like an Argentine tango dancer, and I spun an instant crush on him, fantasizing my way onto the back of his Vespa, careening around corners, whispering French nothings in his ear. I'd be his Catherine Deneuve and he'd be my Jean-Paul Belmondo while we puffed unfiltered Gauloise cigarettes and made out passionately in smoke-filled cafés. I also had my eye on the dashing Persian boy I'd met at a Lycée Jaccard dance, with beautiful brown eyes and jet-black hair. No wonder I'd lost touch with the blond boy back in Hanover.

Our lab teacher's experiments frequently went bad, but he seemed to enjoy having things blow up in front of us. He'd lean over a concoction, daring the ash of his cigarette to drop into the beaker. When it did, the contents would pop and sizzle and he'd hop around the stage like a jackrabbit, talking so fast I couldn't understand a word he said.

"My God," I whispered to Christina, one of the American girls, from Greenwich, Connecticut, though English was forbidden in Chem Lab. "What's he saying?"

"I don't have a clue," she said.

— ❧ —

In October, my father won the Pulitzer Prize for *Selected Poems 1930-1965*. I learned about it secondhand via breathless letters from my mother, who stuffed envelopes full of US newspaper clippings. *The phone hasn't stopped ringing since yesterday,* Mom wrote. *Your father is mighty pleased.* Apparently, my next-door-neighbor in Hanover, Martha Hennessey, then thirteen, got the word from Mom and raced home to announce, "Mr. Eberhart just won the Poet's Surprise!"

The Pulitzer was a turning point for Dad. It was important to him because many of his friends had won it and it made him even more of a household name. The day he won, I learned about it from my American Lit teacher, who'd clipped the foreign wire news from the *Guardian* and *Le Monde*. Dad's win prompted in me an unwanted focus on him for the next month as we studied his poetry in English class. Other students expected me to know more about him than I did. What I knew was that I hadn't thought about him much since I'd left the States. The summer before traveling to Lausanne, I'd noticed him looking at me in ways that made me feel uncomfortable, like I wasn't his daughter. It had rattled me, but I'd put it out of my mind, busy with school in Lausanne.

Mom wrote that Dad was reading his poetry at Carnegie Hall that year as a part of a yearlong international poetry celebration, along with Denise Levertov, Dick Wilbur, Judy Collins, and Jim Dickey. Listing all the famous writers in her letters, I assumed, was meant to impress me. Mostly, I was impressed by all I was seeing and doing in Switzerland, things I could never have seen or done in Hanover.

Later, in my father's archives, I would learn how the book for which Dad won the Pulitzer came about and could understand more fully how the prize changed everything for him. It was his first paperback, an idea Jay Loughlin, his publisher at New Directions Press, floated to my father as a possible innovation, believing it would make Dad's work more accessible to a larger audience and might continue the momentum he'd been gaining since he'd been at the Library of Congress. Jay suggested my father pitch the idea to his primary publisher, Oxford University Press, but Oxford's editors turned down the idea categorically. By their standards, poetry was meant to be between hard covers. Dad returned that news to Jay, who promptly offered to publish it himself at New Directions. That summer, Loughlin, who had planned a monthlong trip to Italy to stay at the home of Ezra Pound, carried all of Dad's books in his luggage and, on arrival at Pound's, pored over them, selecting the poems he thought best for a paperback. The result was a slim volume with good sales from the start. After it received the Pulitzer, it sold thousands of copies per month, leveling off only after its fifteenth year and ninth print run. My father had a good eye for opportunity and took a risk on Jay's foresight. Dad was forever grateful to Jay, and the two would continue as collaborators. I think my father enjoyed pulling that very successful book out of Oxford's ancient hands and giving New Directions a Pulitzer Prize.

— ⚬⚬⚬ —

Brillantmont's bedtime rule was lights out at 10:00 p.m., but Lucy and I broke it regularly. She or I would gather our third-floor mates in her room and whisper into the night, switching back and forth between English and French. We convinced Princess Faisal to unlock her special trunk full of royal garments and jewels. We were impressed. One of those nights, Lucy and I got everyone to strip to our bras and panties and pose for Instamatic camera shots, pretending we were runway models or recruits to the international sex trades. Luce, as I called Lucy, and I were obsessed with the sex trades, on which the press reported widely in Europe and the States. On our afternoons out for shopping in Lausanne and Geneva, we schemed about how we'd avoid being snatched.

"I read all about it in *Cosmo!*" Lucy informed the gang.

"And *Paris Match*," I added. "If we're kidnapped, Luce and I are going only as a pair."

"They'll auction us off to the highest bidders," Lucy said, her arm around me, "from Turkey or Africa, but we'll only be taken together."

Lucy was tall, straight, and thin, with long brown hair down to her waist. I was short, with curves and a curly blond mane. She was Brit, I was Yank. She said things like "bloody" this and "bloody" that, "I don't give a piss," and "what a rat's ass." I'd never met anyone as fully wonderful as she.

"Boarding schools are such a bloody retch!" she whisper-yelled across her bed. She knew firsthand because she'd lived in them most of her life; religious schools, where she'd blown out the sacred candles in the convent and perfected the practice of stealing money from the plate one week to repay it the next. "Take it out of my allowance? That's just bloody stupid!"

One night, Luce and I snuck out of school after 10:00 p.m. Our destination was the little kiosk six blocks down rue Secrétan, with its cigarettes and postcards and piles of Swiss chocolates. We tiptoed down the narrow back stairwell and scaled the eight-foot stone wall with locked gates that surrounded the schoolyard.

"Give me a lift," I whispered.

"Oh, posh," she said, impatiently interlacing her fingers for my foot. I pulled myself up and over and leaned back to give Lucy a hand. We dropped off the other side and raced to the kiosk.

"*Qu'est-ce que vous aimeriez, mes filles?*" the elderly Swiss lady in the kiosk asked, standing inside her six-foot-square store. By second semester, she didn't need to ask. She knew what we wanted.

"*Une tablette de chocolat noir, s'il vous plaît,*" I practically yelled, hoping that confidence in French might get me credit if our headmistress found out.

"*Trois carambars pour nos amies,*" Lucy barked.

"*Et les têtes-de-nègre là. Ils sont mes préférés!*" Although the name of the fluffy marshmallow confection covered in dark Swiss chocolate embarrassed me, it was my favorite.

Back at school, we carried our shoes and tiptoed over the gravel in our bare feet, then pressed our shoulders up the stairwell, *shh*-ing each other to stop giggling. We were convinced we'd be thrown out if caught.

"Back to Hanover? No way!"

"To London and my stepmother? Are you bloody sot?"

For spring break, Brillantmont offered two trips for those of us who couldn't get home—one that would take us through Italy, the other through Egypt. I chose the latter, figuring anyone could get to Italy. My father, preoccupied with his Pulitzer, rarely wrote to me that year, but he was opposed to the trip. *It's too far-flung*, he wrote by hand on a piece of typewriter paper, *and too dangerous*. None of the Middle Easterners I knew in school seemed dangerous, and Mom liked my logic. While thirty-five girls selected Italy, twelve of us picked Egypt, and with two teachers we flew to Cairo. I was instantly shocked by abject poverty next to unimaginable wealth. Legless beggars lay in a gutter across from the brand-new Hilton Hotel, which we convinced our teachers we needed to visit to eat hamburgers. Packs of children chased after us, demanding Swiss francs. Prostitutes circled grand stone monuments, a thousand years old. It was intense and intoxicating. With eyes and ears wide open, I listened to the day's fifth call to prayer, heard across the city, while celebrating my sixteenth birthday in Cairo.

—⁂—

My favorite place in the capital was the Khan el-Khalili souk. Centuries old, with its extensive rabbit warren of alleyways, it was easy to get lost in, among the hundreds of stalls with enormous dye vats standing next to skeins of drying wool; carpets of every color, shape, and size hanging on the stone walls; spices that rocked my senses laid out in rows of baskets; and intricate carvings of alabaster gracing hundreds of shelves. I was mesmerized, but my sense of direction, necessitated by my mind-mapping when out with Mom, was keen, so I quickly figured out how to get around.

On my first day, I happened on a friendly, French-speaking Egyptian tailor named Nagui Azia and struck up an easy friendship in his dress shop, where I ordered two *djellabas*, the traditional men's caftan, one for me and one for Mom, thinking they'd make good nightgowns. Every day of our week in Cairo, I returned to Nagui's shop to try on the garment so he could adjust it. Nagui was well educated and good looking. He promised my djellabas would be ready for our return through Cairo at the end of our trip. We had fun speaking in French, and it was clear we liked each other, though, looking back, maybe he saw in me only a possible escape from the medina.

Over the next two weeks, we saw the rest of Egypt, riding camels across the desert, tenting with Bedouin families, exploring archeological sites at Luxor, and sailing down the Nile to the new dam at Aswan. Back in Cairo, I retrieved my tailoring and bid a fond adieu to Nagui. I doubted I'd ever see him again, but who knew—life was open, and so was I. Two weeks later, in the salon at school, we turned on the scratchy black-and-white TV and watched Israel drop bombs on Nagui's beautiful homeland. It was June 1967, the start of the Six-Day War.

I couldn't make sense of it, nor could my school friends. They educated me on how much war there was in the world, most of which I didn't know and hadn't learned about in Hanover. While Israel was bombing the children of Egypt, I did know that the United States was bombing the children of Vietnam and occupying the Dominican Republic. Girls from Guatemala and Indonesia spoke of wars in their countries as the reason they were sent to school in the safety of Switzerland. Teachers widened my perspective further by detailing atrocities in North Yemen and the Congo. My classmate Carmen's older brother was killed in Vietnam. War was everywhere, I was learning, and it formed a backdrop to the end of my year in Lausanne.

I tuned in to Ayn Rand and stayed up late talking with girls about history and politics. I noted in a letter to Mom, *I want answers about war. What's wrong with you adults? Would you want me blown up? Is ideology more important to parents than their own children?*

Mom's letters cataloged growing unrest in the States, as college students were taking to the streets and police were fighting

back. She'd recently been in San Francisco, visiting Marie Rexroth (then divorced from Kenneth) and sent clippings from the
San Francisco Chronicle of the peace march they'd joined. While
Mom's worldview was progressive, she was also perplexed by the
radical changes taking place around her. Still, her curiosity rarely
failed her. She and Marie spent a day doing their own form of
social research in Haight-Ashbury, interviewing real hippies, as she
called them, to figure out who they were and what they wanted.
She reported on this in a long letter to her college friends that I'd
find decades later in my father's archives. She disliked the *vague
and nameless fears that go with raising the young in this age of LSD,
long hair, strange clothing, and the pill,* but concluded that *the hippies mostly just want peace and love, and what could be wrong with
that?* To me, she wrote, *You're asking all the right questions, Gretch,
and you should continue your education at a US boarding school,
like Concord Academy or Abbot.*

Concord Academy? Abbot? To a small, provincial, girls-only
school? What could they possibly have on Château Brillantmont
and Lausanne? I knew we couldn't afford for me to stay in Lausanne, but I had no interest in American boarding schools. As
the year ended, I was tiring of the cliques in an all-girls school
and I wanted my own bedroom. I would miss Lucy terribly, but I
was ready to go home. I lobbied my case to Mom and to Dikkon,
then a sophomore at Dartmouth, who got dragged into the family
conflict from his dorm room, first reading my letters to him and
then listening, by phone, to our mother's worries. Finally, Dikkon
wrote me a long letter about growing up. *I've been put in the role
of judge in this fight over your future, but I think you should be old
enough to make your own mistakes. And I have faith that you will
make worthwhile ones.* That was what I wanted: to make my own
worthwhile mistakes. I used that in my final argument to Mom: *For
the millionth time, I don't want to go to Abbot or Concord. Everyone
except you and Dad is on my side. What I want most is my own room.
I want my own room.*

In letters, I tried to prepare my parents for who I'd become. I'd traded black watch blouses for European knits. I'd turned in my flat shoes for toeless heels. I'd learned how to apply makeup and style my curly hair. I'd weighed in at forty-six kilos. My body was shaping into that of a young woman. The Persian boy I was dating at Lycée Jaccard was headed to the University of Pennsylvania, and we promised we'd see each other stateside. I continued French flirting with Nagui in Cairo by way of thin blue airmail letters. I'd stamped my passport through a dozen countries. I had no idea where I was headed, but I sensed it was in a new direction. And I was fluent in French, both reading the full text of *Rouge et Noir* by Stendhal and dreaming in my new language. I wanted my mother and father to take notice.

I've changed, I wrote in my last letter before flying back to the States. *Get ready. Don't expect me to be the same.*

Chapter 11:

Biding My Time

There's a picture of me having just landed at JFK on Swissair flight 120 from Geneva on June 30, 1967. I'm dressed in a red corduroy miniskirt and a red-white-and-blue-striped knit shell. My eyelids are shaded sky blue, my lashes brushed in brown. A leather bag I purchased on a shopping trip with Lucy hangs from my shoulder. The look on my face is a mix of confidence and apprehension. Maybe it was the effect of two flutes of champagne on our flight home, the Swiss drinking age being sixteen. The plane was abuzz with American girls returning from our years abroad. We'd dined on chicken cordon bleu and helped a classmate blow out candles on her birthday cake, both prepared fresh onboard.

Mom greeted me with a warm hug and said, "I *love* your new clothes." She'd taken notice.

My father looked me up and down, took me in his arms, tilted me backward, and smacked a long, wet kiss on my lips. Instantly, I knew I was in trouble. His exuberance and charm, once engaging to a little girl, now felt sexual. His eyes gleamed as he said, "Welcome home, our Lausanne sophisticate!" More ingenue than sophisticate, I had no intention of being his pet prize. I'd known I would need to resume watching out for my mom, but, for different reasons, now I had to watch out for Dad, too.

— ∞ —

Mom had painted my bedroom in Hanover a bright, sunny yellow and covered my white spool bed in dotted Swiss. I'd wanted my own room and appreciated her updates; she had made the space feel warm and welcoming.

I spent the next two years in my small and insular hometown. I was more interested in what was going on in the larger world, where Janis Joplin was demanding her place alongside Jagger and Hendrix, college students were shutting down their schools, Aretha Franklin was singing for respect, and Huey Newton and Bobby Seale were feeding poor kids in San Francisco while taking their Black Panther message to the streets. Mass arrests, brutality, and deaths of black men were exploding in ghettos across Newark, Milwaukee, Detroit, and Buffalo. Joan Baez was arrested for blocking the Oakland induction center. Meanwhile, Allen Ginsberg and Gary Snyder were levitating the Pentagon. In 1968, the country to which I'd returned would witness the assassination of Martin Luther King Jr. and would itself massacre five hundred innocent Vietnamese at My Lai. Mom and I hovered over Walter Cronkite every night at six o'clock. The news was disturbing and riveting, and I wanted to be part of it, whatever it was. Lucy wrote from London, asking what was wrong with the "bloody States." My country was at a fever pitch, uncontainable in its present form.

Old friends in Hanover were focused on sports, making out, and stealing each other's boyfriends. In truth, they'd just moved on from me that year, and, equally, I'd moved on from them. While a war raged outside our doors, I had one raging inside me, as my father's wet kiss had been repeated. Hanover High School had just instituted one of the first open campuses in the country, which meant I didn't need to be in the building unless I had class. Dikkon and his theatre-major friends at Dartmouth were welcoming as we hung out at the Hopkins Center drinking Cokes and eating french fries. I wished I could live with them.

New friends Barb and Prue helped get me through. They'd each arrived from other cities and brought with them new ways of being. Barb and I crisscrossed the college campus on our bikes after dark, visually stalking Dartmouth undergrads in their well-lit dorm rooms and building serial crushes. Prue was beautiful and smart and, she'd tell me much later, focused mostly that year on getting laid. I dabbled in local boyfriends but was confused about sex, while Dad kept trying to land his lips on mine. My platonic affair with the Persian boy at Penn was on slow simmer. Nagui Azia wrote loving letters from Cairo in broken French: *Je vous aimez de tous mon Coeur, parce que elle son gentil et joli.*

—⚬—

Mr. Mazroff's patience in Lausanne didn't carry over to my math teacher in Hanover, and I struggled. Next door was Mr. Hennessey, who nearly daily simplified the concepts for me until I understood them. My father was still in high demand from the Pulitzer and frequently away on reading trips. When he was home, I tried to stay out of his way.

During those last years of high school, my father had numerous visits from poets and writers who co-taught his classes or read on the Dartmouth campus, and two of them affected me significantly. The first was Allen Ginsberg, who, with his partner, Peter Orlovsky, appeared unexpectedly at our kitchen door around suppertime after the Hanover Inn turned them away for lodging. With no other option in town, the men walked over to Webster Terrace and knocked on our door.

"What?" Dad said. "How could they turn you away?"

"Well, they did," Peter said. "So, Betty, we are at your mercy."

"It's settled—you'll stay here," Mom said. "Gretch, come help me show Allen and Peter the guest room."

Mom set off at a near run, dashing upstairs while Peter, Allen, and I tried to keep up with her. I showed them the small room off the hallway, with its odd location for a light switch, and the bathroom they'd be sharing with me. I couldn't wait to call Barb and Prue. Ginsberg was a rock star.

That evening over dinner, I settled into an easy conversation with Peter and Allen about our travels. They'd just returned from India and asked probing questions about my year abroad, better questions than anyone had asked since I'd returned home. They were intrigued that I was reading Ayn Rand and had interest in Karl Marx. They asked about my travels to London and Milan, Zurich and Cairo. As New Yorkers, they pined for the precision of Swiss trains and we laughed at the rules I'd broken at school. It was the souk in Cairo they were most interested in, along with the mosques and minarets, and the Bedouins in their tents. I was keen to hear them describe the cacophony in Calcutta, where cows and bicycles and taxis all competed for space on the road. They introduced me to Buddhism. Peter was the warmer and more relatable, and I liked him immediately. Allen was headier, with a fast-moving and fascinating mind, and clearly the smartest one in the room. Listening to Buddhist monks chanting had invoked in his mind the poem-songs of William Blake. That led to a quick back-and-forth with Dad. Except for that exchange, my father recedes into the background in memory of that night. Peter and I talked US politics. Allen had friends to introduce me to. Ginsberg quoted an inspiration he took from Swami Sivananda, who said something like "let your heart be your guru." I felt validated as a young woman for my intelligence and fresh perspectives. Ginsberg and Orlovsky had seen me.

As we cleared dishes together, Peter invited me to New York and Allen recommended I continue my education on world cultures by reading *The Bhagavad Gita* and *The Tibetan Book of the Dead*. Each was present, direct, and authentic—all good characteristics I might have looked for in men.

— ∞ —

I'd learn in my studies at Rauner that my father first met Allen at a poetry reading in New York in the 1940s, when Allen, as Dad wrote to his friends, *came across a smoke-filled room, sat at my feet, and told me how much* [my father's poem] *"The Groundhog" had meant to him.* A decade later and one month after we moved to Hanover in 1956, the *New York Times Book Review* commissioned my father to investigate the West Coast Beat poets to explain to the Eastern literary establishment what they were about. Dad's innate curiosity made him the perfect ambassador.

My father connected with friends he had in the West already, like Theodore Roethke and Kenneth Rexroth, who in turn introduced him to others. *The West Coast is the liveliest spot in the country in poetry today*, my father wrote in "West Coast Rhythms," his article for the *Times Books Review. It is only here that there is a radical group movement of young poets. San Francisco teems with them.*

In San Francisco, my father met Lawrence Ferlinghetti, Kenneth Patchen, and Robinson Jeffers and visited again with William Carlos Williams and Denise Levertov. In Seattle, Roethke connected him with Stanley Kunitz, Carolyn Kizer, William Matchett, and Richard Hugo. Many of those poets were not yet published. My father predicted they wouldn't remain so for long. *However unpublished they may be, many of these young poets have a numerous and enthusiastic audience. They acquire this by their own efforts. Through their many readings they have in some cases a larger audience than more cautiously presented poets in the East. They have exuberance and a young will to kick down the doors of older consciousness and established practice in favor of what they think is vital and new.*

Dad's article praised the twenty-nine-year-old Ginsberg as the most exciting in the group. *The most remarkable poem of the young group, written during the past year, is* Howl. *This poem has created a furor of praise or abuse whenever read or heard. It lays bare the nerves of suffering and spiritual struggle. Its positive force and energy come from a redemptive quality of love, although it destructively catalogs evils of our time, from physical deprivation to madness.*

Before the article came out in the *Times* on September 2, Ginsberg had written to Dad: *Kenneth Rexroth tells me you're writing an article on SF poetry and had asked for a copy of my MSS. I'll send it. I sat listening to you sans objection in the car while you told me what you'd said in Berkeley. I was flattered and egotistically hypnotized by the idea of recognition but really didn't agree with your evaluation of my own poetry. Before you say anything in the* Times, *let me have my say.* On a long bus ride from San Francisco to Portland, Oregon, Allen hand-wrote a thirty-five-page letter to my father, and followed it later with a two-page, typed summary. The handwritten original, which I would read at Rauner Library in 1996, is a recitation of displeasure with Dad's critique of *Howl*, penned with drawings to illustrate his points: *The poem is really built like a brick shithouse. This is the general ground plan—all an accident, organic, but quite symmetrical, surprisingly. It grew out of a desire to build up rhythm using a fixed base to respond to and elongating the response, still, however, containing it within the elastic of one breath or one big streak of thought.*

Despite Allen's and my father's differing interpretations of *Howl*, Dad insisted that Ginsberg and the Beats be recognized for their openness to experimentation and their all-out appreciation of the poetic form. It's possible my father's article launched multiple poetry careers. It helped launch Ginsberg's, as Allen told me over dinner. One month after Dad's article came out in the *Times*, *Howl* was published in a small paperback print run by City Lights Books, the San Francisco bookstore where my father had heard Allen read it. Ten years later, City Lights Books had sold 126,000 copies of *Howl*, an unheard-of accomplishment for a tiny publisher or a contemporary poet at the time. Later translated into twenty-two languages, *Howl* would become one of the most widely read books of the twentieth century.

As my next summer approached, I informed Mom I wouldn't spend it in Maine. While the war raged on the streets outside our walls, the one with my father continued. I'd walk out of my room to find Dad exiting my bathroom, which he used for the tub, with his robe untied and nothing under it. Was he oblivious to me? "Dad," I yelled, and turned back to my room. I didn't want to be at Undercliff with him. He'd never conversed with me about what I'd learned abroad. He didn't inquire about what I was considering for college. I felt isolated and alone in his company. Mom pressed me for a reason I didn't want to go to Maine, and I demurred, insisting I just wanted to do something interesting that summer. Together, she and I found a project for high school students run by the American Friends Service Committee and I spent that summer in Owatonna, Minnesota.

Two weeks into the project, on a Saturday morning, I leaned back against a worn-out sofa, one of a half dozen we'd borrowed for our makeshift meeting room. I looked around at my summer companions and wondered if we were up to the task. Nineteen of us, ages fourteen to eighteen—racially, religiously, and economically different—were holed up in that room, planning a strategy to get us into the migrant work camps owned by the Owatonna Canning Company. Paid two cents per pound, the Mexican-American farm workers were there for the growing season to pick strawberries and asparagus and to work in the canning factory. Any children under age ten were often left on their own and were chronically behind in school. We would tutor them and try to interest their parents in thinking about family planning.

The mayor of Owatonna, along with half the residents in town, the owners of the canning company, all but one of the eighteen Christian churches, and a healthy sector of the local business community, was opposed to our assistance. *A bunch of hippies*, we were called in letters to the editor of the local newspaper, as well as *Hells Angels*, *radicals*, and *weirdos*. The mayor was quoted as saying,

I've got a bet with my buddy that most of the girls will be pregnant by the end of the summer.

Sixty miles south of Minneapolis, Owatonna was a small city of twenty thousand people. Its mayor had proclaimed to a reporter that the town had *no integration problems, no Semitism, no bias of any type*—which seemed to me and my new friends a sure bet that it did. Our group was made up of Jews, Quakers, Christians, agnostics, and atheists. We were brown, black, Asian, and white. That summer became a case study in how to work as a team within a homogeneous town that didn't like the way we looked. My summer family's open decision-making process gave me a new lens for evaluating my family of origin. I'd moved on from the clear structure and rules of Gram's and at boarding school to a group engaged in finding its own structure and rules, with light guidance from our adult leaders.

In the cavernous, abandoned lumber warehouse we'd rented from the Salvation Army, the couches almost looked new. Over the first couple of weeks, while we waited for the canning company to allow our involvement, we did the easy things, like splitting into small teams to take care of our collective needs. We'd set up a weekly budget and planned, shopped for, and prepared our meals. We'd established girls' and boys' dorm rooms in two bays of the warehouse. We'd scrounged furniture for our meeting room and had created a makeshift kitchen. That morning, we still needed an effective strategy to get into the camps.

"We should attack from multiple angles," said Margie, a blond Quaker from Philadelphia.

"Legally, to start," said Scott, our most ardent brother.

"Legally, but also with education," Harvey said, tempering Scott. "We've got to build connections better than we have." I was building a crush on Harvey, a whip-smart Jewish boy from Scarsdale with soft brown eyes and a heart full of compassion.

Slumped nearly horizontal on our circle of sofas, with our bare feet pointed inward, we were just kids in cutoffs and denim work shirts, wedged against each other while we examined the false premise of Owatonna's church-front facade. The local newspaper had taken up our cause, and so had Molly Ivins in her first job out of journalism school, at the *Minneapolis Tribune* (now the *StarTribune*). Ivins had driven sixty miles south to poke around at what was going on in Owatonna. One of her first articles, titled "Hippies or Helpers, Owatonnans Can't Agree," was about us. Her piece generated a firestorm of response in the Minneapolis and Owatonna papers. Residents called us a disgrace to the community, with our long hair and sex-fueled minds. We rarely read support, except for one townsperson who called us a group of youth just trying to do something useful with our summer.

Nancy sat upright, crossed her legs under her, and made a second pitch for starting with legal action. We talked strategy, debated tactics, and mapped out a plan. We broke it into small bites and pledged to evaluate progress at twice-weekly family meetings. I felt liberated by this work, a self-managed conversation between hormonally charged teenagers with high ideals and instant mutual affection. Our leaders, graduate students from the University of Michigan, and a professional community developer, held back until we needed a push or a prod or a broader context; then one of them would lean into our circle and give us their perspective. Once we had our plan mapped out, we split into teams for legal, educational, social, and relational efforts, the sum total of which we hoped would pry open the canning-company gates. We met with the less friendly churches to see if they'd budge, using "love your neighbor" as an argument. They wouldn't. We met with the friendliest one of the churches, which came around and helped us collect tutoring materials for the migrant families' children. We had only eight weeks. That summer I felt like I was living at the Hennesseys' house, where both parents and their kids had voices.

Quickly, the Minnesota ACLU came to our aid and brought with it the US district attorney of Minnesota. He wrote to the canning company, reminding them that *outside visitors are entitled to come into migrant camps if there is no breach of peace and if the migrants welcome them. The canning company has no right to keep them out. Freedom of speech and assembly are involved.* One week after receiving that letter, company management conceded to an agreement with us, but they still believed the migrants didn't want our help. Okay, we said, let us test that theory after you let us in.

— ∞ —

Harvey and I posed a problem for our leaders. Our affection was obvious. I was attracted to his brain and the way he treated me with respect. He liked my humor, as it lightened his intense drive. Our leader, David, pulled the two of us aside one evening after dinner. David had no issue with our friendship but didn't want us separating ourselves from the group. I listened to what he said and how he said it. He conveyed caring for Harvey and me as individuals, and he understood that we were becoming a pair, all the while advocating for the needs of the family at large. I'd never seen or heard such clarity about responsibility in relationships. I took from David that communication mattered in much more than just poetic form.

Halfway through the summer, while a hot sun bore down on southern Minnesota, we flung open the huge doors of our "offices" in the lumberyard, physically removing the barrier between us and the community. Slowly, day by day, people started dropping in to check us out and to talk, just as my mom had done with the hippies in San Francisco. Slowly, the papers stopped reviling us. We'd established a successful tutoring program in the first work camp and were getting a few parents to consider family planning. The migrant workers saw us as trustworthy and confided in us. They weren't happy with their conditions, their wages, or the plight of their children, for whom they wanted better lives. We promised the workers that a community-based committee would carry on our work after we left. Thirty residents of Owatonna expressed interest. We'd collectively managed what had seemed like a daunting set of obstacles and were leaving Owatonna changed. Lieutenant Shelby, of the Salvation Army, a strong supporter of our efforts from the start, would chair the community committee, and we had faith in him. As we departed, he wrote to the mayor of Owatonna, *Molly Ivins earned her brownie points, for she stirred up our community. Local citizens say the migrants are happy as they are. It recalls the old cliché about the happy darkies strumming their banjos in the slave quarters.*

I said good-bye to Harvey and left Owatonna in cutoff jeans, quite unlike what I'd worn coming home from Switzerland. I'd seen firsthand how desperately U.S. farmworkers live and how hard they worked. I'd learned first lessons in building relationships with mutual respect and responsibility, lessons I should have learned at home. I'd seen that I could be a leader and that power came in collaboration and engagement, both in our group and with management of the canning company. On my flight back to New Hampshire from Minneapolis, I was hopeful that the confidence I'd brought from Lausanne, combined with the gritty hard work and team-building skills I'd gained in Owatonna, would serve me well. I would bide my time for one more year in Hanover.

— ✺ —

Dad seemed increasingly unable to deal with me and I felt increasingly out of sorts with his eyes on me. On Thursday nights, when hand-picked seniors sat in our living room for their poetry seminar, I cranked up my record player and listened to Bob Dylan, Joan Baez, Laura Nyro, Jeff Beck—the louder, the better.

"Gretchen Eberhart, turn down that music!" Dad yelled from the bottom of the stairs one evening. I was intentionally interrupting his salon.

Except to teach his classes, my father was frequently out of town. Mom and I cooked dinners together and read aloud long articles in the Sunday *Times Magazine*. We gravitated to the ones about Vietnam, the world, and the waning days of her generation, while I was impatient to get on with mine. After reading *The*

Feminine Mystique, by Betty Friedan, Mom told me the world was mine to conquer. Meritocracy, she assumed, would allow me to be equal with men. I loved my mom but never confided in her. She could be as indiscreet as my father with personal information. Trusting her with what I was really wrestling with about boys, college, sex, and her husband wasn't on my list.

Dad's volume of sonnets written for Louise Hawkes came out that year, and he spent a month at Yaddo, the writing retreat in Saratoga Springs, on whose board he served. He went there whenever he put together poems for a new book; that year it was for *Shifts of Being*. Mom was preparing our house for a presidential campaign stop by Eugene McCarthy. Square-jawed Secret Service men circled our yard, talking into microphones on their wrists. Dad returned from Yaddo just in time for the event. I ran into him in the kitchen, where he was pouring himself a tall bourbon. He turned around and caught me on my mouth. Really? Why was he doing this? I wiped off my lips and stomped out of the room. I had no strategy for dealing with him, except to avoid. He was the center of our gravitational field and no one besides me seemed to notice his behavior.

My friend Pam's parents owned a popular motel across town, and she and I sometimes camped out in one of the rooms when they weren't full. Decades later, at a high school reunion, when I confessed to Pam about my father, I asked if she'd noticed anything. "What I noticed," she said, "was that you never wanted to go home."

One weekend in the early fall of my senior year, Pam introduced me to an out-of-town friend of hers named Jeff. Following a late night of heavy necking in my parents' living room after they'd gone to sleep, he asked me to marry him. Headed to boot camp in Alabama, he wanted a wife. For ten minutes, I considered his proposal. The impulse to leave Hanover was attractive. Maybe I could levitate myself out of the house, I joked to Jeff, the way Ginsberg was levitating the Pentagon. But Jeff was joining the war machine I was against, and besides, was teenage marriage—or any marriage—what I wanted? Weren't we women supposed to do something more important? I wanted to meet more people like the friends I'd made in Owatonna. I wanted to take my fluency in French and classical piano and see what I could make of myself in the world. I wanted away from my father. I told Jeff, no thank you.

Chapter 12:

Poetic License

The day is as clear to me now as it was half a century ago. An unusually warm, late-fall afternoon in Hanover. There was a lot happening that afternoon inside the house, so I'd taken my homework out to Dad's study, separated from the house by a small porch, where I could work alone. I heard laughter coming from outside and opened the room's heavy door to find my father and a small entourage of tweed-jacketed English professors circling Anne Sexton like planets around a literary sun. Anne saw me on the porch and took our steps like she owned them. She was lit up with fame, having won the Pulitzer Prize six months earlier. Striking and exotic, with jet-black hair and eyes, she radiated both sexual and intellectual energy. She brought her cigarette to her red-painted lips, sucking in air.

"Hello, Gretchen!" she said, reaching out her hand for mine, her neck tilted like the mast of a sailboat in a stiff breeze. Her eyes pierced mine. "I'm Anne."

Sexton was wearing a fitted, sleeveless shift and a string of pearls around her neck. A cardigan rested on her shoulders. A poetic Jackie Kennedy. Outside Hanover, women were burning their bras and protesting the patriarchy. Sexton, well-coiffed and prototypically feminine, seemed to carry her weight just fine. She was smoking, breathless, a little fidgety.

There'd been a buzz around the house that afternoon. My father had shown up with the car trunk full of liquor and asked me to help unload. As we carried the boxes inside, he had given me a quick rundown on Sexton, what he thought of her poetry, that she was thirty-nine years old and had already tried to kill herself twice. Dad often underlined alarming facts; his description didn't shock me. Mom's pot roast had been simmering on the stove, its rich broth wafting through the house each time my father and I had opened the door and brought in more boxes of booze.

On the porch, my father's attraction to Anne was obvious, as I noticed him looking at her the same way he'd been looking at me. She seemed attracted, too, but, at twenty-four years his junior, maybe it was like that of a rising star for an elder statesman who'd been kind to her with his words.

The sun barely had enough strength to scale the tall trees around our backyard, but I fixated on their shadows across the porch floor, not sure what to say.

"How are you, Gretchen?" Anne asked, drawing me in. "I hear you're back from school in Switzerland?"

"Yes," I stumbled, taken by her looks and star power.

"What are you studying? Can they possibly equal your French?"

"No." I laughed. "They can't. But they're letting me take French at Dartmouth, so that helps." Dartmouth had an arrangement for town kids to take classes on campus if they'd exhausted what was available at the high school. I'd placed into a senior French seminar with eight boys; Dartmouth was not yet co-ed.

— ∞ —

Many years later, when I'd read through my father's correspondence with Anne, I'd learn that Dad had sent her a congratulatory note on winning her Pulitzer, the year after he'd won his. *What high news today of your Pulitzer!* Dad wrote. *Congratulations! Now we shall lie together on the same page for years to come!* How like my father, I thought, then, as an adult, his innuendo likely intended.

He'd written a blurb for her first book, *All My Pretty Ones*, and had recommended her for a Guggenheim fellowship, which she'd received. *Thank you, thank you, thank you,* Anne wrote to Dad with the same breathlessness I'd witnessed on our back porch. *I got the Guggy!*

I didn't go to her reading that night, but I'd find my father's written introduction to her in his archives. He traced the history of women poets, noting that in the original, 1900 version of *The Oxford Book of English Verse*, which included the best poems from 1250 to 1900, the audience would have to read through 396 poems before it came to the first by a woman. *Today there are so many good women poets that I cannot name them all. They have the franchise, the education, and the imagination to equal men in poetry and this will be true into the future.* Known for his support of up-and-comers like Sexton, Denise Levertov, Maxine Kumin, and Adrienne Rich, he'd also long revered veterans like Marianne Moore, Edna St. Vincent Millay, Gwendolyn Brooks, and Elizabeth Bishop. To Anne's crowd, Dad recounted his first meeting with Sexton and Kumin in a poetry workshop organized by the poet John Holmes, in Cambridge, in the late 1950s. Anne and Maxine were so dedicated to their craft, they put the men to shame. About Sexton's poetry, Dad concluded, *She has been able to penetrate to the centrality of her experience and communicate this directly to us. We get the message. We believe in her because we too are alive and suffer, each in our own way.*

Anne's sex appeal, tied to her equally evident intelligence, gave me an idea that afternoon that something beyond just puppy love might be in my future, too. She tethered the politics of the moment—in which women were demanding their space alongside men—to something I could see, touch, and feel. It wasn't just about burning our bras or marching in the streets, I realized that afternoon; we'd have to *do* something with that power once we seized it.

Later that night, I went down to our living room to say good night to Anne. The house was pressed to the walls with people.

Every room was filled with smoke, and glasses and bottles were everywhere. Anne, who'd been impressed by the Dartmouth students she'd met, was working the room, high from her reading, at the top of her game. Poets and writers, professors and students, friends and unknowns—it was my parents' usual crowd, multiplied by ten. Anne tossed her head back when she saw me, and I felt drawn in. I wish I could have sat her down and asked for advice, for answers to my questions, for something. She craned her long neck, as she had that afternoon. "Oh, Gretchen," she said enthusiastically. "I'm so glad to have met you. Good luck with your French. Good luck in your life!"

There was an electricity in the house that night fueled by Anne's star power, along with a hundred literary-minded people drinking it in. Later, when I would look back from the perspective of many decades, it would be hard for me to imagine how all that energy could possibly have been contained. Just like the world outside Hanover, our house was bursting at the seams. The place was ripe with potential, and the liquor shelf was wide open.

— ∞ —

Upstairs in my room, I closed my bedroom door, turned off my bedside light, and rolled over on my stomach. I pulled the dotted Swiss spread over my shoulders and thought, *I'll be out of here soon.* Sexton had stirred something up, and I challenged myself to figure out who I was and what I could do—to find my place in a world that had been owned by men.

I don't know how long I'd been asleep, but I woke to hall lights illuminating my room and bright laughter pouring in from downstairs. The glare of light and party sounds was jarring. More jarring was my father sitting on the edge of my bed, his thick, square hands having already found my back, waking me from sleep. Caressing me through my bedshirt, his fingers worked my neck and arms. I lay stone still. *What's he doing?* His weight tilted me toward him, and I braced my hip against the mattress to resist the tilt. His hands, still rough from his summer in Maine, moved under my shirt, touching my seventeen-year-old skin still slack from sleep, creating friction, carving paths, then quickly under my chest to cup my breasts. I had yet to take a breath. His hands grazed my belly, pushed aside the elastic of my underpants and began to slide over my hips. *He's not stopping!* I grabbed the spool headboard for ballast and kicked.

Curled into a ball, I felt the warm yellow walls of my bedroom implode as my father sat on the edge of my bed. I felt my love for my father implode. I felt my womanhood implode. Coiled like a snake, my eyes locked shut, my throat sucked dry, I willed him away, willed this not to be true. *Go,* I wish I'd said aloud. *Just go!* He said nothing, just sat quietly. A whiff of bourbon split the air between us. Then he stood, cleared his throat, turned for the door, and chuckled. It was a chuckle I'd heard many times, like when he got caught with his hand in the cookie jar before dinner. It's the chuckle that's stayed with me.

He walked out of my room and closed the door behind him.

Seconds passed. Or minutes? I opened my eyes and stared at the pine trees outside my window, glowing in the party light from downstairs. I could see but not speak. I could hear but not say. I gazed at the pines and locked my eyes on their muscular trunks. My stomach clenched, my hands fisted, my eyes waited, as if for something more to happen. Adrenaline raced through me. I was nauseated and swallowed by a black abyss, swaddled in bright yellow paint and dotted Swiss—an abyss for which I had no name. I stared at the trees—motionless and steady, trustworthy and solid—outside my walls and outside my family. I parked my faith in those deep-green conifers, their earth-brown trunks as steady as my gaze.

In my family with its beautiful words, words had been stolen that night. It was 1967, and all I knew—instinctively, without naming—was that no one in my world had ever experienced anything like this and no one should ever know.

— ∞ —

Years later, I would wonder, was it my budding breasts that night? The intoxication of Anne Sexton? One too many bourbons? None of those mattered. It was just my father's poetic license, the license privileged men have long taken from the women around them.

I wouldn't get to be my own version of Anne Sexton. I wouldn't emerge into womanhood with only myself to consider. What had happened was not tenable; it was unthinkable. Memory shredded into fragments and I buried my father's deeds deep inside. The present evaporated. Meritocracy. Equality. They were a ruse. I was adrift, the Eberhart myths dissolving like a bitter pill in my mouth, while my voice—a young woman's voice, a leader's voice— quickly receded into what would be a long retreat.

Chapter 13:

Family Lexicon

One Monday morning early in 1993, I sat at my desk in the off-site storage building and watched snow fall on the pine trees outside my window. I was forty-two years old, and it was my third year in my father's archives. Dry flakes blew by the window above my desk, before settling on thick branches. The deep snowfall quieted me, and the solid trees took me back to the memory of that high school night when my father molested me. A quarter century had passed, but it haunted me still. It had driven nearly every decision I'd made from seventeen to thirty-five and was wound up in every failure. In 1967, my father, at the peak of his powers and public capital—literary, social, academic—had taken from me what wasn't his. I'd slumped into adulthood, the weight of him like a lead foot against forward momentum.

I'd given up trying to get through every one of Dad's fifty-five thousand letters and had found nothing to pin that experience on him. I envied writer friends who had a single shoebox of cards from their forebearers from which to conjure a story. I was drowning in an ocean of my father's words. Some mornings, I would chase down useless tracks, wasting hours, finding nothing of interest. Other days, I'd uncover a gem like Ginsberg's long letter about *Howl*.

Like a golfer's hole in one, that kind of find kept me coming back. I questioned my obsession. A woman in her forties, heartbroken by her father at seventeen and by her husband at thirty-nine, a woman determined to look inside the gaping hole in her heart and let her anger rage, formless, if it had to, without end.

I leaned back in my chair, pondering the beautiful storm and the snow-covered trees. As a consultant, I'd learned to hunt down salient facts to give my clients new perspective, in order to manage their most perplexing situations. And, I didn't ignore emotion—the ones I felt being inside their companies and the ones I heard expressed to me by them. I'd learned how to tell them a coherent story, one they could use to craft positive change. But, I'd not yet figured a coherent version of my father. I'd taken the energy and learning from my summer in Owatonna into boardrooms and conference rooms as I'd guided executives to open their ears to the voices around them, including those of women, which, in the 1990s, were still largely ignored. My company had passed its five-year mark, a good sign, and was growing rapidly. I'd established a reputation and a sustainable niche in the male-dominated world of executive consulting and coaching. I thought about the dichotomy between the capable woman I was in my work with those men and the frustrated and angry one I was in my search for my father. Which was I? And who was he? Was he the generous friend and mentor to women writers or the abusing father? Was he the father I'd once adored or the one I no longer did? I dug for scraps, restless, unrooted, not knowing if or when I'd ever name a story of him that was true.

———⌘———

At noon that day, I called my friend Ellen to see if she'd meet me for a drink after my digging. I'd been staring at fine print, and my eyes were exhausted. I was wrestling with his words, and with my own. I needed her ear, a friend who didn't know my family and could be objective.

Ellen was waiting for me when I got to the restaurant. She looked pensive. I assumed she had had a long day with her clients. "No," she said with her usual quick laugh, "I just really hate winter!"

We sat at Molly's on Main Street, its window wall looking out on one of Hanover's two intersections. Ellen had picked for herself a glass of California zinfandel in honor of her years in San Francisco, and for me, she'd chosen a French cab. We quickly caught up on our love lives—hers confirmed, mine not yet—and our work. Both of us were bound by codes of confidentiality with our clients; we understood what we could and couldn't share, but Ellen could laugh at anything and she always made me smile, which was what I needed that afternoon. I told her I was reading Wallace Stegner's *Crossing to Safety*, with his smart fictional account of academic couples. "I just learn so much more about life from fiction right now," I said. "It surprises me. Before my divorce, I read only nonfiction."

"Maybe that's because the last few years of your marriage *felt* like fiction," Ellen teased.

I raised my glass to hers and smiled. "You're brilliant."

We ate our bread, and I changed the subject. "Have I told you about the first time I heard the term 'sexual abuse' in connection with what Dad did?"

"No," Ellen said. "Tell me."

"It was seven years ago, at one of those personal-growth workshops everyone was going to. I got paired up with a woman named Susan from Chicago—for an exercise in which we were to tell each other about a life-changing event, either good or bad."

"And you told her about your dad?"

"I think she was the first person outside my ex-husband and my brother whom I ever told. I told her about meeting Anne Sexton, about the booze and the party, about being asleep in my room, about what had happened and the feeling of my life imploding, how I clung with my eyes to the pine trees outside my window." I took a long sip of the rich red wine. "She looked me straight in the eye and said, 'You were sexually abused.' I was floored. I'd never thought of it that way. I'd excused him for years. *He just felt me up,* I'd say, or *It wasn't that bad,* or *Others have had it far worse.* Her words stung. How could they describe my benevolent father? I can't own them, even now." I paused and took another long drink. "By definition, though, she was right."

"It must be so much easier—well, not easier, but clearer— if the abuser is horrible," Ellen offered. "Then you can hate him with all you have. When it's your dad, whom you loved, whom you trusted as a little kid, *and* who's famous and whom you're still protecting, it's gotta be hard to hold those two things about him."

"It is," I said, twisting the end of my napkin into a rope. "He didn't tell me not to tell anyone. He didn't have to. I was conditioned to uphold the family myths."

It was past dark, and the snow was still falling. This would be a big storm. Ellen and I needed to get on the road, back to our homes. But I wasn't quite finished.

"So, last week I was on grand jury duty, right?"

"Right. I remember. How did it go?"

"The jurors were all so different which was interesting. It was challenging to be in a decision-making group that I wasn't facilitating." Ellen laughed, knowing how tough that would be for me. I'd been a leader in every group I'd ever been in; it was my default—the vigilant side of me taking charge, as I'd learned around my mom.

"I worked really hard *not* to be elected foreman," I said, smiling.

"I bet you did."

"We had to weigh the evidence presented by the state, to determine which cases were solid enough to go to trial. Most were drug charges, a few burglaries, but one was for domestic abuse. The state's attorney asked if any of us was uncomfortable hearing the case, and said, if so, we could be excused. I thought about it but decided to stay."

"Were you okay?"

"It was hard to hear, but I was okay. The woman had been assaulted by her boyfriend more than once. She'd let him back in more than once. She'd feared for her life. It seemed likely he'd end up behind bars. That's the image I have of an abuser. Not someone like Dad."

"Aw, hon," Ellen said, reaching for my hand, right when I needed her.

"The attorney gave us a legal definition for 'assault,'" I continued, making air quotes. "'Assault is any unwanted physical touch by another person.'"

I looked at Ellen, my eyes filling with tears.

"Any unwanted physical touch by another person," I repeated. "That's assault. I was in my bed, for Christ's sake. It was more than unwanted. I was asleep. Was he really capable of *assault*? He didn't push or insist; he stopped when I kicked. But, he'd assumed."

We sat at the high table, needing to leave but not wanting to. We watched the late-afternoon traffic wind down. Lights on the corner turned from red to green and back to red. Students threw disintegrating snowballs at each other, while crossing Main Street.

"You know how, with clients, the problem presented isn't always the real problem? I'm thinking that opening myself to all this inner scrutiny isn't just about me and figuring out about Dad. I think it's helping me create more—or better—space for my clients to really look at themselves. I'm not a therapist, but sometimes what I care about most, sitting in their corner office, is how these men look at the power they hold—their privilege—and what they want to use it for. Sure, they're rich and entitled, but are they becoming better *people* while they're there? What did my father do with his privilege? Did he improve his writing? Did he care about his daughter?"

"Maybe that's your gift," Ellen said, having spent enough time with her own consulting clients to know what I was talking about. "I remember you telling me about the guy from London who broke down in tears when he told you he was gay. You do seem to get grown men to cry!"

"Right," I said, "I do." She and I laughed. "I'll never forget that guy, the CEO of a huge company, but he hadn't told anyone at work, he was so closeted. At the end of that conversation, and in our later work, he had a new arena from which he could serve and lead. It was riveting to watch. I feel humbled by what they tell me—wanting to leave a million-dollar job to work for Amnesty International; growing up in a small village in Pakistan decimated by war; feeling shame for having betrayed a colleague. It's amazing how much humanity they can bring to the conversation when they get in touch with their own vulnerability."

I signaled for the bill and paid. I'd need Ellen and many more glasses of wine before I was finished with my father.

"It takes guts to change," Ellen said. "Them, yes. But you, too."

Ellen and I gathered our coats and zipped up. We'd toggle through our clients' growth, or lack thereof, and our own and, over that decade of the 1990s, would become each other's chosen sister. Walking out into the soft falling snow, I was thinking about the term *assault*. I gave her a hug and whispered, "I keep having to add new words to the family lexicon."

Chapter 14:

Clueless in Seattle

Freshman year, University of Washington, 1969. I lay back on the grass and pulled my backpack under my head. The quad was a soft center on a campus built of stone and steel. A cobalt sky hung overhead, and students drifted by in waves, arms around each other as if they didn't have a care in the world. Mark, a friend from Shakespeare class, lay on the grass beside me. We'd bonded over *The Merchant of Venice*, reading it aloud to each other while memorizing Othello's quatrains. I'd drawn the perfect roommate—Jan from Denver, who loved her Broncos and got me hooked on cigarettes—but Mark was my closest other friend that first semester. Around us, trees were tinged with gold. Mount Rainier was rising from the clouds that day, taking my breath away. Like the top of that mountain, my head only occasionally rose above a general fog of malaise. I listened to students chatting and laughing, feeling as if they were a different species. A university of fifty thousand students, I'd figured, should be big enough in which to hide.

Fluency in French had placed me in a small senior seminar with the best professor in the department. Flip side, I sat with five hundred in a cavernous lecture hall for Introduction to Architecture. Anonymity suited me; it allowed me deep immersion in one of the books assigned, *Mont-Saint-Michel and Chartres*, which I read in both English and French while drawing a notebook full of Doric, Ionic, and Corinthian columns, wondering what I was doing with my life. I roamed Seattle's seven hills, outwardly marveling at the Cascades and the Pacific. Looking inward was hard, so I didn't try.

That afternoon, Mark's and my first time together without just studying, he told me he was from Olympia and had already declared his major in English. He wanted to be a writer. He knew I'd made a long trip to UW, and I was sharing a bit about where I was from.

"He's *the* Richard Eberhart?"

"You've heard of him?"

"We studied him last year."

I'd traveled 3,000 miles across Canada by train, 150 miles south from Vancouver by bus, and was still living in the shadow of my father.

I wasn't supposed to be there. UW had turned me down with a single sentence: "We appreciate your interest in our university, but our quota for students from outside Washington is filled." Two days later, I'd written back, "Thank you, but I plan to arrive from New Hampshire in September." Mom had liked my spunk. My father would have preferred Radcliffe or Brandeis. Seattle and UW, he said, were too far away and too big. Far away was fine for me, and big was better. Apparently, the admissions department had second thoughts. A week later, I got their second one-sentence letter: "In that event, we welcome you to the University of Washington."

A week after I'd first hung out on the quad with Mark, we were there again, basking in the sunny September weather and catching up on class requirements. I could see we both felt an attraction. Mark was like no other boyfriend I'd had or could imagine. The opposite of arrogant, not a jock, he was a chronic worrier who stacked the square corners of his notebooks precisely to match the corner of his desk. He lined up his socks in his drawer. He cleaned his room daily. Tucking in his shirt was a meticulous undertaking. His habitual movements fascinated me. Soon, I'd see how his outward control masked a mess inside: digestive problems, he told me hanging out on the quad, maybe an ulcer. Pressing my ear to his belly, I couldn't decipher the sounds but they worried me. Someone in pain who wasn't afraid to talk about it, though—I found that attractive. I couldn't have done the same.

"So, did you know Lowell?" Mark wondered that afternoon, as he traced outlines of a puffy cloud with his outstretched finger. I touched my thumb to his and noticed a spark. "Did you see the article in *Time*? He's *the* best American poet today. Don't you think so, too?"

"He has beautiful eyes; they're the nicest color of blue, like warm seawater," I said. "He's quieter than most of them, shier."

"You know Elizabeth Hardwick, too?"

"Mm-hmm." I pulled his fingers together with mine. "They have a house in Castine, not far from our place in Maine, and they come over for rides on Dad's boat to the islands and to talk poetry."

"Does he really take lithium?"

"I guess." I'd heard Mom and Dad mention the drug, and I knew Lowell was periodically admitted to mental hospitals. "He goes on binges and stays up for days, writing. Then he goes into deep holes and can't get out. Mom worries about him."

"You know Ginsberg?"

"Yeah."

"And Frost?"

"Mm-hmm."

"What about William Carlos Williams?"

"Dad tried to get him to visit Hanover for a reading, but Dartmouth wouldn't pay him enough."

"Those are big names. What's it like?"

"They're just there. Like furniture. Hey," I said, stretching over him and looking into his warm brown eyes. "I came out here to get away from all that."

"Why do you want to get away?"

"Why do you ask so many questions?"

Mark took my hand and kissed it.

"Poets are on such ego trips," I responded. "All they care about is themselves."

"If they didn't have egos, they wouldn't make their art."

"Yeah, well, less ego would be fine with me."

Mark pulled me in and rested my head against his shoulder.

"My parents are pretty preoccupied," I said, as he pulled a Tums from his pocket and popped it in his mouth.

"What do you mean?" he asked.

"Oh, jeez, I don't know. . . ." I paused, until an early example came to me. "Like when I was two and Dad was teaching at UConn. We lived in faculty housing, next door to the Peters family."

"Wait, if you were that little, how do you know this?"

"I've heard the story a hundred times, and Dikkon remembers it, since he was in first grade. It was at night, and snow was falling. Dikkon would wake up when I cried in my crib. He'd wait a few minutes and hear Mom pick me up and settle me back to sleep. I guess one night, I was crying and no one had picked me up. Finally, Dikkon got out of bed and found me balled up in my crib, wailing. He couldn't find Mom and Dad anywhere, so he carried me over to the Peterses."

"Wait, they weren't even at home?"

"Mom's side of the story—which I've heard a million times— was that they had planned to check on us regularly, but when Dikkon rang the doorbell and Mrs. Peters opened the door, the grown-ups were in the living room, drinking and playing cards and ooh-ing and aah-ing over what adorable waifs we were."

"Really?"

"Dikkon was in his pajamas, and I was in a wet diaper. Snow dusted our shoulders and heads—those are the words Mom used in her story. I guess they liked how Dickensian we looked."

Mark adjusted himself on the grass and gave me a hug.

"Dikkon told me he was scared that day and that Mom and Dad were proud of him for doing what he'd done. But, really, the story was about how adorable we were in our bare feet in the falling snow."

Mark squeezed my hand.

"Do you want to be a writer?" he asked.

"Are you kidding? Self-absorbed, like the poets? No way. I thought I'd major in piano, but now maybe architecture."

That night, Mark and I fell into his bed from conversational fatigue and slept platonically. He wasn't ready for sex, and I was okay with that. I slept poorly and woke up repeatedly, hearing sad sounds from his stomach. By morning I saw what was left of his package of Tums—a twisted wrapper.

—⟍⟋—

The summer after high school, seven months after my father molested me, I'd met a guy in New Hampshire, and during that first semester in Seattle, I'd been thinking of him. We'd made no promises, but I felt his pull. My high school graduation had been held in Webster Hall on the Dartmouth campus, now the Rauner Special Collections Library, and the hall was stiflingly hot. My maroon robe—our high school color—stuck to my shoulders, and the dress I was wearing stuck to my legs. Friends were excited about summer jobs and heading off to college. Others were as bewildered as I about what would come next. All I knew was that I was determined not to spend that summer with my parents in Maine.

"I'm not going," I'd told Mom.

"What? Again?" she'd asked.

"I'll stay here."

I was eighteen years old. If Dikkon had wanted to stay in Hanover at that age, I was sure they would have said yes.

"You'll have to have something to do," Mom had said. "You can't just stay here without a job."

"What about summer school?"

I'd already learned I was eligible at Dartmouth and could knock off a couple of classes before heading to Seattle. A few class-mates were doing the same.

Three weeks later, I was standing in line for registration with a check from my parents for Government 101 and a seminar on world religions. The latter would help me make good on Ginsberg's recommended book list, since its syllabus included both *The Bhagavad Gita* and *The Tibetan Book of the Dead*. Registration was taking forever, and I'd struck up a conversation with a gregarious guy named Sheff.

"What are you studying this summer?" I asked him.

"Oh, I'm not. I'm just holding a place for my friend here. I'm a painter."

"You paint houses?" I asked.

"No," Sheff laughed. "I'm a landscape painter. I'm painting this summer at Alex's farm, thirty minutes south of here."

Sheff's thick brown hair kept falling in his eyes, and he'd placed it back behind his ear. He was easy to talk to and had a guttural voice I found interesting, as if his tongue sometimes got stuck in the back of his throat. He was wearing the New England prep school uniform of a frayed oxford shirt tucked into worn khakis.

Alex joined us, and my face immediately warmed. I'd already learned from Sheff that the two had grown up as neighbors in Cambridge, not far from Gram's house, and that Alex's father taught at Harvard Business School. Alex added that his parents had recently divorced and his father now owned the farmhouse south of Hanover where he and his family had spent their summers. Classes at Dartmouth would lighten his senior year at Penn, where he was majoring in sculpture. *Two artists*, I thought. *That's interesting.* At six feet, Alex had a slim build and was noticeably more retiring than Sheff. He wore the same oxford shirt, only tucked into a low-slung pair of well-worn jeans. I liked the way he'd pushed his sleeves up beyond his elbows, revealing strong tendons in his forearms. He reminded me a little of Cal Lowell, with a pack of Camel unfiltereds visible in his chest pocket.

"You should come out to the farm sometime," Sheff said after we'd finished in the registration line and paid our bills. Alex wrote down the phone number on a small piece of paper and gave it to me.

On my first visit, Alex was in the kitchen, steaming lobsters. *A guy who cooks,* I thought. *I like that.* Outside the window, I could see Sheff working on a landscape of the New Hampshire hills fading into the Green Mountains of Vermont.

"You like them, I assume?" Alex asked, knowing I'd spent summers in Maine.

"Of course!"

"So, do you subscribe to putting them in headfirst in boiling water, or do you put them in cold water and bring the temperature up?"

"Headfirst! The latter sounds torturous! And usually in seawater in a big copper kettle on the beach."

"No sea water here, but I did salt it."

I spent that night in the guest room and remember Alex waking me the next morning to be sure I got back to Hanover in time for class. The look between us, he in the doorway, I in bed, was warm and tender. A couple of weeks later, and after a few awkward moments, he was the first man I slept with. Looking back from a distance, it was comforting and hopeful, where I might have imagined it would be confusing or I'd feel numb. And getting to sleep with him through the nights was lovely, as we woke each morning to a cacophony of birds outside our window. I thought how safe I felt, and loved.

Throughout that summer, I spent a few days a week at his place, as my classes allowed. The farm was magic—a refuge in the middle of green waves of beauty, the foothills and mountains in the distance. I worked in the gardens, fed the chickens, swam in the ponds, took long walks on the road, wrote in my journal, and got to know Alex. In early September, as he headed back to Penn and I made my way west to Seattle, we'd made no real commitment. I'd fallen in love and assumed he felt the same way. Practically speaking, he needed to finish school and I needed to begin.

— ⌘ —

In Seattle, first semester, Mark and I were on the same page, recognizing our relationship was best for companionship and Shakespeare. Over time, his anxieties had only piqued mine, but I couldn't have talked about my father or my shame even if I'd had the language for it. Trauma gets fragmented and tunnels deep into our flesh, away from conscious thought, until later when we can handle what it means. I see now that trauma was clearly in control of me, pushing me to find quick safety while also nudging me to experiment with others. My entire time in Seattle I was confused about sex and men—my father had used me, Alex's lack of clear commitment confused me, and going further with Mark made no sense to me. Still, my eyes were open for others.

My last night at Mark's apartment, I slept on his couch and apologized for not seeing more of a future. I hoped we'd remain friends. His forgiveness was a kindness I hadn't expected, nor knew how to accept. It would be a long time before I'd really trust kindness from any man.

I pulled on my white cotton sailor pants, the ones I'd bought at an Army and Navy store with buttons forming an upside-down U on top, along with a navy-blue turtleneck sweater, then shook out my long, thick curls. I felt restless. I didn't know what to think about Alex. I was intimidated about selecting a major. After a dozen years studying classical piano and playing in recitals, I was afraid to audition at UW's music school. What was wrong with me? Three years earlier, I'd set out for Switzerland to become fluent in French and had fallen in love with a Persian. Now I couldn't even set a goal, let alone execute one. That semester, my father mailed me clippings from the *New York Times* about people like me who were "living in sin" and risking our lives using the pill. The envelopes came without personal notes, as if the contents had come directly from the editor and I should therefore take them as truth. I tossed the first few clips in the trash and didn't open the rest.

— ∞ —

Over a quick Christmas break with Alex in Philadelphia, I'd found him focused, nearly entirely, on his final sculptures for his major. His preoccupation, I concluded, was a necessary part of his artistic focus, something familiar I'd grown up with around Dad. Ignoring those early signs of potential trouble, I found friendly conversation with his roommate, Mitch, as he showed me around the dark and filthy streets of West Philly.

Three months into my second semester in Seattle, a sense of spring was in the air as I walked home from campus to my apartment. The misty rains of February and March were receding. The cherry trees on campus were in bloom, and waves of hellebores graced the ground under them. It was cool outside as I felt the weight of my long curls hanging on my neck. I was thinking about Alex; I reminded myself of the challenges of a long-distance relationship and put aside any reticence I was intuiting from him.

Headed in my direction was a small, slim man with a wide smile on his face. His hair was thick and brown, his hands and feet small, but he had a confident stride. In Seattle, strangers often smiled and struck up conversations, something I was getting used to as a New Englander. I liked that he was about my height, that I could look him in the eye. I was pretty sure our encounter wouldn't end with "hello."

"Your hair!" he said, his first words, which, in 1970, was a decent pickup line for a girl like me. I quickly learned he was two years ahead of me at the university, that his name was Darry but his friends called him Flow, and that he hailed from Bakersfield, the hot center of California's agricultural heartland.

"I like your curls," he said, taking my hands. "And your eyes. You're curious."

"I like your hands," I said. "They're warm. You're nice."

We stood on Roosevelt Way and talked for an hour, shifting our weight from foot to foot, saying hi to passersby, enjoying the sunny afternoon. On a bench in a park, we sat for another hour while the sun began to drop into the Pacific. We covered our classes, our professors, our roommates, farmworkers in Minnesota and California, contrasts between East and West Coast weather. . . . Maybe that explained his nickname—two hours with him had just flowed. We turned to Nixon's war and our mutual opposition, to friends who were fighting in it, friends who hadn't come home from it, and friends who'd moved to Canada because of it.

"Another president insinuating himself into another foreign war," Flow said, concluding on Nixon.

Hmm, I thought—a quick insight, then buried, of men insinuating themselves into places they don't belong.

Flow took a lock of my curls and twirled it between his fingers. His eyes sparkled like August sun diamonds on Penobscot Bay. When he kissed me on the bench, I didn't care who noticed. It felt like shelter.

That evening, Flow took me to Lake Union, where most of his friends rented houseboats. Splattered by seagulls and smelling of fuel, these boats were popular rentals for artists and musicians, both students at the university and professionals passing through. In a sunken living room with porthole windows, Flow picked up a dulcimer and handed me a recorder.

"You play?" he asked.

"A little."

We joined in a chorus of voices and instruments weaving together a complex tapestry of sound. I took in the men and women, mostly older than I, from different continents and nations, the houseboat's occupants jamming together till the wee hours of dawn. Seattle and UW had everything I could have hoped for: distance from home; a smorgasbord of options for learning; a young, diverse crowd; a Western world of new ideas. I couldn't then appreciate the likeness of the houseboat to the literary living rooms on Hilliard Place and Webster Terrace, in which I'd grown up; these were my people, and this was my time. Flow and I fueled that night with cheap wine and easy dope, the evidence everywhere in the form of old Mateus bottles turned into candleholders and ashtrays filled with roaches. The room was alive, breathing, as if itself human, with an ever-shifting, syncopated beat, as jazz morphed into blues into Indian sitar into early reggae. I could have done anything at UW, even majored in Sanskrit if I'd wanted. I was glad to have left the cloistered ivy walls of Dartmouth, and Hanover, behind.

Flow and I eased into a sweet tempo, quickly becoming friends. After finishing classes on campus, we'd meet up at one of the houseboats for music. Flow's pursuit was tender, nurturing, and kind. He was all in. Looking back, I should have been, too. But, despite his patience, I could give him little physically. I'd given that part of me to Alex, as nascent as that part of me was.

Occasionally I'd catch a piece of news about Anne Sexton and think of the day I'd imagined my future through her. I'd already failed to live up to that image, failed to seize any power at all. I'd allowed myself to be persuaded by men. With an unclear commitment from Alex, I still couldn't let an entirely normal guy like Flow find the deeper parts of me that were hidden. I was burdened by an existential loss of confidence, a loss of self, extracted for my father's moment of greed. I would lose Flow in time, and everything I'd wanted from the West. It would take decades until I would find my own true, safe ground and, from there, find myself.

— ⌘ —

With Alex's graduation from Penn on the horizon and the summer following freshman year to fill, he and I talked about my joining him in New Hampshire, where he intended to live on his family's farm, assuming he could get out of the draft. The draft hung over all of us like a doomsday we knew would come. If you were male and not in college, you were fair game. Everyone hoped for a high number, or they tried to get out of it entirely. Alex was prepared to move to Canada if he had to. I wasn't sure I'd follow. Eventually, he got out with a medical deferment. With that behind him, Alex prepared for his graduation from Penn, and his move to New Hampshire. His roommate Mitch and a couple with a three-year-old daughter would join him. The couple was looking for a way out of the city, and Mitch needed a place to finish his senior thesis, a study of early twentieth-century communes. A farm in New Hampshire seemed the perfect place for all of them.

Three months before I would leave Seattle for my summer in New Hampshire, a small band of the Weather Underground, a radical group of US college students, accidentally blew up a three-story brick townhouse at 18 West Eleventh Street in Greenwich Village while preparing nail bombs intended to disrupt a noncommissioned officers' dance at Fort Dix. I knew about the Weathermen. Their declaration of war against the US government had already led to acts of violence. Diana Oughton, Terry Robbins, and Ted Gold were killed in the accident. Kathy Boudin and Cathy Wilkerson escaped from the rubble and went underground, where they'd stay for over a decade. They had commandeered the brownstone, owned by Wilkerson's father, while he was out of the country. Cathy's mother, who'd been at Smith College with Mom, owned a house across town from Alex's farm with her second husband. Alex had been summer friends with Cathy's younger sister. When I got to New Hampshire and visited our local post office, Wilkerson's face was on the FBI's Ten Most Wanted list.

In July, we started noticing a click when we made phone calls. Mitch quickly surmised the FBI was tapping our phone, which made a sort of illogical sense, since Alex knew the Wilkersons. A bunch of hippies living on a farm near Cathy's mother might be of interest to them. Cathy did not contact us, but it was stirring to think about a girl, six years older but not unlike me, from a progressive East Coast family who'd gone to Abbot Academy and been admitted to Swarthmore College. We shared certain beliefs—opposition to our government's war in Vietnam; injustice in how we treated the poor and people of color—and were both committed to changing the institutions we thought were holding our country back, only in entirely different ways. I could no more have imagined myself joining the Weathermen than I could joining the Army, even if I'd been able to, back then. I credit both my parents and Gram for that. Still, the possibility of our phone being tapped by the FBI kept the Weathermen on my mind throughout that summer. Eleven years later, Cathy would turn herself in and be sentenced to three years in prison for her crime.

While some were taking to the streets, Alex and I took to the land. We lived simply, trying to build a different life than that of our parents. He and I were in sync that summer, tending a big garden, taking care of his chickens, and riding his horses. We shared kitchen chores with our housemates and smoked joints from a small patch of homegrown weed. While Mitch and I walked the trails through the deep forests around us, Alex fixed things at the farm: the tractor, his jeep, fencing for the animals, a broken toilet. I was attracted to the way he laughed, his telling of stories with backwoods, old-timer accents, and his ability to do practical things with his hands. I saw him as the opposite of Dad.

That summer, I plowed through the books of Helen and Scott Nearing, especially *Living the Good Life*. Helen and Scott lived three miles from our cottage in Maine, where they had established a thriving homestead to which dozens of young people came each summer to work and learn about organic gardening. Helen picked up seaweed off our beach for her compost piles, and my parents bought Nearing vegetables. While Alex and I were visiting Undercliff that summer, we spent a couple of days with the Nearings to learn about gardening, greenhouses, and the good life. Likewise, we spent two days with Eliot and Sue Coleman, Nearing protégés and neighbors. Eliot and Sue showed us how they'd cleared a forest for their house and gardens, how they'd built their spectacular soil for growing exquisite-tasting food, and what it was like raising children on the land. I could see such a life for Alex and me, one that might be filled with the physical work of gardening and house building while also including creative pursuits like sculpture and writing. I journaled regularly and found comfort with a pen in hand, no matter what I'd told Mark when he'd asked.

Alex and I breathed new life into the farm. Communes were sprouting up around us in New Hampshire and Vermont, western Massachusetts, and Maine. Couples were returning to the land to raise their families, bringing with them a new ideology. It was about respect for the land and our environment, for each other, for the bounty of food we grew. In the background, though, violence was everywhere: the brownstone bombing, the four unarmed students at Kent State University gunned down by the Ohio National Guard, UW students and faculty blocking Interstate 5 in protest, and six thousand more American soldiers killed that year in Vietnam. While Marvin Gaye and Tammi Terrell were belting out simple love songs like "Ain't No Mountain High Enough," Jimi Hendrix had written his antiwar anthem, "Machine Gun." In New Hampshire, I felt surrounded by kindred spirits, all of us trying to change the world by living differently. I returned to Seattle in September, full of pastoral memories and hope, even more committed to Alex, though we'd still not made any clear plan for our future.

— ⌀ —

Sophomore year, Jan and I ditched Lander Hall and rented a cheap apartment to share with her boyfriend. I claimed the garret room with its steep, sloping roof, in which, even at five foot two, I could barely stand. My bed was a mattress picked up at Goodwill and flung on the floor. Out our tiny kitchen window, we glimpsed a sliver of Mount Rainier. Jan and I tie-dyed sheets, T-shirts, and laundry bags for friends and learned how to make our own bread, our hands covered in dye and flour, our rooms covered in drying fabric and cooling loaves.

I missed Alex, and I had no will to pick a major. Adrift, I skipped classes, caught afternoon movies on Queen Anne Hill with Jan, hitchhiked around the city, and made a home for my journaling in a corner café at the Pike Place Market. On weekends I borrowed a Volkswagen or hitchhiked twelve hours to Berkeley, where Dikkon was living with his first wife and pursuing a graduate degree. On rainy days in Seattle, I spent long hours writing poems in my garret bedroom, the only time I would ever turn to verse— mostly obtuse stanzas that trailed off in thin lines, heading down dark alleys, offering no clear exit. I was finding it hard to think. I didn't know what or how to feel.

In October, my cousin Eloise visited from Chicago. I'd been El's flower girl in her wedding. Fifteen years older than I, she was an adult I looked up to. After showing her around campus, I heated up water for tea in my tiny kitchen. She asked about Alex and what our intentions were. I wondered if Mom and Dad had sent her as an emissary.

"I don't know. I guess we're figuring it out."

"Do you intend to marry him?"

"Why is marriage important if we're committed to each other? Living together is the same."

"It's not the same," El said, as she launched into reason-able arguments, both civil and religious, as well as generational. I bristled at her lecture and stewed about it for weeks. My parents' marriage had not impressed me. The institution, forged to per-petuate the species, seemed, at its worst, an ownership system for property and bloodlines. What I cared about was freedom and equality, trust and respect. I didn't need the state to condone those things. Marrying seemed part of a larger cultural system I was ambivalent about and an expensive distraction from the real work of building a life with someone.

Late that fall, I had just crossed over Fifteenth Avenue on the edge of the university and was headed down Forty-Second Street toward my apartment on Roosevelt Way. I was looking forward to having the place to myself, knowing that Jan and her boyfriend would be on campus until late that evening. I needed time to think, to toss around my confusions about school, about Alex, and about my future, on the pages of my journal.

Just then, a good-looking guy sidled up to my shoulder from out of nowhere. I'd never seen him before. Even on a huge campus,

I was familiar with people on my routes. As we exited UW, I took in that he was older, maybe in his thirties. His long mane of Jesus hair was thick and hung past his shoulders. In tight black jeans and Frye boots, he was a quick conversationalist, peppering me with questions that I took for interest. Maybe a drifter, I thought, but he showed no sign of menace. He quickly draped his arm around my shoulder, pulling me in tight. I still hadn't asked him for his name. When he pressed his hand firmly against the small of my back, it felt like he had me, and, in my state of confusion, someone leading was too easy to follow. This wasn't tender Mark with his insecurities, nor genuine and potentially long-term Flow. He showed no ambivalence, like Alex had. He wore his wants and his charm as well as he did his black leather jacket. When we got to my apartment, I saw no reason not to invite him through my door. Not that he asked.

"You first," he said after I'd unlocked, a small chivalry. His questions came so fast, there was no time to ask him anything. He pulled me out of my doldrums by drawing out of me where I was from, what I cared about, and what I was doing at UW. He picked out a Stones record and placed it on my turntable. We danced around the floor in small circles, trying not to bump into orange crates Jan and I had used to build our bookshelves, Mick Jagger crooning in the background.

"You like Ginsberg?" he asked, pulling a beer from our fridge. *The Bhagavad Gita* sat on our coffee table. I'd mentioned my dinner with Ginsberg, but why the hell was everyone so interested in the poets? Why weren't they interested in me?

I let go of the day I'd been looking forward to for writing and thinking and let this man fill it. Quick to the mattress in my garret room, I don't think I clearly said yes or no; he just took over. The next morning, he smacked a wet kiss on my lips and left. "See you around," he said. "I'm Chuck."

His wet kiss and hasty exit from my room got packed next to the hollow memories of my past. Not until much later would I see how easy I'd made it for him to reel me in with his words, his charm, his needs to be met. The charms of my father, only in leather and jeans. I was just one more woman on his path, having gotten nothing from him but sex.

I made my own decision to leave Seattle, though I'd wanted it to be mutual with Alex. My academic father was humiliated. My mother was confounded. With classes I'd taken at Dartmouth and three semesters at Washington, I qualified as a junior. I said good-bye to Western friends, packed up my belongings, left my tie-dye equipment with Jan, and flew back to the farm in New Hampshire.

Chapter 15:

Hippieville

I'd spread a blanket on the lawn at Alex's family's farm and cradled my first child in my arms. With a warm, bald head and bright cheeks, he was as beautiful a human as any I'd ever known. Somehow, over the day of his birth, Bastille Day, 1974, he'd singlehandedly drawn me from the past into the present, his urgent needs a pleasure to fill. I was twenty-three years old. In pictures from that day, I'm as tired as any new mom, with both exhaustion and pride all over my face. Ben's middle-of-the-night feedings were a special time, as I watched his breath rise and fall while he nursed. He slept well, always would as a child. When awake, he was eager to explore his new world, quickly searching with his eyes and wrapping his hand around my little finger. The first two weeks of his life had been a tired and happy blur. Our new house next to the farm was not quite finished, and Alex rushed to install a washer and dryer to accommodate the piles of cotton diapers. Until fall, we could use both the farmhouse and our own as we needed.

I laid Ben down on the blanket to nap, and my mother and I got to work shucking peas into a large wooden bowl between us. Mom and Dad, then sixty and seventy, respectively, were excited about their first grandchild and had driven over from Undercliff, in Maine, to meet him. Mom would have done anything I asked her to do, but I needed to prove I could do this mothering thing on my own. It was a sweltering day in late July, and in the shade of the old apple tree there was hardly a whisper of a breeze to scatter a fly.

"He's beautiful, Gretch," Mom said, sweet with love at first sight. She pulled peas from their pods and put some in her mouth and some in the bowl. With a basketful to shuck, I would steam and freeze them later that day. I, too, was proud of my creations, both human and vegetable.

"Yes, Sesame," Mom said to our yellow Lab mutt, "you're beautiful, too. You'll need to be patient, but there's still room for you." Sesame nuzzled Mom, and Mom kissed her back.

My father stood under the apple tree, shifting his weight from foot to foot, looking impatient, as if he had something else on his mind, but he was often impatient when our focus wasn't on him. He let us know he'd gotten another honorary degree that year, from Colgate University. He knocked his pipe on the stone wall, emptied its spent tobacco, and refilled it from his striped pouch. Periodically, he took his handkerchief from his pocket to mop his brow. Without the sea breeze my family was accustomed to in summer, a July river-valley day in New Hampshire could be hot and steamy.

Ben woke briefly, and I picked him up.

"Would you like to hold him?" I asked my father.

Dad, too, was proud of his first grandchild. "What a fine head," he said, after cradling Ben in his strong arms and examining him. Uncomfortable with newborns for more than a few minutes, he handed Ben to Alex and, with a gratified smile, said, "He reminds me of my Irish ancestors."

— ∞ —

Alex's father had given us fifty acres of land as a wedding present two years earlier, acreage that we annexed from the farm. We'd spent the prior two years clearing the land for a large house we intended to build, into which we could grow our family. I had worked at Dartmouth's library for as many hours as they'd give me through those years, while Alex was a carpenter, later an electrician, and taught guitar lessons privately. We'd put nearly all the rest of our energy into planning our house, felling trees for a clearing, and building. I enjoyed thinking about the architecture classes I'd taken in Seattle and using those principles in our design, and I liked the production of making a life on the land.

We'd hired a seventy-year-old local man to skid the logs out of the woods and take them to the mill. We learned from him, as we had from the Nearings and Colemans, about the value of hard physical work and the inherent pride that comes from touching and seeing one's creation. We'd shared our news that we planned to marry.

"See this," he said, pointing to the wedding band on his left hand. I looked at his wrinkly, work-worn finger. "That's fifty years." The ring was nearly invisible, as if the skin on his finger had grown around it, like the barbed-wire fencing we sometimes found buried in the bark of the trees we were felling. He spoke from the wisdom of age, as he welcomed us into the community. I had let go of being against marriage once we had planned to have children. Alex continued to question the need but came around with some persuading. Later, I'd wonder if I'd latched onto marriage as a way to quell the deep questions I still had about who I was and what I wanted to do with my life.

—⚬—

We started construction in April, but June came quickly, and we had to break with our carpentry to bring in the first cutting of hay from the fields. An annual ritual for Alex since he'd been a kid, it became one of my favorite summer pastimes. Predicting the weather was essential—we'd need a three-to-four-day window of low humidity, sun, and breeze to make sure the hay was dry before we loaded it into the barn. If we got it right and did it early enough in the season, we might get a lighter, second cutting, in August. We watched the skies, talked to other farmers, and trusted what little weather reporting we could get. The week we chose was good. Alex drove back and forth across the fields, the cutting bar of his tractor slicing the grass. He knew the curves of that land—where the wet places were, and the rocks. I liked watching his rhythmic cutting when I rose from our garden rows long enough to look.

With the hay cut and the weather on our side, it was dry enough in three days to be raked—another long day of work for Alex, maneuvering the tractor and its rusty circular rake to pick up and fluff the hay into windrows. You couldn't do it too early in the morning, or the hay would be damp. You couldn't leave it too long, for fear of rain. We needed the hay for winter food for our small herd of goats and bedding for the chickens.

Getting the hay in the barn required explicit roles, and we recruited our neighbor Doug to help. While Alex drove the tractor and hay wagon across the field, he and Doug pitched up forkfuls to me inside the wagon while I walked around its inside perimeter, tamping down the hay with my feet.

"Need more over here," I called to Doug, and he threw some up.

"Now over here," I summoned to Alex.

I liked this walking meditation in the confines of the wagon. I liked being in charge of where the timothy and clover fell as we filled up the cart. Even in cutoff jeans and a bikini top, I was covered in sweat; the sun bore down on us all day, heat reflecting off the hay piled around me, and by 8:00 p.m., specks of dry grass and seeds stuck to every inch of my skin. Every three trips, we stopped at the pond for a quick dip to cool off before driving to the barn to unload. Inside the hot barn, the three of us stood in the wagon and pitched hay up into the loft, in a whirling, swirling sauna of hayseeds and grass dust.

Backing the last load of hay into the barn at 9:00 p.m., Alex shut off the tractor. "Let's call it a day," he said. "We'll unload it in the morning."

"Come on, Doug, stay for supper," I said. "I'll scramble some eggs."

I cut a generous handful of fresh chives from our garden and a bunch of small spinach leaves. Inside our kitchen, I whisked fresh eggs from our chickens with cream from Doug's cows, swirled in the chives and spinach, and grated in some local cheddar. Alex's homemade bread rounded out our meal. We popped beers from the fridge and ate like lumberjacks. We were dealing with a wood-chuck in our garden, as was Doug, and we co-invented clever strategies, most of which would fail, for their eradication. By the time Doug left, Alex and I were exhausted and slept well. I think of those days in the fields like a vision—infused with the sweet smell of clover, our bodies as lithe as our timothy stalks, our limbs as strong as our love.

— ∞ —

Once haying season was over, we went back to our jobs and building our house and saw no reason for me to stay on the pill. It had taken my mother five years to get pregnant with each of her children, and, despite my being twenty-two, while she was thirty-seven when she had me, I assumed conception would be genetic. There would be time to ease into the idea of raising kids. We'd get a few years to finish our house, build out our vegetable gardens, and continue with income-producing work. By surprise, I was pregnant in a month.

To his friends, Dad called me a "back-to-the-lander" and a "hippie woman," with a mixture of glee and derision—I never could tell which he felt more. He was delighted that Alex and I had married, that we were building a home on the land, since people like us had been written up in the *New York Times*, and even more so that I was pregnant, but he was embarrassed by having a dropout for a daughter and didn't much trust our slim chances for monetary success.

Dikkon had written a couple of novels in his twenties, and Dad offered his friends for help with promoting them. Once the books were published, Dad enjoyed showing them off, expressing wonder at my brother for writing fiction, a genre Dad had tried once and quickly found too hard. I'd been shown off in my earlier years, but I didn't want to be on display anymore. I didn't want to be an object of desire. And I was tired of self-centered writers. I wanted a simple life in the peace and quiet of our town. If I had no clearly articulated image of the family I wanted to create, I knew it would be different than the one in which I'd grown up. I wasn't alone. Everyone we knew was heading to the woods or the hills. Many of us were privileged, well-educated white kids who shunned cities and hated suburbs. We'd rather *make* what we needed— houses, clothing, and food—than work in city jobs to buy them.

— ∽∞∾ —

There's an entry in my journal from the year I was pregnant with Ben that reads, *Childbearing is not new, but it is new to me.* I was both excited and apprehensive about becoming a mom and serious in my intentions to be the best one I could be. After Ben's birth, I spent two years at home with him, taking care of the house and gardens while he napped, and Alex brought in money. I took long walks down country roads and through the woods with Ben in his front pack and Sesame by our side. I couldn't have imagined giving him over to someone else for care, but I didn't have the wealth of my grandparents or my parents, who'd hired help for their babies.

I'd prop Ben up in his chair for a nap while I weeded a long row of broccoli plants, or, when he was still little, I'd place his chair on the counter in our kitchen while I canned tomatoes and he kicked his arms and legs in glee. We had little money to finish our house, though we were living in it. The raw insulation between studs was depressing to look at, and heavy plastic covered some of the windows. Still, we made it our home, and slowly, over a decade, we got it done. We were settling into marriage and parenting, over- all pleased with the life we'd carved out.

— ∽∞∾ —

Ben and I were in the garden one day, where I was hilling two rows of potato plants. Suddenly, he started crying inconsolably. I tried singing. I gave him toys on his blanket. I fed him crackers and a bottle of water. Maybe it was the heat, I thought, though it wouldn't be any cooler inside our house. Maybe he had a stomachache or was coming down with a summer cold. Maybe he'd picked up on something stirring in me, as children do. I'd been feeling sad lately, hard at work each day planting and weeding, feeding our chickens and collecting their eggs, trying to make a home out of an unfinished house. That afternoon, while Ben cried, I cried, too, the two of us blubbering away in the woods, with no one listening. I hadn't expected to feel so isolated. And I was ashamed of feeling sad. It was confusing, after having an easy pregnancy and an easy baby. I knew nothing of postpartum depression back then, and if I had, I would have denied I had it. I was young and healthy. We'd mostly created the life I'd thought we wanted, but was weeding and canning all I'd do with my life?

— ∞ —

In 1976, shortly after Ben turned two, I ran into a friend in the grocery store. She'd opted to have children while maintaining her job as a school counselor. In addition, she was sitting on the board of a health agency near where we lived. She mentioned a new job at the agency and asked of my interest. I knew nothing about managing health care programs, but I'd known nothing about fluency in French or house design or gardening or being a mom and had figured them out. At the end of a long interview with the board of directors, I was offered the job. Ben was eligible for the best daycare program in the area, and I now had people and money to manage, a new program to implement, and reports to write for my board. I liked pulling together a team and working with a group to accomplish goals. Borrowing from what I'd learned in Owatonna, I experimented with new ways of making decisions and engaging my colleagues in planning.

Mom called me at work one day to invite us for dinner in Hanover. Alex offered to pick Ben up from daycare so I could go on my own. I hadn't seen my parents much except to drop off Ben at their house occasionally while I shopped for food. Michael McCurdy, publisher of Penmaen Press, was in town that day. McCurdy was known for his trademark black-and-white wood engravings; for beautiful broadsides of poems by contemporary poets; and for high-quality, limited-edition books by writers like William Saroyan, Joyce Carol Oates, William Stafford, and my father. Mike wanted to pick Dad's brain about new ideas for his press.

— ◦◦◦ —

Mom didn't like to cook. She'd never learned, since Gram had had help. She'd tried in the Navy years, I'd learn later from reading one of her journals. Dad expected his new wife to have dinner ready when he got home from the Navy base and she described her feelings about it in her journal: *Of course, all French women know how to cook. I can't do it and I don't like it. My main difficulty is a lack of enthusiasm for doing it ever again. I made two loaves of bread yesterday, mostly fun, but I don't care if I ever make them again. That's what I never liked about cooking.*

The writer Jay Parini would tell me later about a dinner he had with my parents in Hanover. The British literary critic I. A. Richards and his wife, Dorothy, were staying with Mom and Dad. Richards had been my father's mentor at Cambridge University. My father had enjoyed long walks through the British countryside with Dorothy and Ivor. The Richardses were regular visitors when they were in the States.

After cocktail hour in the living room, Dad looked at Mom. "Betty, is our dinner ready?"

Mom jumped up from the couch and went to prepare supper. When the group was seated around the dining room table, Mom carried in a big bowl of cooked frozen peas.

"Betty, have you forgotten the rest of the meal?" my father exclaimed. "Don't you have something else for us?" I can see I.A. and Dorothy each peering over their wire-rimmed glasses, in curiosity.

"This is it. We're having peas."

"What? But this is inhospitable to our guests," Dad continued.

"Well, but the British *love* peas!"

Mom could get away with that kind of thing. It was the conversation that mattered, never the food.

— ❧ —

That evening with Mike McCurdy, Mom filled our stomachs with her company pot roast, something she'd told me when I was a teenager didn't really require talent—all you needed to do was cut things up and put them in a pot to cook themselves. I was enjoying being with my parents and McCurdy, as Dad launched into an idea he'd been germinating.

"It's been twenty years since *West Coast Rhythms* came out in the *New York Times*," he said, "and twenty years since Allen wrote his marvelous letter to me about *Howl*. Why don't you bring out a special edition of both together?"

McCurdy was intrigued.

"I could write a retrospective piece," Dad added, "and I don't see why Allen wouldn't agree to do the same."

At the peak of his career, a peak that would span several decades, my father could pretty much call his shots, especially with creative publishers like McCurdy. A year after our dinner together, my father would win the National Book Award for his *Collected Poems, 1930-1976*, and Penmaen Press would publish 1,500 special-edition copies of *To Eberhart from Ginsberg*, 300 of which were hand-numbered and signed by the two poets. The thin volume is now considered a historic document of the Beat generation.

— ❧ —

On the night of December 4, 1979, snow fell as winter rolled in over our hillside. Alex and I had the living room set up as a bedroom for the birth of our second child. We'd planned for the hospital, but I'd learned that the doctor who'd delivered Ben had been charged with inappropriate acts with patients and had resigned from practice. That was enough. I was done with men controlling my body. I wanted an experienced woman by my side, and I wanted to birth my baby on my own terms.

By then I'd risen to associate executive director at the health agency and had gained confidence in my leadership abilities. I got a three-month, unpaid leave, followed by part-time status for the next year, as I'd requested. Alex and I spent my pregnancy speaking with doctors and midwives, reading books on home birth, and working with Ben to understand what we were doing. We hadn't planned for a snowstorm.

The day before, I'd been standing on a ladder, helping screw the last pieces of Sheetrock onto our ceiling, believing I had about two weeks to go. By noon the next day, I was in labor. By 6:00 p.m., I alerted our midwife and we agreed to talk again when my contractions got to her prearranged number, at which point she and her attendant would begin their forty-five-minute drives to our house. Snow was swirling outside, and it was dark early. By 8:00 p.m., we alerted the midwife that we thought it was time for her to get in her car. My work friend Jill, a woman who knew Ben well, would be with us, too. I wanted someone to be focused solely on him.

She arrived quickly. "It's a little slippery out there," she said. "The roads are kind of a mess, but they'll make it. I mean, I did, and I'm from New Jersey!" Ben was asleep upstairs while Jill waited with us for the right moment to wake him.

Alex was keeping our two woodstoves going. By nine thirty, he was beginning to worry about Ruth's late arrival. I was grateful he didn't share this with me until later, when he'd tell me he'd been anxiously trying to remember the details of the emergency-childbirth chapters we'd read. I lay on the couch, oblivious to that concern, focusing on my breathing. Jill periodically peered out the window, looking for car lights, and said, "It's really coming down!"

Throughout that evening, I was focused front and center on my increasingly regular and intensifying contractions. I'd taken a yoga class while pregnant with Ben and knew a little about breathing. Jill turned on some music, and later we tried watching TV. Neither helped. I needed to find my own zone, intuiting what my body was asking for. Mostly what it seemed to ask for was deep, slow breaths through each contraction.

Around 11:00 p.m., still no midwife, and I'd lost my rhythm. Then I heard this faint voice inside me saying, "Mom, I'm coming out. Pay attention!" Contractions washed over me and I felt like I'd suspended myself above my body, neither frightened nor anxious, just communing with the power of the moment. I found a low gear and breathed, in rhythm with the poetry of birth. That night will stand as one of the most powerful I've known. Power not over, but with. Power in sync with my body and what it was doing. While Alex and Jill filled the woodstoves, I was focused wholly on ushering this new person into the world. Sesame knew something was up. She kept nuzzling me, and between contractions I attended to her a little, too.

Ruth and her assistant finally showed up, both cars arriving at 11:45 p.m. At that moment, all hell was breaking loose. Ruth sized up immediately that I was in transition and needed to keep my focus. Meanwhile, she gave orders to everyone in the room, with confidence and empathy both.

"Get the temperature up—we need it at eighty-six degrees," she said to Alex.

"Get water on to boil," she told her assistant, who was laying out instruments.

"It's time to wake up Ben," she coached Jill. Jill ran upstairs and coaxed Ben awake. From the moment we'd told him he'd have a baby brother or sister, he'd wanted to be part of the birth. he'd witnessed births of goats and lambs, calves and pigs. We'd explored child-oriented books on labor and delivery and discussed with him what it might be like. We'd asked him regularly throughout the pregnancy what he thought. He didn't want to miss the arrival of his sibling. Still, a four-and-a-half-year-old waking in the middle of the night to the intensity of a birth scene must have been quite an experience—which I'd hear about much later, when it became clear to him as a young adult that no one else he knew had witnessed such a thing.

I was breathing heavily and drew Ben near me briefly, reminding him of what we'd talked about, how proud I was of him, how excited we were for him to have a sibling, and that he'd know who it was very soon. Then Jill took over with him, shielding him from much of the view while sharing the experience with him. Again, I heard that voice inside me, this time saying, "I'm almost there. We can do this. We have everything we need." Those words sustained me as I rode the final waves of transition.

Suddenly, my breathing got ragged and I was sweating profusely. Frantically, my eyes searched for Ruth, who put her face six inches from mine, warmth written in her smile, and said, "Look at me, Gretchen, and breathe. Stay right here. We're almost there. Just look at me and push. Hard!"

Without the drama of a hospital, our new baby was out, peacefully. Wide-open eyes. Immediately present and inquisitive. Unafraid. The alertness surprised me. Resting on my belly, our baby turned its eyes on Ben and held them there. In that raw moment, I knew that if anything ever happened to Alex and me, our children would have each other, which was all I could ask for.

Ruth busied herself with cleaning up while five minutes passed. Suddenly, I asked the obvious. "Well, what is it?"

"Oh, it's a girl," Ruth said, laughing.

I smiled. Of course. I'd thought it had been a she who had spoken to me.

We wrapped Molly in a soft blanket and laid her on the bed while we hung out and celebrated her real birthday. We passed presents to Ben and Jill, to Ruth and her assistant. Jill had brought a carrot cake with a single candle, and Ben blew it out. I was proud of Molly for bringing her quiet wisdom to this world and of Ben for revealing his full heart that night. Later, I'd think of Ruth as I further developed my leadership skills and consulted with clients—her equal parts force and compassion, a view of a woman in her power.

"It was rough getting up the hill!" Ruth laughed once the fires were restoked. She had performed the usual tests, and Molly scored high on all of them. "I hadn't put on my snow tires yet and had to gun the engine to get up here. But I would have walked if I'd needed to!"

Later, I'd learn from Alex that as Molly was coming out, the cord was wrapped twice around her neck and her body was blue. He was grateful that Ruth had arrived just in time to slip that cord over Molly's head. That fact would give me much pause about home births, but only later. We were having a lazy, fun celebration that night, lit by fatigue and euphoria.

Molly was born just after midnight on December 5, 1979. Ben finally got back to bed around 2:00 a.m., and for the next six months, he checked on her each morning. Alex and I had planned this together, just as we'd planned Ben's birth and the design and construction of our home and gardens. We were capable of a lot. What stays with me, beyond the great gift of each of our children, is the power I found inside me. I'd found it by allowing myself to be vulnerable, while fully present for what was. That was a lesson I'd forget and have to relearn on more than one occasion.

— ∞ —

While Alex and I were living simply on the land and raising our children, my father was a supernova, receiving one accolade after another, including honorary degrees nearly every year. In 1974, he was invited to teach winter term at the University of Florida, in Gainesville. At seventy, he also kept fall term for teaching at Dartmouth. Three years later, he was awarded the President's Medallion by the University of Florida and a line item in the university's budget to return for as long as he wanted. In 1978, he welcomed the Russian poet Andrei Voznesensky, whom he'd met in Washington, to Hanover. In 1979, the year Molly was born, Dad was named poet laureate of New Hampshire, a post he'd hold for the next five years.

In Hanover, poets and writers came, as they always had, but we saw my parents less, as they wintered in Florida and summered in Maine and had only a few months nearby each year. When I visited, no matter the location, their houses were full of writers and I'd compare my own meager writing with theirs, always coming up short. The wager I'd made the day I met Anne Sexton still bubbled inside me: What would I do with power if I ever had it? After Molly's birth, I'd begun to wonder how I could translate that into something more? I thought about writing, but at a party at my parents' house in the early 1980s, I scanned the room and realized that nearly everyone had won a Pulitzer or a National Book Award. If that was the standard, I knew I'd never meet it, so I put it aside.

I had more practical matters to attend to. I had work that made ends meet. I enjoyed tending our gardens and playing with the kids. With a job and a second car, I felt less isolated. A group of women friends and I carved out long weekends to hike in the White Mountains. Leaving our kids with their dads, we'd set out, into the wilds, scrambling up rocky peaks, talking nonstop, and doling out leg massages at the end of each day. With bottles of wine in our packs, we enjoyed the high huts of the Appalachian Mountain Club, where we were fed well and bunked on wooden platforms, slowly checking off the forty-eight peaks over 4000 feet in elevation in the small state of New Hampshire. Those long weekends were sacred, as each of us dreamed up what we wanted in our lives and supported each other in achieving it. A circle of women, as I'd witnessed around Gram's and Mom's women friends, along with physical exertion in wild places would be essential to seizing all I'd learned and doing with it what I could.

— ✺ —

In August 1980, we took the kids to Undercliff for a week. My father taught Ben how to handle the outboard motor, and Mom showed him how to catch crabs with a string and a piece of bacon. Molly toddled around, pulling whole flowers from Mom's gardens. It was important to me that my kids loved the Maine that I had loved, that they understood the feel of freedom there, along with the beauty of the sea and the islands, even if it was hard for me to spend long periods with my own parents. The big sky overhead, the sunshine, the echoing gulls—all were a part of me, and it was a legacy I hoped to pass on.

There was a new guest with us at Undercliff that year, whose name was Joy. An English professor at the University of Florida, she floated easily between literary conversations with my father and his friends and dinner preparations with my mother. In the midst of a divorce, she had several children around my age. Not until the end of our week did I catch Mom rolling her eyes at Joy, but I chalked it up to nothing. The next day, we gathered our vacation-scattered belongings, the special rocks and sea urchin shells we'd found, and Alex and I drove our family back to New Hampshire.

Chapter 16:

The Sunshine State

In 1984, I took my kids—then ten and six—to Gainesville for their February school vacation. Alex's work would keep him home, where he'd tend our woodstoves and keep the animals fed, making it easier for me and the kids to be away.

On our ascent out of Boston, the kids and I looked forward to a full week of sun, leaving behind the bitter cold of New Hampshire. Settling into an easy trip south, Molly befriended the flight attendants and Ben watched the contours of the eastern coastline from thirty thousand feet. He and I tried to name each state en route by its terrain.

Mom and Dad had invited their friend Jay Parini for the week, too, which had surprised me. Three years older than I, Jay had started his academic teaching career at Dartmouth, and my father had welcomed him warmly to the English department. Years later, Jay would describe his first meeting with Dad. "I hadn't occupied my office for more than a week when a knock came at the door, and it was Dick. I'd read and admired his work since college," Jay wrote in a tribute to Dad, "and still remember a dramatic reading of his harrowing poem 'The Cancer Cells.' Dick came into my office like a burst of light, a short, chubby man with the face of a baby, an angelic nature, and a wildly energetic manner. He smoked a pipe continuously. He invited me to dinner that night, and I went. In fact, I kept going for decades."

Mom and Dad became something of surrogate parents to Jay, a successful poet and novelist in his own right who could accompany my father on rides to readings, as he shared similar tastes and interests. For this trip, though, I'd assumed it would be just the kids and me.

We settled into our rooms in my parents' furnished rental apartment, dropped our winter clothes on the floor, and put on our bathing suits. It was getting late for dinner, but the kids couldn't wait to get in the pool.

The next morning, Molly asked Mom, "Gumma, will you teach me to knit?"

Mom pulled out her basket of yarn and helped Molly learn the basics of holding needles and looping stitches. By the end of that week, she'd knitted a solid square. Meanwhile, Dad toured Ben around the university's extensive athletic facilities, including its football stadium. Returning from their adventure, they were trying to figure out how many Dartmouth football stadiums would fit inside the gigantic one in Gainesville.

We rendezvoused over lunch, and while Mom, Dad, and Jay had things they were doing that afternoon, I took the kids out to the pool for our first full afternoon in the sun. We tossed balls around in the water and dove for coins, Molly in the shallow end, Ben in the twelve-foot deep end. The pool had a small diving board, and Ben thundered us with cannonballs while Molly demonstrated the crawl she was learning on her swim team. Ben made bets with his sister and me on who could hold our breath at the bottom the longest. Leaving the pool to them, I laid out a towel on a lounge chair, and watched the kids enjoy themselves. They were growing so fast, I'd barely noticed, their limbs long and lanky. The sun felt good on my winter legs. My joints unstiffened from our travel. The health agency I was running by then had grown, and I'd been elected to serve on the boards of a health care coalition and an innovation consortium. My children's laughter made the responsibilities of home and work fade away as I dozed off for a few minutes, happy to be on vacation.

At thirty-three, I'd completed my undergraduate degree at the University of New Hampshire in health policy and management, a program I could pursue primarily off-campus while continuing to work full-time. Not to lose momentum, I went on for my MBA. I'd soon be named executive director of the agency and was put in charge of a hundred staff. We had a significant budget and ours was the largest and most sophisticated agency of its kind in our region. It was like running a small company. I was chief strategist, chief finance officer, chief revenue generator, and chief team leader. It got me reading and thinking about organizational systems and how they functioned well or poorly based on how people inside them carried out their duties.

There were small signs that Alex and I were growing apart. Decisions became time-consuming. We'd lost the flexible, positive approach and excitement of our early days. I chalked it up to a then-twelve-year-old marriage going through a stretch of its own adolescence. A week in the sun was just what I needed.

After their afternoon in the pool, the kids were occupied with baseball cards and knitting and I was chatting with Mom and Jay over glasses of iced tea. Dad was smoking his pipe on the balcony, a tropical breeze blowing through the screen door from the deck. I felt my breath deepen and lengthen, as if I could let go of all tension on this break.

"I'm going out for my swim," Mom announced around 4:00 p.m., heading off to change into her bathing suit.

"I'll join you!" I called. "Meet you out there." Dad, catching up on his preparation for his seminar at UF, was happy to keep an eye on my kids so I could have time with Mom. My relationship with her had softened. No longer trying to prove myself as a mother, I could laugh with her about the challenges of raising children while reveling in the fun of it. She was still not a confidant, but our relationship was easy on the surface. She so adored my children, she'd have done anything for them, and I appreciated that devotion.

Ten minutes later, I bounded down the six flights of outdoor concrete steps, stopping once to watch a mourning dove in the rustling palm trees. The apartment building was quiet, its occupants mostly workers at the university, not yet returned from their jobs. I turned the corner toward the pool and saw Mom facedown in the aqua water, her bathing suit skirt floating around her hips, her heels pointing up to the sky.

"Mom!" I screamed, jumping into the deep end, where she was. I tried pushing her up out of the water and failed. I tried turning her over and failed. The dead weight of my mother's body was sinking. I finally got her face out of the water, but my thrashing legs were nearly useless. Fully clothed, with sneakers on, I was barely treading water with her in my arms. We were in trouble. I yelled, but no one heard me. Just then, unexpectedly, Jay came out of the elevator and jumped in. He knew her seizures—no explanation needed. Together we finally got Mom to the shallow end and dragged her out of the pool, scraping her leg badly over the concrete lip, just as I'd scraped her leg on Boylston Street. Her gashes were angry with blood, but they could wait. She wasn't breathing. I pounded her back with my hands. "Breathe! Breathe!"

"Breathe, Betty!" Jay yelled, helping me rearrange her, but we were making no progress. Long before I knew anything about CPR, time lost meaning. We yelled and pounded, but nothing happened. Finally, when it seemed to have been far too long, Mom choked up water and gasped for breath.

Jay and I exhaled, exhausted. My mother was back again, one more time.

— ∞ —

After getting Mom upstairs and in bed for a nap, I dropped my wet clothes on the bathroom floor where they created puddles. Standing in the hot guest shower, my hands shook, and my knees quivered. I was freezing in the dead heat of Florida. What if Jay hadn't been invited for that week? What if he hadn't come out to the pool? What if my mother had died in my arms? I let the hot water pound my back as hard as I'd pounded my mother's. As I wept, a memory surfaced, jolting me. I was five at the time, my brother ten. We were on the beach at Undercliff at dusk. The grown-ups were having a party at the top of the beach, bottles of beer in their hands or bourbon in paper cups. A spontaneous feast was spread out on a picnic table. A powerful storm had blown through Penobscot Bay the night before, rolling in a set of full-length logs that were still bobbing around at midtide in the dusk. Dikkon and his friends were balancing on them in the water as the evening sky turned dark. Somehow, I managed to get myself on top of a log, though I couldn't swim. Within seconds, the log rolled over and I went under, sinking into the murky sea. Surrounded by storm-whipped water the color of chartreuse and jade, it felt peaceful, as if I were in a dream.

Just then, Dikkon dove down and grabbed me, bringing me back up to the air. Mom ran down the beach as I coughed and sputtered.

My brother's version of the story has me on a log with him; he claims that it rolled, tossing us both over, and that he pulled me up immediately. He may be right, though I remember the peace and quiet of water all around me, and feeling not yet afraid, taking it all in. I've been told that's something akin to what drowning can feel like. My parents' story, as told and retold around beach fires in Maine, played out like a heroic myth wherein the damsel goes under and at the last moment is saved from the jaws of the sea by a hero—male, naturally. Sobbing in the shower, I saw no charm in their romanticized tale. Mom had nearly drowned in the pool. I had nearly drowned off our beach. I saw my parents then as reckless people assuming a generous fate would take care of what they ignored. I was hot with fury, enveloped in steam.

— ⋙ —

That night, after cleaning up from supper and putting the kids to bed, Jay and I sat in the living room with my parents. Everyone was worried, but Mom had shrugged off her near drowning, blaming it, once again, on her damnable disease. That was no longer good enough for me. I was done with bearing the cost of my parents' denial, the cost of their inattention. I needed Mom to be my children's grandmother. I still needed her to be my mom.

"Look me in the eye," I said to Mom. "I don't want you to die, and I especially don't want you to die by *drowning*. You have to promise me you'll never swim alone again."

Mom shook her head and stared at her lap, her brain ahead of mine, knowing what that would mean. My fiercely independent mother had had to give up so much to live with her disease. When I was ten, my news about our near car accident had caused her to rip up her license. At thirty-three, I was causing her not to swim on her own, a pleasure I knew she loved. She agreed.

"Dad, you have to agree, too," I said. Sitting at a distance from Jay and Mom and me, my father was smoking his pipe near the screen door, conveniently removed from our hot center of emotion. "Mom has to be able to swim. But you need to be with her. If you can't be, you need to make sure someone else is." My face was hot with passion and from the Florida sun. I knew this was an imperfect solution. Even if someone were present, there was no guarantee that person could get my mother out of the deep end of a pool. I hadn't been able to. But it was the only thing I had. Dad tugged on air, his pipe tobacco spent. He shrugged his shoulders, acquiescing; he, too, knew this was a change that would affect him.

I slept poorly that night, rehashing what had happened. My father had the words to describe Mom's disease and never wrote a single poem about it. He was frequently perplexed by her epilepsy, even though her seizures were common. Years later, when I had dinner with Jay in Middlebury, Vermont, I wanted his take on Mom's near drowning. He'd been there as my big brother that day in Gainesville, one I could trust, no explanation needed; like a member of my family. Jay followed up on our conversation by email. *Your father was always in denial about Betty's seizures, at least on some level,* he wrote. *He really wanted the world to be as he imagined it.*

— ∞ —

Three years later, in 1987, when the kids were thirteen and eight and my cousin Susan Butcher had won her second Iditarod race, I planned another trip to Gainesville with Ben and Molly. It had been a year since I'd left the health agency to start my own consulting company. Mom and I were on the phone, confirming dates for the kids' vacation week. She offered to rent a beach condo at Cedar Keys, accurately predicting they'd enjoy the warm ocean while she and I had time together, watching.

"What about Dad?" I asked.

"If his teaching schedule cooperates," Mom said, "he'll come, too."

A month later, the kids and I walked into that condo on the eighth floor of a typical tourist rental, all white, with three bedrooms in a line down a long hall and craft items decorating the living room. Wooden signs on ledges proclaimed GONE FISHIN' and THE SEA FLOWS IN AND OUT AND CALMS US AS IN ITS WAKE. I stepped out onto the large deck overlooking the sea and caught a squadron of pelicans, with their enormous gullets, gliding in front of a long, low wave before disappearing out of sight.

Aside from being with my kids, I had only one goal that week: to get some uninterrupted reading time, and not about business strategy or team building, which was all I'd been consuming for a year. The kids would sleep in, and I could set my alarm for 5:00 a.m. to enjoy a couple hours of alone time. I'd brought Natalie

Goldberg's *Writing Down the Bones*, which looked like something I could open and close as needed. I still harbored ideas about writing, but with two growing kids, my work going well, and a small entourage of farm animals, neither Alex nor I got much time to ourselves.

At seven o'clock on the second morning, around the time I expected to hear Molly wake up first, my father abruptly pushed through my bedroom door. His bathrobe was untied around his pajamas, reminding me of his nakedness when I was growing up. He looked like he'd just woken, his face weary. I stared at him as he approached me; I had no idea why he was in my room.

He walked around the end of the bed and sat down on the white chenille spread. "Betty's had a spell," he said. Mom regularly had spells; this was nothing new.

I squinted at him as bright sunlight spilled from the hallway through my open door and his weight on my bed tilted me toward him. Some neural magnet scooped up long-buried and disowned fragments of memory, like they were small metal shards, coalescing them in one clear recollection after seventeen years in hiding. The sights and sounds had fueled its emergence—my senses acutely aware of the past—the light spilling in my door taking me back to my bedroom in Hanover, the noise of the party for Anne Sexton, the feeling of my father's hands under my shirt. A sucker punch of shame I'd never had a name for came in full force. Sitting on my bed, my eyes open and staring at my father, I flashed back to that night when I was seventeen years old, but this time I was wide awake.

"Get out," I said, throwing Natalie Goldberg to the foot of my bed.

My father looked startled.

"I'll check on Mom when I get up, but I mean it, Dad! Get out!" My voice was back.

— ∞ —

That visit in Florida was the existential pivot I needed after long years of denial: I was entering new emotional territory and would require new teachers and new skills. I knew how to do isolation and loneliness, and how to hold a deep family secret. I didn't know what I would need to put myself ahead of my father, to free myself from his shadow. My father's fame, his fabulous friends, my beautiful family mattered not—this was *his* failing, not mine. Saving *myself* had to be my first order of business.

I got the kids out of bed, fixed them breakfast, called our airline for an earlier flight, and went to find my mom.

"Are you okay?" I asked, kneeling on the floor next to her bed.

She shook her head in disgust at epilepsy. "It's just this disease."

"I know, Mom. I'm so sorry you have to go through this. I hate that you have epilepsy."

Mom squeezed my hand and said she'd get up soon.

"It's okay. The kids will be in to see you in a minute, and then you can sleep as long as you want. But something's come up and we need to leave earlier than expected. I just got us on a flight for later today."

"What? Is everything okay?"

"Everything's fine, Mom," I said. My second-best lie. "I just think it'll be good to get home and have the rest of the weekend before the kids head back to school."

Part of me wanted to confront Dad then and there. But the memory was too fresh, too confusing, too overwhelming. I could barely look at him. I knew I needed time, and help. I felt bad for leaving Mom, and the kids were confused, but I rationalized they'd like a day at home before school and that Alex was missing them. I could not have stayed in that condo with my father for another night.

— ⌘ —

A soft snow squall swirled around us when we landed in New Hampshire, and I felt different already. My skin had changed. It had gone from prickly to porous, like I'd lost all my defenses and was suddenly vulnerable and raw. Denial had been useful. Without it, the terrifying truth was nearly unbelievable. My eyes had been opened in the Sunshine State, the state that had nearly claimed my mother and had awakened me to family information I could no longer bear in silence. The next day, I called my physician, Mark, and in his office I spilled what had happened in Florida, and what I remembered from my bedroom in Hanover. He listened carefully and said all the things I needed to hear. He urged me to find good support and offered the name of someone he knew who could help. That evening, I called my first therapist.

Chapter 17:

Things Fall Apart

Her office was a sunny second-floor room with three walls of windows and its own entrance off the driveway. A homey space with comfortably worn chairs; I liked the light. She was soft bodied, with gray hair, and greeted me warmly. A slight scent of salty soup infused the air, perhaps something on the stove she could check between clients. In her comfortable shoes and with a purple scarf around her shoulders, she was motherly, in ways I probably needed. But how could I possibly fill an hour? I didn't even know her. I'd given her a thumbnail sketch—recent memory of abuse—by phone, but that was all.

"How are you doing?" she asked.

I broke into tears.

Questions tumbled out of me like spring snowmelt gushing over granite ledges. Why did he leave my bedroom door ajar? Why did he chuckle? What was he thinking? *Was* he thinking? Did he remember? Why me?

The two sides of Dad—the generous, kindhearted friend, and the narcissistic, self-serving man—made the sound of a clashing gong inside my head. I didn't see myself as a victim. I saw myself as a mistake. It was my fault; everyone loved both my father and my mother. It couldn't have been him. Thirty-six years of confusion flooded her room. In my work and in my community, I was viewed as capable, trustworthy, bold; inside that room, I was infantile, uneducated, bewildered.

By the end of our first fifty-minute session, I'd learned that denial had protected me against what I couldn't yet handle. She suggested books, and I read them all—on sexual abuse, narcissism, shame, and anger—poring over statistics and anguishing stories far worse than mine. I couldn't sleep. I wanted to understand my disappointment, anger, embarrassment, resentment, fear. So many new feelings, and so much to learn. Over the next months, this deep dive took on focus, as if I'd started a second company, requiring drive, commitment, and resolve similar to that of consulting, only this one I kept to myself. I was in hazy pursuit of diffused, tangled layers. It was more a feeling than a goal. Years later, working with Marshall Goldsmith at a business school in its executive education program, I was introduced to the signature line he gave to leaders on their way up the ladder, "What got you here won't get you there." It summed up for me the pivot I had needed, from old habits to new intention. The years of entertainment from my parents' stories, of putting my father on a pedestal of perfection, of believing his words—they were behind me.

Without denial as my cover, my nerve endings lay bare on my skin. My family had sold me a bill of goods. If we were so special, then what was this? In her room, no question was left off the table. In my journals, I spared no words. From clarity, I built resolve. The walls of her room became my skin. And as I changed myself, I intuited there'd have to be changes in my marriage if Alex and I we were to integrate the new me.

— ∽⊗∾ —

Six months into this hard look in the mirror, during the fall of 1987, and at the end of a killer week of work with multiple consulting clients and multiple flights, I was looking forward to a weekend full of kids' activities spread across several towns. I headed up to my home office early on Saturday morning, and felt a pain in my chest. A whisper at first, then a severe burning; then a stabbing. My heart raced, and I thought I might pass out. Pain shot down my arm. My palms were covered in sweat. I tried to ignore it but couldn't, and called Mark, who told me to meet him in his office. Alex would watch the kids.

Mark was that rare physician with whom I could work professionally—we served on a hospital board together—while seeking from him my medical care. He asked questions and ran tests. It wasn't a heart attack, he said, assuring me that would be unlikely, given my lack of risk factors. He suggested I sit down across from him at his desk. He leaned back in his chair, his Saturday L.L.Bean flannel shirt comforting me for the moment. Then there was a pause.

"I think your heart is fine," he said.

"Well, that's good. So, what's wrong with me?"

"I think it's post-traumatic stress," he continued. "The same thing soldiers have. Sexual abuse survivors experience it, too."

Me? PTSD? He offered suggestions: that I spend more time outdoors, that I enjoy my kids, that I scale back my commitment to work. I nodded, already doing the first two as well as I could, and pretty sure the third wasn't in the cards. I enjoyed working with smart, interesting people, and I liked that we had more money.

"How's the therapy going? he asked.

"Hard. Good."

"She's very good. Stick with it. I know you very well. You'll come through this stronger on the other side. You may not believe me today, but you will. But you can't go back to who you were. You have to find out who you are now."

His confidence was like a charm I held in my pocket and pulled out when I threatened to retreat from my personal work. I wasn't afraid to ask the tough questions. Had Dad been drunk? Did it matter? Did anyone else know? What did he want when he saw I was asleep, in Hanover? What did he want when he entered my bedroom in Florida?

"You pushed him away," my therapist said. "And then you pushed him away again. That took courage." It didn't feel like courage. Courage was what my cousin Susan was displaying in running a twelve-hundred-mile sled dog race in blizzards in Alaska, for which she was named Female Athlete of the Year. What I'd done was what anyone would do if their house was burning down: run like hell and try to save your life if you could.

———— ✺ ————

One year into therapy, I needed to hear from someone who knew my father and would give me his honest opinion. John Hennessey, my next-door neighbor while growing up in Hanover, was my first choice. His wife, Jean, was my mother's best friend, and John, then dean of the business school at Dartmouth, had mentored me in math as a kid, advised me through finishing college, and encouraged me to get my MBA. We'd become friends as adults. I felt close to him but we'd never had this kind of conversation.

Jean came to the door after I rang the bell.

"Gretchie," she bellowed, using my family nickname, and poured me a cup of tea. "I know you're meeting with John, but do stop by again and see us both sometime. We'd love it. Right now, I have an election to win and I'm calling every person I know." Jean, one of the *grande dames* of New Hampshire democratic politics, was working feverishly for Michael Dukakis's bid for president.

John showed me into his gracious home office, with its floor-to-ceiling bookshelves and Oriental rug. Impeccably dressed in gray flannels, a tweed jacket, an oxford shirt and tie—even on Saturday—he had the requisite Dartmouth mementos on his shelves, along with pictures of his two children, whom I'd grown up with, and his first two grandchildren, who were the same ages as my kids. I stumbled through my story, ashamed to be telling him, embarrassed to be so intimate. John held a steady gaze without interrupting. He had long championed equal rights for women, to the point of telling Dartmouth he wouldn't take its offer of making him dean at the Tuck School of Business unless the college started admitting women as undergrads. When he spoke to me, he didn't mince words.

"The way your father looked at you just wasn't right," he said. "He had you on a pedestal, not as a well-loved child, but more as an object. It was troubling to both Jean and me."

"I can't believe you're saying this. That's exactly how I felt."

"It was uncomfortable to watch."

"It's like he had a version of me that was never me. He never really *knew* me."

"This information is very concerning to me," John said, in his quiet, gentlemanly way. "I'm honored that you've trusted me. Now, tell me, who else knows?"

"Alex, of course."

He nodded.

"And Dikkon."

"And what was his response?"

"He listened to me but hasn't mentioned it since."

"You'll need good people to help you through this. I will always be here for you, but do you feel you have good friends whom you can trust?"

"I have incredible friends, along with my cousins, Kate and Susan, Eloise and Lil." John knew these cousins and nodded his head. "You'll tell them in time. When you're ready. I will not speak of this to anyone else."

"I'm okay if you tell Jean."

"She, too, will be saddened by this, but I can't say that I'm surprised."

— ∞ —

Sexual abuse hides underground, dwelling in the shadow world of families. Thirty percent of us never reveal our truth to anyone. We let the abuser win his intimate battle, sometimes to save him or our families, sometimes to save ourselves. I was determined not to be in that 30 percent, but I had no clue what that might mean, nor when or where I'd feel safe enough to speak. If I couldn't trust my father, then, really, whom could I trust? It's the things we don't see that deceive us and I'd not seen a lot. Deeply buried secrets only prolonged my suffering. Silence is isolation, as bad as the abuse itself.

As a consultant, I'd been inside dozens of companies by then. I'd looked around and asked questions. I'd listened. I'd gotten a feel for the way employees talked about where they worked—whether they could be honest, whether they felt it was safe to raise legitimate concerns. It was the culture at NASA that had prevented engineers from voicing their concern about the O-rings in the Space Shuttle Challenger. I'd witnessed leaders resisting voiced concerns while others welcomed them and, with new information, were capable of change. I preferred working in the companies whose actions day in and day out lived up to the pretty words posted on their walls. In corner suites, I listened to the stories of CEOs and saw, in real time, how hard it was for some of them to change. No matter how many books I read, I'd learn the most about culture inside a company from observation, as I had, circling the poets when I was a kid. I considered confronting my father—but didn't believe he'd have more to give me than a shrug. Instead, I focused on how to shed the shame I carried, how my own brand of self-centeredness and denial had brought me only so far and wouldn't get me where I wanted to go

— ∞ —

In October 1989, I heard about a three-day workshop designed for finding our "essential" selves. It sounded woo-woo, but colleagues I trusted had suggested it. I figured it couldn't hurt. It was there that I first had to connect the term *sexual abuse* with my father. The workshop allowed me another forum—with strangers—in which to confront my darkness, and I thought about my marriage with Alex. I thought we were okay, despite occasional rough patches. The kids were growing and doing well. We sometimes got away on our own. We were involved in our community in meaningful ways. Now, I wanted to be sure Alex and I weren't withholding things from each other, that we were addressing our problems as they arose and strengthening our bond.

Home from the retreat, full of new ideas and some lessening of grief about Dad, I felt deep love for Alex and a full commitment to our marriage. We'd made it through twenty years together, eighteen of them married. With kids who were fifteen and ten, I thought, we had time to integrate the new me.

His band was scheduled to play at a Halloween party that night. We carved out time for me to give him the headlines from my weekend, before we had dinner. I'd missed the kids over those three days and opted to stay home that evening. The four of us gathered for a quick dinner before Alex picked up his guitars and headed out.

Three months later, in late January 1990, Alex confessed he'd met someone at the Halloween party, a woman twenty years younger, dressed in a toga—the love of his life, he said—and they'd been seeing each other since then. Four months after that, he announced to me, and then to the kids, he wanted a trial separation.

Chapter 18:

Body, Breath, and Belief

Spring 1990, I was on my own with the kids in our family home. It was a Friday morning, after Ben and Molly were off to school, when I touched my toe tentatively to my sticky yoga mat under the skylight, as if I were testing the ocean temperature in Maine. My toe symbolized a question. Could I commit to this practice? Was I all in this morning? I'd carved out this hour before I would launch into a day on the phone with clients. Commitment beyond the next hour or two felt like a stretch.

Recovery from trauma, I was learning, had to start in my body. It was where the trauma had found its hold. Cellular, not intellectual, it was bound up in neurons. It couldn't all be talked through in therapy or with friends. Its roots were tangled and buried in crevices, its screaming hold knotted in synapse and sinew, its journey to light trapped first under muscle and bone. Among other things, I was humiliated by my husband's departure; it felt like one more traumatic blow for my body to absorb. As the one remaining in our home and in our tightknit community, it was I who had to answer everyone's questions—*What? You seemed the perfect pair; what was he thinking? Did you know this was coming?*—only adding insult to injury.

I stood on my mat, eyes closed, and allowed my office—full of blinking lights and to-do lists—to recede from my mind. I let go of the thinking I'd been doing in therapy. Later, I would look back on the first half of 1990 as a shapeless, surreal time between marital separation and I knew not what. I circled in loops, asking myself if I should hope for a new beginning or prepare for an end. I didn't know. I got no clear signal.

Shoulders back and knees soft, I rooted myself to the mat and stood in mountain, the deceivingly simple pose that wakes me up whenever I am in it fully. My feet were tentacles digging through the soft outer layer of earth. My head was a cloud reaching for the sky. There were no critics there on my mat, no man telling me who I was or what I should do, no judgment, no blame. There was only room for body, breath, and belief. That slow practice was a far cry from how I normally lived in my body, which was moving at high speed. I took to the hills that May and June as fast as my legs and bike could carry me. My biking buddy, Sharon, and I had planned a Saturday ride, for a loop around Mount Ascutney. We would leave from her house near me for a sixty-mile circuit—my first serious test in the early biking season. I'd signed up for a century ride in July, and I needed miles.

I biked to stay in shape, to feel free, to visit with women friends, and, especially that year, to burn off anger and steam unleashed by the separation. The rolling hills of New Hampshire and Vermont provided miles of challenging terrain, and a rhythm to mastering my gears. I'd checked in with Sharon the night before to finalize our plans.

"I don't want to do sixty," she'd declared. "I'll do fifty with you, but not sixty."

"I need sixty," I said. Sharon was training for a much tougher ride, up Mount Washington in August—a ride started in 1973 for elite cyclists from around the world. At 7.6 miles, it's not its distance but its pitch. And Mt. Washington's notorious weather can dish up record wind, rain, sleet, snow, or ice, even in August.

"Too many miles this week already," she said, "My legs are shot."

"Okay, I'll tack on ten at the end."

Our route took us south along the river, before crossing into Vermont and climbing the south flank of Mount Ascutney. Temperature in the mid-sixties, little wind, bright sun. Two friends on four wheels, talking about our gardens, our kids, and our miles, then in long meditative periods, riding single file. A whiff of newly mown grass caught my nose as we passed sleepy cows and frantic chickens along the way. Forty-five miles later, we'd made our final turn back toward Sharon's house. Downshifting, we headed up the last hill into our town.

"Oh, all right," Sharon called back to me, "I'll do another ten."

"I knew you would! It'll be our best." We sprinted five miles south of town and back, before pulling into Sharon's driveway. We checked our computers: fifty-nine miles.

"Huh? Really? I want sixty."

Sharon laughed. "You're on your own." We hugged over our bikes. "I'm headed to the hammock," she said.

I clicked into my pedals and did a quick sprint out and back until I saw 60 on my computer. I was thinking about power, the power of my quads and glutes, to move my bike. I'd been getting nowhere on a temporary separation agreement with my husband, just a simple list of things we needed to agree on about the kids and money, but I'd gotten my miles, something within my control.

— ◊ —

In August of that year, I took the kids to Europe for a trip we'd planned as a family. I couldn't afford it, almost canceled, but went anyway, hoping the distance would provide perspective. Molly and Ben were eleven and sixteen. We scoured London from the top of double-decker buses and mastered the Underground. Together, we took tea at Kensington Gardens and sang our way through *The Buddy Holly Story* at the Victoria Palace Theatre. In Paris, I forked over the best $50 I'd spent in months for one Coke, one limonade, and one beer on the Champs-Élysées, in exchange for two free hours of street theater. From our four-hundred-year-old stone rental in Beaucaire, the kids could practice their French by picking up pastries and fruit for breakfast, and again when I sent them out for baguettes, *jambon*, and *fromage* for sandwiches. Over two weeks, Molly and I played in the Mediterranean while Ben and a buddy from Seattle, whose parents owned a house in Beaucaire, rode their bikes to the Pont du Gard to swim. (Years later, I'd learn that the boys, taking advantage of the sixteen-year-old French drinking age, had snuck out regularly after dark to play *boule* with elderly Frenchmen in the square who spoke no English.) We hiked up and around Les Baux-de-Provence and drove through fields of late lavender and sunflowers with the windows down in our rental car, belting out Buddy Holly and immersing ourselves in the beauty of the countryside.

Despite an underlying sadness to that trip, the wide Atlantic cushioned the shock of separation and gave me some peace. Ancient French towns provided a longer arc of history with which to look at the day-to-day dramas of my falling-apart marriage. I devoured Alice Walker's *The Temple of My Familiar*, fell in love with her main character, and signed on to the Gospel According to Shug: *Helped are those who love others unsplit off from their own faults. Helped are those who strive to give up anger.* My anger dissipated by being in those old French towns. Shug had given me hope.

On our return to New Hampshire, buoyed by our respite, the kids were ready for a new school year and I was looking at a full calendar of consulting work, aware that Alex and I had a lot to figure out if we were to reunite. I assumed that was the option we'd focus on first, and I was ready for that work. A few days after our return from France, he came to the house with a request for divorce.

— ∞ —

In early September, pulled to memory in muscle and bone, I stood on my mat and breathed in autumn, a season of change. I took deep, slow, steady breaths, filling my lungs with what belief I still had—in my kids, in my circle of women friends, in my work with clients—and reached out for warrior. Arm level to the ground, legs holding firm, my core pulled in, I scanned the four decades of my life—through poetry-filled living rooms, through the early idyll that had been Undercliff, through the hopes and betrayals of growing up in my family, through the dream of Alex's and my home and our children in New Hampshire. I turned my *drishti* toward a small statue of Buddha, letting my mind wander through the public squares and gardens of London, the wild beaches of southern France, my schoolmates Lucy and Sarah in Lausanne, the beggars and prostitutes in Cairo, dinner with Ginsberg, the promise of Sexton, the forested trails right outside my door. I leaned into the moment, in warrior pose, and realized I was fine in the here and now but was stuck when looking ahead. I saw nothing.

Grief had no boundary that year. Harvey, my boyfriend in Owatonna, died in a car crash in May. Molly's puppy died in July. Gram died in September. Grief stalked me each day and hung its hat on my head at night. It burrowed into the weave of my clothes until I finally told it to get out. It made me nearly nod off in business meetings and ride much too fast on my bike. The two most important men in my life had betrayed me. And I had failed—failed to do whatever it was that would have kept them from betraying me. I was still tied to that lingering shame of it all being my fault.

—⊷—

In mid-October, I was driving south toward Hanover after a chilly bike ride. Through inconsolable tears, I was racked with emotion. Angry and confused, terrified and sad, I couldn't stop crying. A cop pulled me over.

"Do you realize you were going forty-five in a thirty, ma'am?"

"I'm so sorry," I said through tears. "I'm going through a divorce. I didn't see the sign."

"I need you to sit tight while I check your license. I'll be right back."

Quickly, I pulled my fingers through my hair, slipped a sweater over my bike shirt, and dabbed water from my bike bottle on my face, hoping to make the splotches go away. I watched as the cop got out of his car and walked back to mine. I couldn't afford a $100 ticket, and I couldn't afford points on my license, since I drove long miles for some of my work.

"All right, ma'am, I see you have no other violations. I'm just giving you a warning this time. But be careful on the road and watch the speed limits. We don't want you to get hurt."

"Thank you, Officer. I appreciate it. I'm really sorry."

"I hope things work out for you," he said, tapping the frame of my window. "I'm sure they will in time."

He handed me a piece of paper with the phone number of a local agency that could help if I needed it. This small act of kindness from a cop marked a U-turn. I'd spent enough time slogging through the past, but he'd helped me look forward—not very far, but forward. It was up to me to construct what that forward would mean. Up to me to seize what I'd built so far—two growing adolescents, a growing company—and see where I could take them.

—⚬—

In January 1991, my mother-in-law, Rita, died of a recurrence of cancer. It was heartbreaking not to be with her, but Alex wanted to go on his own with our kids.

Divorce was brutal. It took forever to make simple agreements. I was raw, had trouble breathing; my jaw stayed clenched. I lost my appetite. Friends confused what they saw as beauty in slimness for what it really was: a deep and wrenching emptiness. I thought of the message I'd picked up from Mom about true love, a high-stakes game in which you had to strategize and manipulate to win, and wanted no more of that, but still had to ensure my soon-to-be ex did his share. On my mat each morning, I made a daily commitment—to my children, to the day, to our future. Toggling between these two spaces—grief and commitment—I folded into sitting forward bend. Suddenly, in that pose, it occurred to me that not eating, driving and biking too fast, and being depressed were lousy strategies for a life. Plus, there was a lot of good going on, cracks of clear sunshine piercing the black door of my mind. Long conversations with Ben late at night by the woodstove after hockey practice. Girl time shopping with Molly. Each of them making their first pies from scratch—pumpkin and apple—for the first Thanksgiving we celebrated on our own. They were making smart decisions in their high school lives, and I marveled at their strength and resilience, their ability to talk things through. They were the kids I'd wanted when I'd thought about having children: strong, independent, compassionate, honest, and wise.

A circle of women was there when I needed them. Business colleagues were flying me across the country and around the world to work with enormous companies at extravagant resorts in beautiful cities. My own clients were adding up to more work than I could handle, enabling me to build a real business. Positive changes stared down the devouring maw of divorce and reminded me that life could be good, that there was new opportunity in this change.

What did it mean to start over? On my mat, I began to identify threads of my past to carry forward—the inquisitiveness and generosity I'd learned from both my father and my mother, the emotional independence I'd learned after my separation from Alex, the physical ability I'd found in my legs and core, the power of voice I'd begun to discover when fully present with a client's innermost thoughts, the moral compass Gram had set for me. What if I claimed all that? Where might it take me?

— ᴥ —

One morning in the spring of 1991, I woke from a bad dream at 2:30 a.m. In the dream, Sharon and I were biking up a long, gradual ascent on Route 118. It was a beautiful day, when an eighteen-wheeler appeared out of nowhere and wiped me off the road. I was dead in the ditch when I woke up.

I called Sharon and told her about my dream. We were supposed to go on that ride later in the morning. "Do you think we should cancel?"

"No," Sharon said, "but we better keep our eyes out for eighteen-wheelers. Make sure you've got your mirror."

This would be a new route, one we'd done parts of but had never strung together. We rode the rail trail east to Canaan and stopped to stretch and hydrate. Sharon pulled out her first attempt at homemade power bars.

"What? No white-chocolate brownies today?"

"I'm off sugar. What do you think?"

"Not bad for spelt and dried fruit."

"I threw in a little seaweed."

"Wish you hadn't told me that!"

Back on our bikes, we battled a severe headwind when I caught in my mirror our first eighteen-wheeler, pulling steadily toward us, his double trailer loaded with logs. My chest tightened. I kept my eye on him and watched his behavior in my mirror. Long before he approached us, he pulled wide, so I held my ground, twelve inches from the edge of the road, with a ditch to my right. After he passed, I exhaled.

"I guess it was a dream!" I yelled at Sharon.

My date with divorce court was three months away, in October, and the period leading up to it would be excruciating, like a confrontation with a bear, as fierce and relentless as anything I'd ever known. While riding with Sharon that day, I could admit to withholding on both sides, to the fact that I'd carried into my marriage the denial I'd learned as a coping strategy in my first family. Alex and I were equally at fault for different things.

We rode twenty miles up Route 118 against a relentless headwind.

"We'll lose it on Twenty-Five," Sharon promised.

"Right!" I yelled ahead. "When does that ever happen?"

On Route 25, the wind came at our sides, making it tough to stay upright, pushing our lightweight bikes in its gusty crossfire.

"Perfect training for Mount Washington, right?" I yelled back to Sharon.

"Right."

Turning west to climb Mount Cube, we came to Lower Baker Pond and I yelled, "Want to stop?"

The pond was a quiet mirror of water, a secluded place, where when I looked at my reflection I saw a strong woman beside a good friend, reclaiming her life. We stretched, stripped, and swam, the lake to ourselves. We snapped back into our pedals and headed up Mount Cube to earn our payoff on the other side: five miles of rolling descent and an entire surface of new pavement. I took that ribbon of black satin as a positive sign.

During our last stretch, on a beautiful country road along the Connecticut River, surrounded by gracious New England homes, a flock of starlings darted in front of us and we rolled through a symphony of peony colors on both sides of the road. A baby fawn and its mother leaped through the meadow grass. At one with my bike, gears shifting in perfect cadence with my heart, leg muscles in harmony with every kink in the road, I had to let life in. No logistics or legalities to sift and sort. That day, I replaced hurt with love and found Zen in the midst of chaos.

— ⌇ —

In late October, my friend Katie wanted to throw me a divorce party a few days before I had to appear in court. Against my protest, she prevailed: *Gretchen reclaiming her life*, she'd written to a dozen of my favorite women. Katie had been divorced a year before and had become a close confidant and friend through our mutual marital changes. Over potluck food and wine that evening, our group laughed and shared stories of my early marriage. I cried.

Earlier that day, Katie had helped me take down the photographs and last reminders of my husband. We packed the memories into a box—wedding photos, letters, marriage certificate, my wedding dress, my ring—and sealed it with tape. I'd thought her idea silly, but she'd persisted, saying I wouldn't really know, perhaps until years from then, what I wanted to do with the stuff. We labeled the box HISTORY and placed it on the highest shelf of a storage closet.

I was sad for my kids. Sad that they wouldn't know a forever marriage between their parents. Sad they'd heard and witnessed too much. Sad in all the ways I'd failed them as a mom. But I knew them. I believed in them. Failure opens us to greater opportunity, to things we couldn't even envision before.

The day the state of New Hampshire made our divorce official, following nineteen years of marriage, I came home emotionally spent, pulled on my yoga tights, and went directly to my mat. I'd arranged for the kids to be with their friends that afternoon, knowing I'd need some time on my own. I sat on my heels and bent forward as far as I could, stretching my arms into child's pose. I thought of Mary Oliver's words in her poem "Wild Geese," about letting the soft animal of our body love what it loves. I loved my children, my friends, my home, my work, and the lifelong camaraderie of being outdoors on skis, on a bike, in hiking boots, with each of my favorite people. I scooped up memories of places I'd loved: the rocky coastline of Penobscot Bay; the snow-swept Swiss Alps; the Bedouin families outside Cairo tucking in their camels for the night; Parisian merchants laying out their fruit each morning; tuk-tuk drivers in the chaos of central Bangkok, where I'd recently been going on business trips; our local store unfurling its flag. Neither Mom nor Dad had shown me the hard work of love, the truthfulness and mutual respect that are essential over a long marriage. Neither had prepared me to address deceitfulness and betrayal, nor how to make my way in a world still governed by men.

—⌇⌇—

Post marriage, on consulting trips out of town and country, I covered my hotel-room bed with sheets of paper, slowly constructing a spreadsheet—pre-Excel—tallying up income on one side and subtracting expenses on the other. Consulting revenue was my only reliable source of income, regardless of what the court had decreed my ex would provide, and that source was entirely dependent on my producing good work and selling more. I couldn't yet see when the income and expenses would match, and I'd had to assume debt I hadn't known we had. I slashed expenses and sold more work. All I wanted—still—was to know what was real. Honest financial and emotional balance sheets. No deceit. Nothing withheld.

Over that year and into the next two, my ledger sessions began showing progress. I was good at selling, bringing to the task my father's curiosity and generosity and my mother's timing and wit. I built long-term relationships with clients, which quickly led to multiyear contracts for large-scale projects. The company I'd started on a whim was thriving. I was looking ahead, and it looked like I'd make it.

Over the handlebars of our bikes and bottles of wine in restaurants, women friends helped me extract lessons from my marriage as they opened up about the things they thought had made theirs successful. I listened. Mostly, it was the obvious things, like doing what you say you'll do, carving out time for genuine connection, apologizing when you're wrong. I should have learned all that from my family of origin. I'd used them to build my company, but they'd gone missing in the later years of my marriage. I'd failed in some of these. Looking back, I could see that Alex had had one foot out the door for longer than I'd known. My inherited familial denial had gotten in the way of what I should have seen.

We'd done the best we could with what we brought to our marriage. We'd been kids, really, when we started, and, albeit hidden deep in my body back then, sexual abuse had been there alongside us. Closets, whether we put ourselves in them or others put us there, are dark and lonely places. What I needed was light. I was no longer the person I'd been when he'd met me, and, with eyes now fully open, I saw he wasn't the same, either.

— ∞ —

The afternoon of my divorce, I stretched out on my mat and did an hour of asanas, before slowly finding my way to corpse pose. It seemed ironically fitting for that day. The light was fading, and my sweat was cooling. The kids would be home soon. Eyes closed, I laid out a simple plan for the next year: support my children as well as I knew how; care for my business clients honestly and straightforwardly; take the trust and intimacy I was finding in corner suites, mostly with male executives, and see what I could do with it in my social life. There was no rush. I breathed in deeply and let go.

I rolled up my mat, anticipating a favorite pasta dish I'd make for supper, a salad of fresh greens, the crusty bread I'd picked up at the bakery on my way home from court. I would set a nice table for myself and my kids and have fun with them, sharing their day's activities. The past was done. I was ready for what lay ahead.

Chapter 19:

A Man Named Bill

I passed a $20 bill to the driver as I stepped out of his cab, and told him to keep the change. It was 1992, and I had little cash to spare, but I was running late. The skirt of my new, navy-blue suit from Joseph A. Banks had ridden up in the backseat, and I nudged it down. Four years earlier when I was in business school, we'd been told we needed to fit in with men, and that the best way to do that was to dress like them, talk like them, and laugh at their jokes. Consulting was a different world than the one I'd known running a nonprofit health agency, and one of the requisite changes I'd had to accept was wearing suits. My appointment that day was with a prospective client who had sounded friendly on the phone.

"I've heard great things about you," he'd said.

"I've heard the same about you. Thanks for setting this up."

I needed the work. Equally important, I needed to feel better, though a sales call could take me either way.

Inside his lobby, I hitched my briefcase over my shoulder and listened to my heels clicking on the marble floor, causing the outer ring of Bill's protectors to look up from their desks.

"I'm his next appointment," I said to his assistant, introducing myself. She was better coiffed and clothed than I was. She let me through to the CEO's outer waiting room, and I felt butterflies take lift in my stomach. The plush burgundy velveteen of his sofa felt soft under my hands. *What am I doing here? And what do I know about his industry? And what does a middle-aged man need from his forty-one-year-old consultant?* The sofa and the beautiful Asian carpet under my feet were like nothing I'd ever owned. Mahogany wainscoting lined the walls, and subdued lighting relaxed my busy mind. I could have parked myself there for a few days just for the quiet. Despite my strengthening resolve on my yoga mat and bike, a keening sorrow still hollowed my heart.

I picked up an industry puff piece and read its headline, "Privilege and Fame"—apparently a reference to the two gray-haired men in navy-blue suits on its cover. I just hoped my matching skirt and jacket would get me a pass through this CEO's door. I was still not getting regular sleep. I hoped CoverGirl was concealing my tired eyes.

I had three goals for that meeting. Listen and find rapport. Leave something of value. Don't fumble over my daily rate. The third was still hard, but over time I would figure out exactly what to charge and would place rates at the high end of the market to reflect the value I was being told I provided. That day, I just hoped I didn't choke on the number.

The door to Bill's office opened, interrupting my reverie. He was precisely on time. Tailored suit, not from Joseph A. Banks. Fifteen years older than I? Boyish brown hair, highlighted by sun. Confident in his skin.

"Hi, Gretchen. I'm Bill. I've been looking forward to our visit. How was your flight?" He led me into his office and pointed to the seat on the other side of his desk. "Mind if I take off my jacket?"

I had less than a minute to make a first impression, so I scanned his credenza for something to say. A photograph of a shingled house on a bluff caught my eye. Nantucket, maybe? We'd been told not to talk about a man's family, so I couldn't use that. A row of business books, most of which I'd read, were kept upright between two brass sailboats.

I eyed the recent bestseller *In Search of Excellence.*

"Do you like it?" Bill asked.

"I don't love it," I said. My office copy was dog-eared and underlined because everyone in every company was reading it, even if it couldn't hold a candle to what I'd learned about business from Mario Puzo and Chinua Achebe, or about life from Toni Morrison and Russell Banks.

"That makes two of us," Bill said. "I seem to be the only person I know who didn't get that much from it. We're already clear on our mission and understand our market. I took this job because my wife and I like what the company stands for."

"Has it been a good decision?" I asked, noting his reference to his wife.

"It has. But I've been here long enough, a year now, to know what the problems are, and the first thing I want to talk about is one of the vice presidents I inherited."

I liked that he'd cut to the chase.

"Tell me about him," I said, relying on the fact that most senior teams back then were composed of men.

"He's bright. Maybe too bright." Bill ticked off the VP's impressive résumé: Harvard undergrad, Wharton MBA, ten years at a Wall Street bank. "Technically, he's as good as they get. His wife's family's from Buffalo, that brought them here two years ago. He's good at everything we ask of him." Bill leaned back in his chair, searching for words, carefully threading a needle between candor and discretion. I suspected he felt uncomfortable talking about someone who wasn't in the room. I respected that. "But he's making life miserable for every person around him. He's high-strung. Is that the right way to say it? He drives us all nuts, including me." Bill combed his fingers through his hair, a trait I would notice him employ when he was nervous.

"Tell me more," I said.

"Do you sail?" Bill asked, gesturing to a photograph on the wall. It was Nantucket.

"Every summer as a kid," I said, explaining that my family had summered in Maine. "But colder water. Penobscot Bay. My first sailboat was an eight-foot pram named *Ozzie*. It especially liked going backward."

Bill laughed. "Then you know how it is when you're out on the water, enjoying a light breeze, and an enormous powerboat steams by, ignoring you, throwing a big wake. He's like that, and I'm left cleaning up his messes. People are starting to call him arrogant."

"I know the type," I said, which was factually correct, if not entirely about executives yet. Arrogance was sprinkled through the men in my family and most of the writers around whom I'd grown up. I knew what it felt like to be around that trait. It was unlikely to feel different dressed in a suit.

"Can you help me with him?"

Bill was frustrated with not having succeeded himself, and this moment of vulnerability was exactly what I was looking for.

"I'll want to meet him and the people around him before drawing conclusions," I hedged, "but, yes, I can help you with that." I was thinking ahead to the interviews I would want to do and the feedback I might have to give Bill. I'd had success inside a short list of companies, and I was interested in what he presented, but I had to feel out whether he could accept honest feedback.

"You'll meet everyone," Bill said, easing my sales job. "Then you can decide. If you think I should let him go, I'll listen, but really, I hope we can help him, because he's got more talent than most of us and he'll be expensive to replace." There were his motivations. Bill sat back in his chair and allowed a pause in our conversation. I'd read that execs spent about fifteen minutes on any given task, but he was taking his time, digging in, trying to figure things out.

"So, other than your VP, what keeps you up at night?"

Bill stared into space for a few seconds, before returning his eyes to mine. He ran through a detailed history of how the bank had become what it was: its successful hundred-year run, its reputation in its market, its consistent earnings, its contributions to the region it served. But the world had changed, and his managers were ill-equipped to lead without gaining new skills. They deferred too much to Bill. They were smart and loyal, but not sophisticated. There was an opportunity there, I thought. The recession was squeezing his margins, and the future looked far less certain.

"How do you change a hundred-year-old company?" he mused.

"A friend of mine says it's not the company that changes but the people inside it who do," I offered.

"I like that. We've brought in consultants, but they have so little real experience. They give us their recommendations and leave. I heard you have solid business skills and are a quick learner. Really, I'm looking for someone to work alongside us as we reset our course and build for the future." I liked that he was thinking long-term. I didn't know much about his industry, but that was learnable. I knew something about change: how hard it is, and why we resist it.

"What worries me most," he continued, "is this very talented guy whom no one wants to work with. Let's start with him."

"And what about you?" I asked. "What's your contribution to this? What could you do differently?"

"Whatever I'm doing now hasn't worked." He smiled. "Honestly, I'm frustrated. And being frustrated isn't helping. If you've got ideas, I'm open. This place is different. Better than the big banks, but I don't have in-house consultants here."

Bill's vulnerability stood in contrast with the men I'd known in my family of origin and in my first marriage. He didn't defend himself or walk out. He took each question as seriously as I'd intended it. In an era when male CEOs were just beginning to bring women onto their management teams and boards, Bill was ahead of the curve, since he already had two women on his board, a female commercial lender, and was considering me as his consultant. He wanted someone with whom he could share problems candidly, weigh his options before making change, and not have to worry about internal politics while he did.

"By the way," Bill said, as he wrapped up our first meeting, "this was a great conversation. I have plenty of advisors, but they don't ask me questions like these. I've never really talked about any of these things with anyone but my wife."

"Thanks." I smiled, realizing we'd passed each other's tests. "Will we need a contract?"

"No," Bill said, extending his hand. "Our handshake is good enough."

On the flight home, I scribbled notes for a simple follow-up letter. I checked my calendar for a block of days I could spend inside his company. Looking out the window of the plane, I thought of a male colleague on the hospital board I was on. He was the chief operating officer of an award-winning manufacturing company, and one of a dozen people I'd sought out for advice when I'd first considered going into consulting. "Being a woman will impede you," he'd said, "and I think it will be tough to get into corporate consulting after working in a nonprofit." I'd left his office not only angry but incensed that in 1987, that kind of thinking was still the norm. I would prove him wrong. I'd already learned that being a woman was not an impediment. Over time, I'd come to see it as an asset. Bill and others like him could open up more with me than with their male advisors. What was important in that meeting was Bill's trust, a commodity I'd found, in my personal life, in short supply. In Bill's quiet corner suite, we had started what would become a dozen-year partnership. I didn't know it on that flight home, but what we'd put in motion that day was a crash course in how I'd build my company. One executive at a time, starting where they wanted to start and encouraging them to bring their whole selves to the job. They were no different than I. Their core questions were often the same: Who am I? What's important to me? How should I proceed? Watching me in a room with their employees, they got comfortable seeing a woman lead. With their companies as background, it was their personal growth that fascinated me. I was humbled by their stories and their marked difference from my father and ex-husband. As they expected me to own my power, I encouraged them to think about theirs. How did they want to use it? What could they accomplish with it that would make a difference in the world? To be of service I would need to continue doing my own personal work. It would take another decade to understand my early attraction to working with teams at the top of organizations. As a kid, I'd been around writers at the top of their field, and hadn't been welcomed in. Now, I was being offered a seat at the men's table.

Chapter 20:

Falling for Real

Just before midnight on a Saturday in the spring of 1992, one year after my divorce and two years into my reading of Dad's letters, A Roomful of Blues was finishing its final, brassy set before packing up its instruments and heading back to Providence. The hundred-foot-long hardwood floor at the American Legion hall was plastered with dancers. Michael and I had been swinging and jiving since the first song. I hadn't had such fun in years.

Michael smiled as he pulled me in and swung me out, building moves to the rhythm of the blues. If he had some Prince in him that night, albeit dressed in loose linens, maybe I had a little Fonda-fit, Joplin sass.

— ᛒ —

On a bike ride the prior autumn, I'd been telling Sharon how not ready I was to get into any kind of relationship with anyone. I had plenty to do with my two children, my work and my circle of friends. But companionship might be okay. "I'd just like to have dinner with someone nice or maybe go to a movie," I'd said.

"Maybe you and Michael should get together," Sharon called to me as we legged our way up a hill during a long afternoon on our bikes. "He's in the same place."

"Which is?"

"In between."

I knew Michael as Sharon's brother, but I'd seen him only at big parties, where we'd said quick hellos. I wasn't holding my breath. The men I'd dated so far had fallen into three categories: boring, needy, or angry. None of those qualities appealed to me, as if the first group thought their monologues passed for communication; the second group needed the next woman to take care of them, either emotionally or financially, or both; and the third group thought their anger at their kids, exes, bosses, the world, should be taken for passion and make them attractive. I had just about sworn off dating altogether.

— ∞ —

"It's Michael," he said when he called my house a few months after Sharon had suggested him to me. A voice over my old-fashioned phone, the kind that hung on a wall by the refrigerator with a coiling cord long enough to walk across the room. I cradled the handset against my shoulder and continued washing the dishes stacked by the sink, my two busy teenagers alighting for food and dashing off to study halls, team practices, and hanging out with their friends. I ran the hot water and squeezed in more soap.

"How 'bout I come over and say hello?" he asked.

I scanned the hockey bag–strewn kitchen and the clothes I had on. Well, why not? I was only looking for a friend. Sharon had invited us to go skiing at Killington that day, a date I'd bailed on that morning, complaining of an aching lower back. Which was true—I did have a chronically aching back that year.

Thirty minutes later, Michael was sitting at my kitchen counter.

"How's your back, by the way?" he asked. We were sitting on hard wooden stools across from each other—not exactly good treatment for tight muscles—but I'd already noticed that the soreness had receded. "We had a good day skiing. Sorry you didn't make it."

"To be honest," I confessed, "it seemed like a long first date. Kind of scared me."

Michael smiled. We'd both seen it as a date. We quickly covered the two businesses we ran, my kids, his siblings, his ex and mine. I liked the way he didn't take himself too seriously. He was up front about things he'd had to change in his life, and he'd gained insight from therapy. He wasn't boring or needy and didn't seem angry. He seemed—could it be? I wondered—*normal.*

"It's been a tough few years," I admitted, considering Michael's clear blue eyes, "and denial built a shaky foundation. It's amazing how you can't see it when you're inside it."

"I know that one," he said, offering a beacon.

I laid out the CliffsNotes of the past couple years and mentioned that things were improving, that Ben and Molly were busy in their lives and had wonderful friends, and that consulting colleagues had recently invited me to do work overseas.

"Sounds like you're coming through it," Michael said, perhaps hopefully.

"Maybe, but I lost faith in a lot of good things, like trust and the future and especially men."

My remark didn't seem to deter him. "How about dinner next Friday? There's a dance we could go to. I can pick you up at seven."

Our first conversation felt like a clear border around a fuzzy puzzle I'd been trying to piece together in the aftermath of my divorce, in which I fantasized that two adults could share both a romantic life together and family logistics. Michael was attractive and open-minded and sounded responsible. Our first date, the following Saturday, started a long dance to fast music—taking us through a winter of snowstorms and a summer of heat waves— punctuated by work and kids and community boards we both served on, as we found our way into each other's hearts, to a backbeat of blues and swing.

— ∞ —

By the time we were wrapping up at the American Legion hall, a full year had passed. I was sweating off any last questions that remained about Michael. He'd already told me about every skeleton in his closet, as I had told him about mine. He knew how much my father had harmed me, how betrayed I'd felt by my ex. He'd checked me out with mutual acquaintances, and I'd done the same for him. There was only one Michael, I kept hearing. He is who you see he is; fun to be around and really solid since he's found himself.

On the dance floor, he didn't always lock my gaze like a great dance lead should. If we occasionally bumped shoulders with other couples, it was because we were swept up in the feel of a song, nuzzled in our own cocoon. Everything he'd done through that year and every word he'd said had proven true. That was new for me. He was like the best of my clients—smart, intensely interesting, and fun—only with a dose of sexiness thrown in. He made it easy for me to feel romantic again. I'd already learned he could fix everything I'd handed him—broken lamps, stubborn vacuum cleaners—now, I realized, he'd also fixed my broken heart.

That night, we'd found wider spins and more complex sequences. As we spun away from each other and returned, our hands met just where we knew they'd be. Michael dipped me so far back, my hair swept the hardwood floor, but his strong arm around the small of my back said what I'd been waiting my entire life to hear: *I got you, babe.* I was letting go, not holding back. I felt protected and safe.

"They're looking at us," I said after he lifted me off the floor.

"Are you spent?"

"Not quite. You?"

The band tuned up a Temptations cover, and Michael hummed the first lines of "My Girl" in my ear. With closed eyes, I imagined the two of us circling an elegant ballroom in New York with chandeliers and a beautiful hardwood floor that went on forever. Waiters in tuxes were serving fancy cocktails to beautifully dressed couples, and the big band was kicking into a tango. I saw myself in a sexy black cocktail dress with super-high heels, my bike-strong leg wrapped around Michael's waist. He was in tails, holding a perfect frame, his eyes locked on mine. We owned that floor. Quickly, I shook off my vision. I liked us even better in linen and jeans. No more myths. No more fantasies.

Opening my eyes, I noticed that the crowd had separated and formed a circle around our dance. Michael and I were grinning at each other when the horns hit an earsplitting crescendo to end the night.

Breathless and sweaty, I felt vulnerable with so many eyes on us yet certain in what we had. We'd both fallen for real. With Michael, I'd found my true, safe ground.

A younger dancer, whose kicks and flips we'd envied for months, came over and embraced us. "You guys are amazing. You're so fun to watch!" she said.

"We're not that good." Michael laughed.

"He steps on my toes." I blushed. "And I miss his lead."

"It's true," Michael added. "I do and she does."

"It's not about technique," she said. "It's about your love!"

Michael wrapped his arm around me and steered me outside, where the cool spring air pinched my skin. A sea of stars floated overhead as we stood in the parking lot outside the hall. I leaned against his beating chest and pulled at his shirt to wipe the sweat off my face. "You don't mind, right?"

"It's as wet as you are—be my guest."

On tiptoes, I whispered in his ear, "How'd we ever find each other in this godforsaken town?"

"Sometimes," he said, "we just get lucky."

Chapter 21:

Intrusion

In 1996, I flew to Hong Kong for a half-day consultation with one of the world's largest banks. A hundred managers had flown in from across Asia, eager to learn Western-style team building. The bank's global head of human resources, Dave, had come to observe. It was an easy morning after twenty-four hours in the air.

Dave joined us over lunch, our courses laid out on an engraved menu with characters I couldn't read. Ignoring what was on it, I dove into a starter placed in front of me, made of celery, thinly sliced on an angle, the color of celadon, its taste infused with sesame oil and a hint of red pepper. Lightly toasted sesame seeds were sprinkled on top. Light and delicate.

"Save yourself," Dave said, leaning over to flip the menu, English on the other side.

"Oh, thirteen courses?"

"This will go on for a while."

Each new business I worked with required learning a new set of jargon and rules, rituals and expectations. Each was like stamping my passport on entering a new country. History and leadership had shaped its culture and what it felt like to work there. Observing company cultures gave me a sharper lens on my family of origin in which Dad held the public power while we revolved around his

schedule and his needs. Mom, too, held power, but often by rebel-
lion—sometimes humorously, like when she fed the Richardses
peas for dinner; sometimes, with intention, like when she told Dad
she could use her own money to do what she wanted. Our rituals
revolved around the endless swirl of people they gathered around
them, moving from one house to another, hardly staying put long
enough to make solid friends, and a fully open-door policy for
visitors. All was in service to my parents' preferred lifestyle and my
father's career. It could be fun a lot of the time, but when something
went wrong—Percy's abuse, my father's sexual violations—we had
no practice for managing our feelings. Denial and avoidance were
our go-tos.

By the time I flew home from Hong Kong, my parents were
wrapping up one of their last winters in Gainesville. Mom had broken
her hip the year before, teaching us that forty years on Dilantin,
which had never really quelled her seizures, had caused osteoporosis.
Ben and Molly, and my brother's first two children, Lena and James,
were intrigued with the pins and plate Mom described were holding
her hip together. She created a book about her experience for her
grandchildren, illustrated with her fanciful watercolors.

"Will I break my hip, too, Gumma?" Molly asked.

"No," Mom said. "I only broke mine because I'm old."

"How old are you?" Molly asked, and Mom reminded her:
seventy.

"That's old!" Molly said.

"When you get old like I am," Mom explained, "things
happen that you don't have control over. It's not very much fun
getting old."

"Well, Gumma," Molly said, cheerfully encouraging her
grandmother, "you *are* old, but you're not dead yet!"

—◊◊◊—

Over lunch in Hong Kong, as one course turned into another,
Dave and I brainstormed ways to help make corporate interest in

building teams across the globe stick in Asia, where hierarchy was strongly protected. As we built a list of next steps, I plucked one succulent morsel after another from each course.

"You use them well," Dave noted, referring to my chopsticks.

"My father taught me," I said. "He took us to a lot of Chinese restaurants."

Dave got me thinking about a dinner in 1962, soon after Dad had won the Bollingen Prize. A round table full of his fans was having dinner in Boston, and, at ten, I'd claimed a seat next to him.

"First you take one stick, like this," Dad had instructed me. I watched as he placed a chopstick against the notch between his thumb and forefinger. The pale sticks felt good against my skin. My father's sparkling eyes and vigorous energy buoyed my learning.

"The next one goes here," he said, resting the second stick against the back of his thumb, on top of the first. I fumbled until I got the two sticks anchored right. My father spun the lazy Susan and spooned himself something from every platter. Then he reached for morsels from my plate. He'd learned how to use chopsticks in 1927, when he'd taken the job on the *S.S. Faralong* before attending Cambridge University. For him, using chopsticks was a sign of respect, a way to learn about a different culture. Halfway around the globe, I could see a quality in my father that I liked in myself.

— ⌇ —

Returning from Hong Kong, Michael and I were creating our own customs and moving easily between his hip loft, with a deck cantilevered over the Mascoma River, and my home in the country, twenty minutes away. Before long, we realized he hadn't left my house in two weeks.

"Shall we call it official?" he asked one morning.

"Okay by me," I said, and nuzzled against him.

By then, Ben was in college and Molly was a sophomore in high school. Michael and I made decisions easily. This version of love didn't require strategy or winning; it wasn't hard. He was a welcome shock to my outdated family system. Two years post divorce, the two sides of me that I'd believed would always be separate—the public me and the private me—had merged.

— ∞ —

Half-way through the 1990s, feeling better in my life, I liked having my Monday mornings carved out for Rauner as I continued in my father's archives. With help from Sarah Hartwell, I was fine-tuning what I wanted to see. Rauner is considered one of the most accessible special collections in the country. I could touch and feel original letters. Along with my father's collection, it holds the first edition of *The Book of Mormon*, the original version of *David Copperfield*, Shakespeare's first folio, Robert Frost's papers, a collection of George Washington's papers, and a large sample of archival materials by Dartmouth graduate Dr. Seuss. It's a beautiful space with high paned windows reaching for the sky, a dozen enormous oak study tables, and a hermetically sealed interior designed for the long-term storage of valuable paper documents.

I wanted to see if there were letters pertaining to a long affair my father had had. What Sarah pulled together for me was a surprise: a box full of letters between my father and his lover. Their affair had consumed a full decade of my parents' marriage, between 1974, the year Ben was born, and 1984, five years after the birth of Molly.

"Jesus," I said audibly, standing at one of Rauner's reading tables after Sarah left me with the folders. The student monitor at the desk in front of me looked up. "Sorry," I whispered, waving at her.

My father had met Joy in Gainesville the first winter he'd taught at the University of Florida. A children's literature professor, she'd warmly welcomed both my parents to town. Twenty years younger than Dad, she was perhaps starstruck by his friendship with famous children's book authors, like Robert McCloskey, who wrote *Make Way for Ducklings*, *One Morning in Maine*, and *Blueberries for Sal*. The McCloskeys lived on Scott Island, a regular picnic spot when we were out on Penobscot Bay. Or his friend E.

B. White, author of *Stuart Little* and *Charlotte's Web*. As a kid, I'd
swung on the long swing in White's barn and dreamed of Charlotte.

If my parents' mutual friendship with Joy had been carried
out in our public home, it hadn't sunk in for several years that it
might be more than that. I'd been busy raising my kids, finishing
college and graduate school, and working full-time. The summer
I first met Joy, I cast her as a friend on my parents' stage, like so
many they enjoyed. The fact that she spent two weeks at Undercliff
each August just seemed like a good opportunity for a colleague to
get out of steamy Florida. As I leafed through the letters to quickly
get their scope, I was dumbfounded by the pair's audacity, and
by the relationship's endurance. Their affair read like a misshapen
bell curve, rapidly ascending through four years before gradually
declining over the next six.

"Jesus," I repeated, this time under my breath.

On June 16, 1974, Dad sent his first letter to Joy from Hanover,
shortly after he and my mother had returned from his teaching term
in Gainesville. *What a joy it was to know you and yours! I have written letters but never put them down, elicitations of every beautiful
aspect of our goings and comings. I tried to stop time and live the
magnificent past as present. I laughed at philosophy. I wish it were
all to do again. . . . Will it be the warm pool or the cool pool? Shall we
go to Ichetucknee or Rainbow or Manatee?*

I looked up from the page, thinking of a trip to Gainesville
when my children and I had floated in inner tubes at Ichetucknee,
realizing Mom and Dad, and Joy, had been with us.

All these and so many memories flood in on me, his letter
continued, *with the greatest pleasure. New England is cool, in
every way, and Dartmouth is somber, rich, and established. What
a difference from the fresh democratic leaps of the northern and
university Floridians.*

Dad noted my first pregnancy and how uncertainty about
my delivery date complicated their travel plans. This infuriated me.
Gretch is quite far out, beautiful, and strong. I thought back to that

roasting summer of 1974, working hard in our vegetable gardens, my pregnant belly sometimes canting me forward, and late afternoon rests with an ice cube balanced in the notch of my throat.

My father wanted Joy to visit him in Maine and suggested a strategy he and she would use over the next four summers, triangulating my mother into their affair: *You might write Betty, saying you would love to visit us and would the first two weeks of August be good?*

Really, Dad? You dragged Mom into this? Jesus, I whispered.

On June 22, Joy replied from Gainesville. *Your letter brought me a sensuous, warm wave of pleasure and delight. Like you, I relive the beautiful moments of our goings and comings. We had wondered aloud whether separation might diminish the intensity of our feelings. And it has not, I think—who knows—perhaps it has increased it?*

Dad warned Joy of capricious Maine weather that might get in the way of a possible cruise with her on Rêve. *I love to fit into capricious weather,* Joy wrote. *It makes me feel resourceful to show the sky and the clouds that I am up to their tricks. P.S. You should destroy this letter, love.*

My neck hurt and my eyes throbbed. Why hadn't he destroyed that letter and the rest of them, as she'd requested? Did he realize that preserving them in his archives meant that anyone, including a curious daughter, could read them? I couldn't fathom my father.

Joy's intimate letters to Dad were interlaced with chatty notes to him and Mom together. She wrote about her children, about her hope for tenure at the university, about wishing her soon-to-be-ex-husband would get out of her house. On June 27, she wrote to my parents, *Thank you so much for your kind and generous invitation to have me visit you. I will love it!* The following week, she wrote to my father, *Thank you, darling, for your letter and for the teacher's aid. I miss you more each day. It will be wonderful to go yachting on Rêve. I have more stamina as a sailor than probably many men!*

He was sending her money? My penny-pinching father? Another maddening surprise.

On the morning of July 14, the day Ben was born, my father wrote to Joy from Maine, *See this week's* New Yorker *for a poem of mine* and, a few hours later, added, *Good news. It's a boy! This solves [our] problem. You should come on August 3 to Bangor.*

My pregnancy had confused them? How dare they, I thought.

I sat back in the heavy wooden chair. My shoulders collapsed. So that was the root of my father's impatience the day he had met his first grandchild, that hot July afternoon when Mom and I shucked peas under the apple tree. My father had seemed more antsy than usual then. Now I knew why.

Damn you, Dad, I said to myself. Joy spent two weeks at Undercliff that summer, taking over what had been my brother's bedroom, down the stairs from the room my father shared with my mother.

On August 28, after returning to Gainesville, Joy wrote to my parents together, *Did I dream Maine? Those glorious blue-sky days—the island explorations, the plunges into swiftly moving water, the voyage through fog, sunset in Southwest Harbor. No, of course it was not a dream—it only seems so now that I am back in the South, where the days are slow and sluggish. . . . Divorce proceedings have begun.*

On August 30, she wrote, *My love—I think of you constantly, the past month is still very much with me—a brilliant collage of memories. I think about the joy of being with you—and miss the warmth of your love. I have never experienced such completeness in body, mind, and spirit.*

I felt sick to my stomach and needed air. I couldn't believe these letters were made public through his archives. Did he have no shame? I couldn't believe I was reading them. Outside, students were criss-crossing the Dartmouth green, and I walked around the quad three times. I sat on the stone steps outside Rauner and called Ellen with an update. I returned calls from Ben about his next semester classes and from Molly about that afternoon's lacrosse practice pickup. I spoke with Michael and told him how hard a time I was having.

"You don't have to read them, honey," he said.

"I know, but I think I do."

Back inside the library, I picked up another letter. It was October when Joy sent a message to my parents together: *I am happy—very—to be considered a part of you, family and friends. And as with family, it would be almost impossible to shake me off now! Too late!*

That fall term, my father guest-taught at the University of California, Davis. He and Mom had told me they'd enjoyed being there. They'd reunited with both Kenneth Rexroth and Marie Rexroth, then divorced, before returning east. In January, he'd taught an intensive course at Columbia. I gazed at the far wall and thought of a phone call with Mom that winter. She and Dad were staying with Gram in Cambridge while he taught in Manhattan. It had made no sense to me that they were basing themselves in Cambridge.

"Why are you and Dad staying at Gram's?" I asked, juggling the phone against my ear with my six-month-old on my hip.

"I'm visiting with Mother," Mom said, sounding dejected.

"But why aren't you both in New York? I thought you'd be staying at Julie's."

"Your father is busy."

"But it would be easier for both of you."

"Maybe it's just better this way."

I didn't know about the affair then, so I left her remarks where they stood. Ensnarled in the letters, I thought of that interchange and Dad having Joy in New York and Mom in Cambridge. I was sick of this. I stared up at the sky through the tall glass windowpanes, and tears flowed silently—tears for my mom and for the never-ending loss of a father I'd never really had.

———

On September 10, Joy wrote to my parents, *I wish to thank you both so much for your hospitality to me, and I'm sorry for the times I complicated your lives! Complications seem to live with me.* Six days later, she wrote to Dad, *I feel desolate that you will be so far away. It was a lovely time there—bittersweet, in a way, because it was fraught with so many human involvements. I loved being with you, but I am truly sorry to have caused Betty pain and agonizing.* Joy pressured my father to make up his mind about her, presumably urging him to leave my mother. Dad didn't respond. He continued to send Joy money, which she described as *poor-professor support.*

On May 7, 1976, Joy wrote to my father from Gainesville after the publication of his book *Florida Poems*: *I won't badger you about writing me passionate letters anymore, my love. I would much rather have your poems. "The Swinging Bridge" affected me deeply— as you probably knew it would. Besides it being a very personal affirmation of our love . . . I remember that enchanted afternoon with the Spanish moss swaying in a gray-green stillness and we were the only two people within sight or sound. I thought it lovely beyond words—and yet you found words.* Joy continued her letter: *Are you sure I should come to Maine in August? It may be better for Betty if she has a summer without me.*

My father replied, *I don't know that you would be happy to come this summer. It is a different time and mood. Two years of high, now the feeling is low. Betty is jealous of your youth, beauty, and ability.*

Dad, really? I said to myself.

I think she would like to be let off the hook this summer, his letter continued, *but then another time she said she could put up with it.*

Mom, you're putting up with this? Now I was mad at her, too.

If only we were friends, my father wrote, *it would be different. My two-year energetic idea that things could change gives way to having to accept things as they are.* Three days later, he added a postscript before mailing the letter: *I wrote this in a low mood, the weather was bad. Now it is brighter, however. You can put all the pieces together and decide what you want to do. Today B asked me if I had written to you, I said no, she said to tell you to come, how does one figure it all out?* That summer, Joy returned to Maine but stayed in a cabin down the road.

Alex and I had visited Undercliff that summer, and the

tensions both between Mom and Joy and between my parents were palpable. Somehow we went through the motions of daily boat trips, island picnics, roasting marshmallows on the beach, and climbing the cliff behind the house. On our drive back to New Hampshire, I told Alex I wouldn't return to Undercliff the following year. Joy's presence had made for a gloomy summer vacation.

After returning to Gainesville, Joy wrote to my father, *I believe we were not meant to see each other this summer. You were right—we had a high for two years, and somehow I think there was a thought (not ours) that we would "get over" our affliction. . . . But the strange thing is that I have a stronger desire than ever to be with you. . . . We manipulate many things, but we find it difficult to arrange our lives in order to be together. Sometimes I find that depressing. I just want to be with you.*

In 1977, the fourth year of their affair, my father received the President's Medal for outstanding service from the University of Florida. He won the National Book Award for *Collected Poems: 1930–1976.* Cal Lowell died of a heart attack that year while riding in a taxicab in New York City. Cal's passing, at sixty years old, left my father in mourning for weeks, and inspired his poem called "Death in a Taxi." Meanwhile, Dad continued sending Joy money *for whatever you like,* and in August she visited Undercliff again, staying at a farmhouse nearby.

After her Maine visit, Joy wrote to my father from Gainesville, *I loved being near you and relished the cool isolation and chance to do some of my own work. But I must be perfectly honest with you— I did not like one bit the icy New England freeze I received from Betty and I don't think I deserved it.*

I was incredulous. Joy didn't think she deserved my mother's icy freeze? Who was this person?

I can understand her feelings of jealousy, Joy's letter continued, *but I will never understand lack of compassion for the human condition. There is no way that you and I will be kept from seeing and loving each other. We know that. But I think we can no longer delude ourselves into thinking we can fit this into ordinary social contexts. I would rather see you alone, as I did in New York—with people who are accepting, rather than condemning.*

Why had my mother not kicked Joy out of her house? Did she have to let Dad do this? Was it her epilepsy that caused dependence on him? Resting on those questions, I realized that was how we were around him. In the end, he'd get his way, not by yelling or demanding or joint decision, but by assuming. I found it hard to fathom how my mother survived that decade.

On July 27, Joy again pressed my father about their future: *Dick, you have to stop thinking about things that happen to you . . . and make things happen for you.* I laughed over that letter, because Mom used to tell Dad the same thing. He was so proactive in his literary life and so maddeningly passive in his personal one, especially in emotional matters of the heart. I thought of his inability to make a commitment to Louise Hawkes and his ambivalence in proposing to Mom. Now, he was doing the same with Joy.

In midsummer 1978, Joy did not return to Maine, but my father invited her to join him in Hanover at the end of July, when he would return to Hanover to introduce Saul Bellow at a Dartmouth event; she turned him down. On August 1, he wrote to Donald Hall, *I am much enjoying the Bellows. Came over to introduce Saul at a dinner Sunday night. He had a packed audience. Betty stayed on the coast. I fly back now.*

Dad planned for another term at the University of Florida during the winter of 1979 while his affair with Joy was on simmer, but it was the first year I noticed Mom returning from Gainesville earlier than him. She'd stay with Gram for a couple of weeks while he finished up his work in Florida. During one of those next years, Dikkon, then married to his second wife and living in Brookline, Massachusetts, offered to pick up our father at Logan Airport and give him a ride to Gram's. On their drive to Cambridge, Dad asked Dikkon if he'd like to know what was really going on between him and Joy. Dikkon said no. This prompted the only conversation my

brother and I had during those years about the affair. I didn't want
to know either.

In 1980, one year after Molly was born, Dad was named New
Hampshire's poet laureate, a post he'd hold for five years. In 1984,
Joy wrote to my parents together but stayed clear of Maine. Mom
transplanted a dozen rugosa rose bushes from Pond Island into her
garden that summer while my father worked on the proofs for his
next book, *The Long Reach: New and Collected Works 1948–1984*,
his third with New Directions Press and his twentieth overall. He
was inducted into the inner circle of the American Academy of Arts
and Letters that year, an honor reserved for only fifty living artists.
That July, my family and I visited Maine and saw clear fault lines
between my parents. At eighty and seventy, they seemed far apart.

— ∞ —

On my parents' return to Gainesville the following winter, Joy had
taken up with another man. Later that spring, after my parents
returned to Hanover, she wrote to Dad, *I'm writing my memoirs,
including about you and me. I won't name you, darling, I'll just say
"a famous poet"—won't that be fun?*

Joy's last letter to Dad, written on September 8, 1984, a full
decade after her first, included a request that he nominate her for
a Fulbright award. On September 13, my father agreed and sent his
last note to Joy: *We all too soon begin to belong to the past, as you
are happily yet too young to realize. But the past will come, and we
will go. You are now going strong in the world and I hope you will
go to Spain-Portugal for a Fulbright.*

I had skimmed through the box of letters in one day and
then had needed a three-month break before I could tackle them
again. I was furious at my father for hurting Mom, for sullying
Undercliff, for being so stupid and self-centered. If I'd been a different researcher, I might have enjoyed the exchange and chalked
up their letters to a steamy literary romance, noting the arrogance
of both protagonists and its predictable downturn. But this was

my father. Narcissism, like denial, I was learning, is obvious when you're outside it and crazy-making when you're inside it.

Artists, perhaps especially poets, have long been given a pass for bad behavior. My friend Mark in Seattle had said as much when we conversed on the quad. If they weren't self-centered, he'd said, they wouldn't make their art. Maybe their art is, in the end, all. Sitting in that stone-silent library, I wondered if it's their true intimacy, the relationship in which they feel most creative, engaged, and vulnerable. Most alive. Maybe their marriages, their children, their lovers, are mere way stations on their paths, as they ideally save their best for communing with their muses. I'd admired and known about artists for whom this seemed true. But, they weren't my father, my mother's husband, the grandfather of my children. I hadn't ever named this in the context of better understanding my father.

I'd scheduled a dinner with Ellen for the evening after my second read-through. We met at the Canoe Club. Ellen was giddy that day as she told me she and her husband would be moving back to the Bay Area. I reveled in her excitement, though I'd miss her terribly. After our salads, I turned to what I'd been reading all day.

"Why did Dad hang on to those letters?" I asked. "Joy even asked him not to. Was he being sentimental? Was he trying to impress future researchers with his virility?"

"I can't imagine it," Ellen said. "I don't understand why."

"Maybe at his core he was just indifferent to the people he claimed to love the most—especially Mom, but my brother and me, too. I certainly felt his indifference when he'd shrug his shoulders when something wasn't important to him. Shit!" I realized, just then. "The way he chuckled when he walked out my bedroom door. That was *indifference*."

Ellen reached for my hand.

"I cried through those letters the first time," I said, waving her off. "Even skimming them was tough to take, but today I saw something new: He was an opportunist, privileged by both gender and fame. He was like that Jesus guy I spent one night with in Seattle—they each had the same male charm and charisma to pull you in."

"Wait, Chuck, you mean?" Ellen said.

"Yeah. Joy showed up in Dad's life as he turned seventy. Joy was young enough and self-centered enough herself—the perfect person to catch his eye."

"Ugh," Ellen said. "I'm sorry you had to read all that."

"What's interesting," I said, "is that I now see myself as just another, albeit teenage, woman on his path." I paused to absorb my own words. "What that means is that it really wasn't *about* me. His intrusion in my bedroom had nothing to do with me. I could have been anyone. But, Jesus, it was my room and he had to take two turns upstairs to get there!"

Ellen nodded, leaning back against her chair.

"I'm done carrying his sins. I'm shedding the weight of him and moving on."

Ellen raised her glass as I toasted her move to Oakland, and she toasted me shedding the weight of my father I'd carried for so long. As strange as it sounded even to me, I was glad my father had kept the letters. His doing so helped me understand the social context for privileged and famous men, their bad behavior so entrenched and allowed, I had no idea how it would ever end. I felt bad for my mom and grateful for the relationships I'd established in my work, and with Michael and my children.

"I think there's one more thing I need to explore before I can call this decade-long research done," I said. "It can wait a few months, but I need to ask Sarah to find me whatever she can about my father's teenage years in Minnesota, especially anything about his relationship with his mother."

"Let's get together again soon, but definitely after that."

Driving home that evening, I felt lighter, as if the ball and chain of shame had finally been cut and I could walk on my own.

It took months to shake off the effects of reading about Dad's affair. Even after the proof of it, I'd seen it as nothing but a selfish and petty act by my father. It embarrassed me. Over time, it also became true that the relationship must have had meaning for them both to have lasted so long. I couldn't toss it off so cavalierly. Complex people create complex lives. I wondered, if after a long life together, might my parents have come to some sort of agreement on this? Not what I would want, but I had to consider the possibility. My father was flawed. My mother was pragmatic. What they'd lived through was, I had to accept, of their choosing.

Chapter 22:

Apple Buds

The stories my father told me about growing up in Austin, Minnesota, were the ones I loved most. Vivid in emotions and sensory details, it was a place he never took me, in person, but that I knew well from his tales. As I sat on the floor and listened, he'd tell of his boyhood exploits with his beloved older brother, Dryden, and his equally loved younger sister, Elizabeth. His stories about his father, Alpha LaRue Eberhart, and his mother, Lena Lowenstein Eberhart, were moving, intense, and hard for a child to fully understand. My Eberhart grandparents died long before I was born, but my father's stories had brought them alive. Through my grandparents' letters to each other, their friends, and their family, that Sarah found for me in Dad's archives, I developed a genuine love for them both.

Austin itself was nearly mythic in Dad's telling—a small city in the American Midwest in the early 1900s, during a time of economic expansion, where men with big ideas brought their talents from the East to build a company under the wide-open skies of Minnesota. It was a place where a young boy could test his wits and ingenuity as widely as he could imagine. Trudging through four-foot blizzards to school; hiking up the Red Cedar River to secret camping places; hopping on ice cakes in spring and riding them downriver until, just before going over the dam in Austin, he'd grab an overhanging tree branch and watch the cake split into a hundred pieces below him. Dad, along with Dryden and a gang of close boyhood friends, had a great early life.

In 1900, my grandfather—A.L., as he was called—and his new bride, Lena, moved to Austin at the invitation of George A. Hormel, founder of what is now the $4-billion food conglomerate Hormel Foods. George Hormel, a stocky German immigrant from Toledo, Ohio, had a grand vision that belied his small meat shop on Main Street. His plan was to create a meat-merchandising powerhouse, something unheard of on the grasslands of southern Minnesota. Chicago was "the hog butcher of the world," as Upton Sinclair had written in his seminal book, *The Jungle.* Yet George Hormel was a tenacious competitor and believed in his vision. What he needed was exceptional sales leadership and he knew he'd find just that in my grandfather.

A.L. Eberhart had been working for the giant meatpacker Swift and Company, running its sales offices in St. Paul. An entrepreneur at heart, A.L. was captivated by Hormel's unlikely vision, and confident in his ability to sell. Over the next twenty years, my grandfather would help increase Hormel's sales by 4,000 percent, opening a dozen sales offices across the country and creating new markets for Hormel meats. By 1920, he was among the best-known and most well-liked meat executives in the country.

A.L. stood six feet tall. *Six feet of a man,* my father would write in his poem "In the Orchard," *and not a mark of fear.* With perfect posture and a patrician face, A.L. was an avid outdoorsman, and enjoyed hunting and fishing expeditions with his sons and customers in the boundary waters between northern Minnesota and Canada. He liked a good cigar, a stiff brandy, bespoke suits. For his family's home, in Austin, he lavished $50,000 on its renovation and named his estate Burr Oaks, for the species of tree that grew along the banks of the Red Cedar River. The Eberharts enjoyed forty acres of sprawling lawns, peony gardens, and apple orchards. With a population of five thousand people, A.L. was likely the second wealthiest man in town.

My grandmother Lena, by contrast, was five foot two, a soft-spoken and cultured woman who cared deeply for all people. She helped found the Austin Public Library and its garden club, one of the first in the country. She introduced my father to poetry by way of a leather-bound set of Alfred Lloyd Tennyson. She ensured that he attend Austin's annual *chautauqua*, where Dad could take in Shakespearean theater and listen to the best oratories of the day.

All of this and more, I'd heard from Dad and by trading stories with my Eberhart cousins, Eloise, Lil, Betty, and Suzanne. The rest I would learn through research in my father's archives and on trips I took to Austin, myself.

The Eberhart family fortune was tied to annual additions of Hormel stock A.L. received, sometimes in lieu of an increase in salary, plus the stock's ever-increasing value. As the company grew, the Hormel family and the Eberharts prospered. Through two decades of remarkable growth, both the company and my grandfather found it easy to secure bank loans which, in A.L.'s case, afforded him the purchase of large tracts of land and herds of prize-winning cattle. Both the company's and my grandfather's financial conditions seemed solid as their assets far outpaced their liabilities. By 1921, A.L. had risen to executive vice president and secretary of the board.

Through 1920, Hormel company management, including Grandfather Eberhart, had been concerned about the company's cash position. Cash is frequently in shorter supply during periods of strong growth, but still, something felt off. The accounting firm, Ernst & Ernst, was called in to perform a full audit and reported that everything was fine.

Jay Hormel, George's son who worked in the company, continued to be concerned and took it upon himself to spend one Saturday combing over the books. What he found astonished him. An embezzlement had been taking place for a full decade, and all counted would total $1.2 million (or more than $15 million in today's dollars). The stealing had been done by the company's star bookkeeper Ransome J. Tompson, both hired and admired by George Hormel for his determination and smarts. Once discovered, the value of Hormel company stock plummeted, effectively to zero, overnight. The company was in financial free fall. All banks connected to Hormel immediately sought payment for their loans. My grandfather's substantial investment portfolio, too, was in ruins.

While the embezzler was carted off to jail, where he'd remain for fifteen years, Mr. Hormel and my grandfather spent every hour of the second half of 1921 trying to salvage the Hormel company, as A.L. also tried desperately to stave off personal bankruptcy. Worse than his financial mess, though, A.L. faced another calamity the summer of 1921 in the sudden onset of a serious illness that struck his wife, Lena.

—⌘—

By the time I discovered the Austin records in Dad's archives, I was settled into my life with Michael and had read widely about the transfer of trauma from one generation to the next. I knew my own trauma had lodged deep inside me, had manifested in the form of headaches and backaches, and had literally changed the wiring in my brain. As an adult, I'd had a conversation with Dad the year he turned eighty, and I'd been struck by how outsized his grief seemed for events that had occurred sixty years earlier. As I came to understand my father better, that period of his life piqued my interest. Even well into his nineties, Dad was easily overcome with tears by the mention of his mother's early death and the Hormel embezzlement's impact on his family. Where he'd often boasted of his idyllic childhood on the Red Cedar River, his continued suffering over the fate of his parents made me realize how very traumatic those events had been for him. I dove into the Austin records.

George Hormel required A.L.'s full focus on helping him get the company back on its feet and to hold off the bankers who were making life miserable for both of them. A.L. was well-admired and known for the kind of sales he could generate if given a chance. His preoccupation on behalf of Mr. Hormel led him to hold my father back from freshman year at the University of Minnesota, where Dad's brother Dryden was a junior. Instead, my father was put in charge of Burr Oaks, his grandparents and their home next door, his eleven-year-old sister, Elizabeth, and his ill mother.

I hadn't known that Dad had kept a personal journal of that time, but it surfaced in his archives, a version of his hand-written original, typed up in the spring of 1939, when he was thirty-five years old. The original covered the period from August 1921 until June 1922, during which time my father was immersed in his mother's care.

On November 7, 1921, his first entry reads, *Oh! God, if I am any comfort to her, I am thankful.* He called for doctors and nurses around the clock as Lena's illness quickly worsened between September and November. Lena was provided needles of morphine and unspecific pills for her pain as family members were called to visit her from Buffalo, New York, and Whitehall, Illinois, first to cheer her up, and later to say goodbye. Dad spent most evenings with Lena reading from the *Saturday Evening Post* before recording the days' events and conversations. *It certainly was a wonderful day,* he wrote in late November. *Mother's praise of our efforts and my work was too much, but I let her know I did it primarily for her.*

A.L. spent long hours at Hormel headquarters across the river, returning for his midday meal and late at night. He played the piano for Lena and reminisced about their happy, early married life in St. Paul. The laughter only caused Lena discomfort. *Oh, I wish I could do it without hurting,* my father wrote that she had said.

Morphine seemed to have little effect on her increasing pain but was administered routinely. She vomited regularly and struggled for breath, a case of pleurisy settling in along with her cancer, as Dad had told me her illness was. My father anguished over her every wince, while, in moments of close companionship, he rejoiced in her love. On November 15, he wrote, *Just as I now finished that sentence, I heard a "good night, son," and turned around to see Mother walking into our room to see me. It was so good. She said, "I thought I'd surprise you a little" and kissed me, in the middle of the room. She certainly is one wonderful little mother.*

As fall turned to winter, my father turned from being Lena's constant companion to being her confidant. He faced her illness directly. He listened to her wavering faith in a cure. With few breaks and little sleep, he chopped wood for her fireplace, fixed her windows, ran her errands, emptied her fireplace ashes, and cleaned her bedpans. In November, he wrote, *I will never forget the embrace that I received from Mother. This was her banner day. We were alone and I held her hand in mine. Then she said, "You certainly love your Muddy, don't you, Dicky Boy?" and she turned and hugged me and her kiss I shall never forget. And I told her she would always be my inspiration and I loved her so.*

During the week leading up to Thanksgiving that year, Lena was confined to her bed and slept fitfully. It dismayed her not to be in charge of the holiday meal. My father struggled to cope, keeping vigil night and day. *As Mother's chin quivered, she had a hard time controlling herself.* She told the doctor she had a crying spell and "got discouraged" this morning. "*I don't think I'm getting well fast enough.*"

Each morning brought bitter cold, but on sunny winter days Dad carried Lena into the hall so that she could feel the sun on her face through the windows and look out at the snow-covered beauty around Burr Oaks. They could see the Cedar River, frozen over, and the Hormel factory in the distance on the other side. *Mother's face, so cold, so pretty*, Dad wrote on November 20.

Thanksgiving morning, Lena woke from a poor night of sleep and asked my father for a *heart-to-heart little talk*. Through tears, she asked him to bathe her and, after her bath, to rub her with alcohol, a crude form of pain relief. She told him not to tell others that she'd been crying and that she was tired of taking so many pills.

Dad carried the Thanksgiving turkey upstairs so his mother could add spices to the bowl of dressing. *The morning was a busy one preparing for the dinner*, Dad noted. *At 11:30 I broke into her room and beheld the most joyous sight I have witnessed. There stood Mother, fully dressed in her black dress, her hair combed and a smile on her face that will never die. Oh God, she looked as well as ever— and her face shone so with the glory of it.*

After the holiday meal, A.L. returned to the factory while my father bathed his mother again and got her to bed. Dryden was home from college for the holiday, and Lena called her three children to her side to make her personal will. Her diamond pin would go to Elizabeth, and her leather-bound set of Shakespeare to my father. She gave her pearl engagement ring to Dad and another one to Dryden, reasoning they'd marry one day and could use the rings for their engagements.

The next day, Lena turned forty-eight. Surrounded by hundreds of birthday cards and dozens of boxes of flowers from friends and family across the country, she said, *Seems too bad I can't get well. Elizabeth needs me. If there's anything in prayer, I certainly ought to get well.*

The following day, A.L. consulted with Will and Charlie Mayo in Rochester, who had recently opened their "clinic in the cornfield." The brothers prescribed daily X-ray treatments for Lena's care and her pain. A.L. immediately installed an X-ray machine in the basement gymnasium at Burr Oaks. Dad carried his tiny mother down two flights of stairs each day for treatments, some of them lasting as long as forty-five minutes. They seemed to do little good and only increased her nausea and distress.

My father summoned a nurse whenever Lena was in significant pain. The nurse increased the dosage of morphine and gave Lena injections regularly. As Dad noted in his diary, *This has been Mother's hardest and worst day.* He sought new ways to soothe her suffering, becoming increasingly intimate. He nuzzled her on her bed and whispered in her ear. He continued rubbing alcohol on her and listened to her questions.

"Do you fear disease or have any fear of this?" Lena asked my father.

I said no and went on to tell why, my father wrote.

"You know I have no fear at all of this," Lena told her son. *"When I was so sick the other day, I would just as soon have passed on as not, but I had no fear. There is this about it, when one thinks of not being with your family and also the suffering . . . but I guess when one's time comes, it is all right. It's only something that everyone goes through. I tell you, after you've been sick months and months, as I have, you realize what your family means."*

We talked of things we were thankful for, my father wrote, *as I kissed her and she loved me.*

Riveted to the pages in this journal, I tuned out all sound at Rauner Library and felt transported to Austin, watching these weeks unfold. I stared at the tall windows and thought about Dad. While his father faced financial ruin and pledged his time to George Hormel, over the months, Dad's relationship with his mother became more profound. This new view gave me context for the emotions he felt when he spoke of Grandmother Lena. I'd heard critics and writers describe Lena as my father's poetic muse. Now I understood that he'd been searching all his life to replace that original love.

When I turned back to Dad's diary, it was late December 1921 and A.L. had learned of a medical procedure available only in Chicago. He took a train to consult with the lung specialist there. My father moved into his parents' room and slept on Lena's bed while A.L. was out of town. A.L. returned from his trip with sobering news. Lena might recover with a treatment developed in Germany, but if it didn't cure her, it would likely kill her. Eighty thousand volts of X-ray would be administered over a single, six-hour period.

The weight of deciding what to do bore heavily on the entire family. Dryden was called home from college and involved in the discussions. Lena didn't want to go through with the extreme procedure, but her pain had become nearly unbearable and she knew her children needed her. She confided in Dad that this treatment would be her last resort. She no longer expected her lung to heal on its own, nor for her faith to cure her. In the end, it was her decision to go to Chicago.

That night, my father turned off her bedside lamp and lit candles on a small, and early, Christmas tree. *Oh, the joy on her face!* Dad wrote. *I'll never forget how we children sat around dear Mother while she read the verses we had written and opened the boxes. Oh, the emotion of that little scene can never be described.* Later that night, when he and Lena were alone in her room, she said, *"I'll miss you, honey. You've been the greatest comfort to me. Whatever comes or goes, you'll be working for me here."*

On Thursday, December 16, my father dressed Lena in her sealskin coat and A.L. carried her down to the waiting ambulance. The family left together for the train station, and while Lena lay in her stateroom, she waved to her children, who stood on the platform in tears. *We hope God will bring me back*, she called out the window. As the train pulled out of Austin, the town was awash in puffy flakes of snow. Dryden returned to the University of Minnesota, and my father and Elizabeth attended a high school basketball game that evening. Their parents returned from Chicago, ten days later.

— ∞ —

George A. Hormel was a thick-necked and stern butcher by trade. I've been told he could cleave a hog with a single blow. After weeks of effort, A.L. and Mr. Hormel, with the company's lawyer, tried to persuade the bankers to give the company a three-year extension on its loans in order to rebuild. Convinced a general depression would have settled over southern Minnesota if the company went under, the Austin banks were quick to agree to this deal while the big banks in Chicago and Boston took convincing, but agreed over time. Mr. Hormel must have been mightily shamed by an embezzlement that had been carried out by one of his favorite employees right under his nose. In January, only two weeks after my grandparents returned from Lena's treatment in Chicago, Mr. Hormel forced A.L.'s resignation from the company, claiming he'd become too soft on his employees. A.L. was the only non-family member of the Hormel management group and became its sacrificial lamb.

As his current debts mounted and the cost of his wife's medical care rose at an alarming rate, A.L. needed to find new work immediately. Through friends in the industry, he quickly picked up an executive position at Dold Packing Company in Omaha, but it required him to be there through each week and to return for only one night in Austin. My father's journal ends after his parents' return from Chicago, but it's apparent that his position in the household and his care for his mother continued until her end.

On June 22, 1922, Lena succumbed to her disease with my father by her side. He'd cared for her for nearly a year. When he typed up the diary at age thirty-five, he added this postscript:

I cannot recall why I did not keep the journal up after Mother's return from Chicago. The treatments probably added a few months to her life, but the pain increased with time. Since cancer was never mentioned among any of us, I have usually thought that she did not know the nature of her illness. But even in reading this old journal, it would seem as if so intelligent a person must have known—to herself at least. I remember filling her room, the north guest room, with pussy willows in the early spring of 1922. In early June we took her downstairs for the last time. I remember when she gave Father back his wedding ring. She talked with each of us children personally in turn. On the night of June 22, the twenty-fourth anniversary of her marriage, I remember lying on the other bed next to hers in the north room. At about 9:30 p.m., in the luminous stillness, some strange exaltation of spirit caused me to write a poem to her. I helped her take a sip of water from a glass tube in a water glass. Then the nurse told me to run for the doctor. I remember careening through the streets in the big, heavy Cadillac at 70 miles an hour, down the

hill and over the bridge to Lafayette Park, where Chautauqua was in
session, and called for the doctor. I remember the last kiss.

—⊱⊰—

In the ensuing months, A.L. would be forced to sell everything he
owned to pay back his loans. My grandfather eventually remar-
ried and went on to hold other executive positions at meatpacking
companies, including Dold and Arnold, but never came close to
regaining the fortune he'd amassed in Austin. He died five years
later, on June 5, 1927, at the age of sixty-two, when his car slammed
into an elevated pier in downtown Chicago. My cousin Eloise and I
have speculated about whether it was intentional, but as I've come
to know my grandfather through hundreds of his letters and by
way of articles written about him in trade journals, I think he was
too level-headed and too genuinely positive a person for it to have
been at his own hand.

I'd long wondered how Lena contracted her illness, which
Dad described as lung cancer, if she'd never smoked and lived away
from the prevailing winds of the Hormel factory. Doctors have told
me that Dad's descriptions of his mother's pain emanating from her
shoulder, may have meant she contracted breast cancer which later
metastasized to her lungs. A psychiatrist read my father's journal
and suspected his relationship with his mother was unusual, even
for the era, and at the time of a mother's death. What I concluded
was that A.L. left his son to care for his wife in the same way my
father left me to care for Mom, each of us given responsibility we
weren't prepared for, his, of course, far greater than mine. It made
me wonder why Dad couldn't have told me as a little girl that he
knew what it was like to care for someone you loved, that it was an
important role I needed to play, and that I could come to him with
concerns. That wasn't my father.

As I thought about Dad's progression in love—from Lena
to Louise Hawkes to Mom to Joy and others—I could understand
better the yearning he had to replace his mother—her adoration

of him and her stalwart belief in his gifts. Maybe it was no wonder he didn't close my bedroom door the night he molested me. Maybe it was no wonder he'd felt permitted to enter my bedroom in the Florida condo. Maybe a door was just an inanimate variation of a familial boundary he'd already crossed. Perhaps when I was seventeen, his behavior toward me was an echo through the generations of what he'd experienced when he was the same age.

— ∞ —

In the story my father told me about Lena's illness, he cast himself as responsible. In a football game just before Lena became sick, in September 1921, he said, he rushed the football down the field for a touchdown, skimming the sideline and knocking Lena over as she stood and watched the game.

"But, Dad," I said the last of many times he told me this, "that couldn't have caused her cancer. You can't blame yourself for her illness."

"But how can we ever know for sure?"

What I knew, finishing with his diary, was that I was done with family secrets, done with covering for my father, done with negating my own life in favor of his. I was ready to throw the doors open on my family and let a clearing breeze blow through. I had told my brother what Dad had done. I had told my children and Michael. I had told my closest friends and doctors. I just didn't know when I'd be ready to tell the world.

Chapter 23:

Cleaning Out the Study

I heaved open the heavy wooden door to my father's study in June 1995 and was bombarded by smells from my childhood—the sweet, redolent residue of leftover pipe tobacco, the almond-like scent of old books, the whiff of my father's sweat—all mixed up with cracked leather furniture and dust. As a little girl, I'd sat on the desk in this room and peered into Dad's Smith Corona while he typed out his poems. At seventeen, I'd met Anne Sexton on the porch outside that door. Now, at forty-four years old, as my kids turned into caring and responsible young adults, I had been heating up the local dance floors with Michael. We were designing a new house we would build together—a tree house for grown-ups, as Ben and Molly would later call it. I was proud of those two, their wisdom and bravery taking them places I never could have imagined.

Dikkon and I had set aside ten days to clean out our parents' ten-room, forty-year home in Hanover in preparation for selling it. My mother had died the year before, at eighty, and Dad had fared better in the transition than we'd thought he might. At ninety-one, he planned to live to one hundred. There was no good reason why he couldn't. Cleaning out the house seemed like an enormous task, and we knew Dad's study would be the hardest, even though he'd already donated the majority of his literary collection to Dartmouth. My brother and I had set aside our final three days for his study.

Going through the house, we had made easy decisions, unlike so many siblings. We took from our childhood home the things we wanted, never considering relative monetary value. Our tastes were different enough—I was interested in the work of several artists, while he liked the furniture and could use it in his home. The rest we sold, gave away, or had hauled to the dump.

Being in Hanover that week made me wonder how the town had held my parents' imagination for as long as it had. A likely part of it, for Dad, was that his big presence on a small campus was meaningful. Hanover is an unusual place for an elite college—tucked between green hills, the region a mixture of excellent academics, medical care, and entrepreneurial companies amid towns and villages with sizable poverty. It hadn't changed much since I'd lived there as a kid, which had been a great time to grow up in Hanover. As a kid, I could walk or ride my bike anywhere I wanted, and if I stopped in any store on Main Street, it was likely owned by the father of a classmate or friend. It was a safe place for Mom, as everyone knew she had epilepsy. If she had a seizure downtown, someone would call an ambulance and get her to the hospital, where, at least, she'd be safe.

The hardwood floor under our feet creaked as Dikkon and I took a few steps around the study and considered where to begin. The place looked like Dad had just left one day without looking back. His tendency to keep every scrap of paper sent to him or sent by him to others was evident. We couldn't fling it all in the Dumpster we'd ordered for the backyard. What if we found more letters from Ginsberg or James Dickey?

I hadn't liked Dickey when I'd met him, after returning to New Hampshire from Seattle to live with Alex, even if I had appreciated his book *Deliverance*. My brother and father were starstruck. Dickey was named US poet laureate in 1966. In 1972, he visited Mom and Dad in Hanover, the year *Deliverance* was being made into a movie. Dickey bellied up to my father's bar cabinet in the kitchen, full of himself, his lips loosening with every drink, after which he turned his whiskey-soaked eyes on me. He made me wonder, *Are all middle-aged men the same?*

Dad's study was cramped with wooden desks jumbled together. The rattan daybed he'd napped on (after pushing aside piles of the *New York Times Book Review*) was the one Grandmother Lena had slept on at Burr Oaks the year she died. Its fabric now faded to the color of ancient brick. I could picture her in her long black dress, reclining in the winter sun of Minnesota, her quiet smile warming my father's face.

The Smith Corona commanded the best view in the room, as it overlooked the back lawn where I'd turned cartwheels. The gazebo still hung over the bank to the Connecticut River, and I could see Frost, Lowell, Hall, I.A. Richards—and more—sitting on its circular wooden bench. I felt like I'd stepped into a loosely bound volume of my father's life—each shelf, closet, and work surface a scene with characters.

Dikkon and I had no strategy our first day in the study. We dug in randomly, my brother attending to the drawers of a desk while I cased the inside of a closet, where stacks of files teetered five feet high like a paper skyline of a small city. In that closet I found third-class mail forwarded to his winter addresses in Gainesville each year, then mailed back to New Hampshire three months later at first-class rates. I found credit card slips and canceled checks jammed up against newspaper clippings of his Pulitzer Prize. Inside poetry books my father had been asked to review, we found $10 and $20 bills used as bookmarks. "Found another one," Dikkon said, holding high a twenty. "Me, too," I answered. By the time we left the study three days later, we'd accumulated $1,460 and split the unexpected proceeds, thinking we'd earned it.

A 1979 tax return slipped from a file I was holding, reminding me of the year Molly was born, when the IRS audited my parents. "It's absurd," Dad had said at the time. "Why would they waste their time auditing a poet?" The audit turned on a single check, written for a conspicuous amount of money, made out to "Churches," and labeled by my father as a charitable donation. When the IRS agent brought it to my parents' attention, Mom laughed heartily, knowing well that Churches was a popular children's clothing store in Hanover where she and Dad had picked out baby clothes for their new granddaughter. "Richie," I remember Mom telling me she'd said at the time, "you're the one who's caused our trouble!"

"Remember that?" I asked Dikkon with a smile. "Our absentminded father was claiming Molly's onesies for charity!"

Everywhere we found pipe cleaners and worn-out pipe stems, half-used bags of tobacco, and enough pages of the *New York Times* to reforest a small woodlot. This was the detritus of my father's literary life. By the end of our first day, we were dirty and tired, and I'd slowly turned grouchy. I wanted to go home. I wanted no more cleaning up of my father's messes—either physical or emotional. As dust swirled, I went outside to toss the leftover pizza we'd ordered for lunch in the dumpster. By the time I returned to the room, I was swearing. "The hell with them leaving all this to us. I'm sick of it. I will *never* leave such a mess for my kids."

Dikkon, who'd been head-down cleaning, looked at me, startled. "What's wrong, Gretch?"

"And there won't be any surprises," I said, bypassing his question.

"What do you mean?" he asked.

"They'll know me as I am," I said, "for good or bad. They won't waste their adult lives trying to figure me out."

— ∾∾ —

I was grieving my mother's death that year and being in her home had made me sad. I felt guilty for not having been with her at the end. I should have recognized that she was going downhill. When Gram was seventy-nine, she could snowshoe down Lakeview Avenue in a snowstorm. When Mom was seventy-nine, she was in a wheelchair. I'd been so caught up in my own life—divorce, new love, working with clients, two growing children—I'd hardly noticed a decline in my mother.

The week before Mom died, Michael and I had gone to Undercliff with the kids for vacation. It was the first summer my parents chose not to go. While there, I'd learned from one of Mom's summer friends that a year earlier, on the morning of my parents' fiftieth anniversary, their cottage friends from around the cove had hung a white sheet on the front of the house facing the sea, proclaiming HAPPY ANNIVERSARY BETTY AND DICK #50 in preparation for the usual end-of-summer celebration planned for later that day. That morning, as the sun rose high enough to scale the cliff, the sounds of a fight my parents were having carried across the water to Mom's friend's cottage. In frustration, the friend told me, Mom had suddenly turned away from Dad and rolled her ankle, then fallen on her hip. I was heartbroken to hear this story, but it corroborated the view I'd had of my parents not being in synch as they aged.

The morning after I returned with my family from Undercliff, our phone rang downstairs at 5:30 a.m., and I rolled over. "It's a robo-call," I said to Michael. "We can ignore it."

The phone rang again a half hour later, and I went downstairs to answer.

"I am sorry to call you," one of my mom's nurses started to say.

"What do you mean, she's gone? I just saw her last week."

"I think you need to come in to be with your dad."

Be with my dad? I stared out the window. *I still needed my mom.*

"You wake up the kids and tell them," Michael said. "I'll make breakfast."

After consoling Molly and Ben and helping them into their days, I called my brother, then my uncle Charlie. I was spent. I didn't know how I could go to be with my dad. I just wanted Mom to be alive.

In Hanover, my father sat in a green wingback chair next to Mom's bed, where she was covered in a white blanket. She looked at peace.

"Come here," Dad said, "and hold her hand."

I reached for my mother. Her skin was cool. A nurse came in to ask about our plans.

"Plans?" I said. "My brother won't be here for three hours. We have no plans." Testy, in shock, I'd been vigilant my entire life around Mom, pulling her out of subway trains, removing cigarettes from her fingers, helping to rescue her from drowning. But I'd entirely missed her dying. This time, she wasn't coming back.

My father and I sat and waited while Dikkon drove over from his home in Maine. Occasionally, Dad would lean toward the bed and take Mom's hand.

"See," he'd say, circling her thin wrist with his fingers. "If I hold on to her, I can make her warm again."

As Jay Parini had summarized to me, he did always want the world to be as he imagined it.

———— ✵ ————

On our second day in the study, Dikkon and I cleared out a bookshelf against the back wall where we could accumulate items we thought important enough for Dartmouth to look at, things that Dad had written or that had been written about him. We'd already boxed up the dozens of letters we'd found from poets and writers and would deliver those to the college. Around noon, I came across a sheaf of original Mary Oliver poems, fifteen verses, each typed on a page, sealed in a brown envelope with a personal note asking Dad for comments. Mom had scotch-taped her own note on top of the envelope: *Dick, please get back to Mary on these.* A fan of Oliver's, I savored her poems on a short break. Later, I would mail them back to Mary with an apology for her not having heard from my father.

By the end of our third day, we had sifted through each volume and page by hand. I'd dipped into my father's way of doing things, the business of his poetry, the way he ran his kingdom. I'd grinned at reading his letters to editors, exhorting them to take a poem or admonishing them for not doing so. I could see how he'd built his career. He'd understood that the work of a writer is about much more than the writing, that any business is about relationships made, nurtured, and kept. He'd built long relationships with his editors and publishers, and he'd delivered well enough that they'd come back for more. I thought back to his years at the Library of Congress, when, against the better judgment of the professionals, my father had accepted every invitation he got to read. Before we ever started applying the term to individuals, he'd intuitively and actively developed his brand. As his ever-expanding fame led to better paid readings, which led to selling more books, he'd created a seventy-year career that would keep him in royalties through the rest of his life and beyond. He insisted on being heard, on being known.

I stared out the window at the tall pines that still ringed my cartwheeling gymnasium. Maybe, I thought, when he'd told me that my only job as a writer was to tell the truth, he'd been telling me the truth was okay to tell, and that my story was okay to be known. Dad once wrote, *If some wound in the soul were healed, there would be no need to write poems.* I'd witnessed his wounds up close—personally, and from reading about them at Rauner—his intimacy and felt abandonment by the early death of his mother; his intense loyalty to his father; his voracious need for the comfort of women, both inside and outside his marriage; his erotic greediness. In not liking him for years, I'd given away my own power.

I pulled myself into mountain pose without thinking, staring out his window, straightening my back and rooting my feet to the floor. With my eyes on the tall pines, I drew in a long, slow, yogic breath of forgiveness, feeling my body relax and my beliefs shift. I'd never get over what he'd done to me, but Dad had taken the gifts and wounds from his own childhood and ridden them to the top of his field. He'd done the best he could with what he had. What he had to give me just wasn't what I'd needed. As I cleared out the stuff of our filial home, I was clearing out the final paternal cobwebs still strung up inside my heart.

It was 3:00 p.m. on Sunday, and Dikkon and I needed to get on the road, back to our families. I put my hand on my brother's shoulder, and, together, we took in the depth and breadth of the bookshelf we'd filled. Seven hundred items—books, biographies, published lectures, essays, and articles, every one of them written by or about our father. I now understood better his contribution to American letters, and, for the first time in my adult life, I could feel proud of him.

Chapter 24:

Ginsberg's Gift

On November 21, 1996, a year after cleaning out my father's study, I picked up Dad at his retirement community and drove him across town to the Dartmouth campus. The college had invited nine of his friends to pay him tribute at an event that had received a lot of press. Dad was ninety-two, and I'd planned on getting him to the auditorium early, but a half hour before the event was to start, 105 Dartmouth Hall was already full. Standers crammed into every corner and were five deep against the walls. Students straggled in with weighty backpacks and all-night faces and had to sit with photographers and reporters on the floor below the stage. It was a week before Thanksgiving, and two adjoining foyers competed for overflow. Cleopatra Mathis, then my father's successor as poet-in-residence at Dartmouth, had to call for audio piped into a classroom upstairs to finally accommodate the crowd.

Downstairs in one of the college's most iconic buildings, 105 Dartmouth is an intimate space. With a low ceiling and a stage close to the front row of seats, it was my father's favorite hall, a place where he'd enjoyed the *throwing about of youthful brains*, as he'd once referred to his Creative Writing undergrads.

Earlier that morning, I'd called his occasional helper to make sure she'd have him ready for the event. "He doesn't want to do this," she'd told me. In the car, he'd said the same to me, adding, "They should have done this five years ago, when I could cope with it."

I just hoped he would rise to the occasion once he got there.

— ∞ —

Six months earlier, around the beginning of June, Cleopatra had called me with her idea for the tribute. "I give full credit to Galway," she had said, "but I think it's a wonderful idea." The poet Galway Kinnell may have had the inspiration, but Cleopatra would pull it off in style. She and I had gotten to know each other after my mother died, since I was the one she'd call with questions pertaining to Dad and Dartmouth. With her Louisiana drawl and her thick blond curls, she was the first woman poet-in-residence at Dartmouth and I was glad to be working with her on this tribute.

"We've got a starting list of writers we're inviting," Cleopatra had said, "but I want your input in case we missed anyone important." Her Who's Who list of American poets, including Richard Wilbur, Donald Hall, and Maxine Kumin, was impressive, but I noted a missing name. For the prior several weeks, I'd been reading through letters between my father and Allen Ginsberg. As my fingers flipped through their correspondence, I'd enjoyed reacquainting myself with Allen, while remembering the evening I'd spent with him when I was seventeen.

"What about Ginsberg?" I ventured.

"Terrific. I have no idea if we can get him, but we'll try."

— ∞ —

Sitting in the first row with Dad, I was nervous for him. Or was it for me? I'd become accustomed to the role of my father's surrogate after Mom died, but he hadn't been in front of a public crowd like this for a decade, and his energy wasn't what it had been. I worried maybe he'd been right—it was a lot to expect. As for me, when the role of surrogate required it, I'd played the proud daughter. As I'd come to terms with his abuse, that role had increasingly felt like an act. His fans wanted to hear of my pride in him, not my shame in his behavior. Meanwhile, the ambience of my father's favorite college hall, filled with poets and students, brought me back to my childhood living room. I took in a few long breaths and let my worries go.

"The poets are accounted for," Cleopatra announced to Dad and me, "but Maxine is looking for a parking space and Allen is tied up at the airport." I wondered if the crowd might get antsy, but everyone seemed to be enjoying themselves. There was a palpable buzz in the air. Molly had been excused from her high school classes that afternoon, and Ben had driven up from his college.

"How are you doing?" Cleopatra asked Dad.

"Why, marvelous," he said, holding out his hand to hers.

It seemed he would be fine. He looked well in his new suit, sporting the tiny purple silk insignia pin in his lapel that indicated his membership in the inner circle of the American Academy of Arts and Letters.

A few minutes later, Maxine had found herself a parking space, and Allen and Peter Orlovsky were on their way. The moment Ginsberg and Orlovsky arrived in the hall, reporters and photographers surrounded them. I relaxed further, realizing all the attention would not be on Dad. I thought of the Eberhart story of how the Hanover Inn had turned down Allen and Peter for lodging because they were barefoot, when I'd known it was because they were gay. I never understood my parents' invention, nor why they kept the fiction going. Instead of advocating for their friends, they'd covered for the inn, making a farce of Allen's and Peter's experience. This was one of Dad's stories I liked least.

Once the poets were accounted for, Cleopatra opened the tribute. Dad leaned forward with his right ear canted toward the lectern. Over the next two hours, one award-winning writer after another carried us through a verbal tour of twentieth-century American literature, using my father's poems and his literary milestones for illustration.

Ginsberg had been selected to close the program, and he introduced his remarks by referring to the Eberhart article in the *Times* about the West Coast Beats. "Richard shocked some in the East Coast literary scene when he supported us," Allen said. I noted an uptick in camera clicks as he spoke—he was still the rock star in this group. "It was an early salvo," he continued. "Dick took the side of radicals and open-form poets in kicking down the doors of the establishment. He was a great elder ally and sustainer of morale." Allen, too, sported the purple pin of the inner Academy—earned, he told the audience—because my father and Kenneth Rexroth had used a "can opener to pry open a space." My father grinned at the memory. I was glad we'd been able to bring these two poets together again.

To a rapt audience, Ginsberg finished his remarks by reading "The Groundhog" and thanked my father "for giving it to the world, a poem that takes a focused camera look at the events of a decaying groundhog out to panoramic awareness, as close an approximation of a real mystical experience as you can find in contemporary literature." Allen stepped down from the stage, kissed Dad on the cheek, and reached for his hands.

"I'll see you at the inn?" he asked, turning to me.

"You will."

— 〜〜 —

Across campus, the spacious dining room upstairs at the Hanover Inn was lit by chandeliers and high windows overlooking Dartmouth's green. Cleopatra and I were pleased at how well the event had gone. Even my father had made it onto the stage to read a poem and to receive what would be his final, sustained and standing, ovation.

A week earlier, Cleopatra had called me with a dilemma. "If I place any of the poets next to the wrong person," she'd confided, "I won't hear the end of it. I need you to take care of the seating arrangements."

Really? We need to worry about this? I thought of Mom telling me that poets were a sensitive lot who needed special care and feeding, and that they could be petty and competitive with each other. In my final year of high school, Dad had been morose when his new book didn't win him a second Pulitzer Prize.

"Don't be silly, Dick," my mother admonished, "you've already won a Pulitzer."

"Frost won four of them," Dad grumbled. "And Lowell has two."

My mother would have relished Cleopatra's seating challenge, purposely putting the warring poets side by side and reminding them, "If the United States can sit down with Russia, then you two can do the same."

I took a different tack, prioritizing my kids. I paired Donald Hall, a passionate follower of baseball, next to Ben, then a college pitcher. I put Ginsberg and Orlovsky next to Molly and my niece Lena, as each was studying *Howl* in her respective English class. I put Ernie Hebert, a member of Dartmouth's English department, next to Stephen Corey, a poet from Florida, three years my senior. Corey had snubbed me on multiple occasions when I'd seen him in Gainesville while visiting my parents. Ernie could handle him. I placed my father next to Dartmouth's then president, James Friedman, with whom Dad had a warm friendship. There were seventy-five people to seat, including cousins who'd flown in from Toronto and Chicago and all six of Dad's grandchildren.

Halfway through the entrée course, I floated around the elegant dining room, checking on the poets. No one seemed to be warring with anyone. Peter and Allen were filling in Molly and Lena on life in Greenwich Village in the 1960s while Allen penned each of them an ink drawing of Buddha. Don Hall and Ben were sitting near my father and me. Grief etched Don's face, and his eyes were less bright than usual. He was mourning his wife, the poet Jane Kenyon, who had died eighteen months earlier. As the waitstaff cleared our dinner plates, Don perked up when he got into a lively banter with Ben about batting averages and baseball statistics. I accepted a second glass of wine.

During a lull in the meal, Ginsberg crossed the room to talk to Don and Dad. Without forethought, I drew Allen and my father away from the table. While the servers brought out dessert, the two poets had a chance to catch up with each other. In their unlikely friendship, Allen and Dad had stoked a decades-long correspondence and a mutual admiration as each worked in his own way to be noticed artistically. They cared for each other; saw in each other an ally, a transcendent spirit, and a unique mind; they made sure to see each other whenever both were in New York.

While the two reminisced, I thought it time to air the Ginsberg story. My parents' fiction of the couple being turned down at the Inn had been amplified and enhanced so many times, it had turned into something wholly false.

"So, I told Allen and Peter," Mom would say. "'Why didn't you just put on your shoes?'"

"What's wrong with Dartmouth, anyway?" my father would cry. "They were my honored guests, on behalf of the College."

"Well, it was the Hanover *Inn,* not the *College,*" Mom would quip. "It's not the same."

"But the Inn is *owned* by the College," Dad would conclude, nursing his drink. "It *is* the same."

When I faulted Mom and Dad for their invention and for side-stepping the truth, they'd shake me off. Over time, their version had hardened into Eberhart lore. I wanted to set the record straight.

"So, Allen, do you remember the first time we met?"

"Certainly. You'd been to Switzerland, and Peter and I had returned from India. I remember the evening well."

"So, is it true that you and Peter were barefoot and dressed in robes when you tried to register at the inn, and that's why they turned you down?"

My father stared at the floor, looking sheepish.

"That's inaccurate," Allen said, looking directly at Dad. "You've been saying that for years, Dick, and it's simply not true. We never would have done anything so trivial."

My father lifted his eyebrows and shrugged.

The inn had welcomed Allen and Peter that afternoon, and Allen was making it clear to his friend that he couldn't use the ruse anymore. It may have been adolescent of me to orchestrate the interchange, but I was tired of Dad using Allen's and Peter's experience for entertainment.

Later, after the toasts wrapped up and the event was closing, I said goodbye to Allen and Peter, embracing each of them.

"Thank you for straightening Dad out," I said to Allen.

"It was time," he said.

"You must come see us in New York," Peter added.

I looked forward to such a visit. Allen had taken photographs throughout the evening, and I hoped he would send some to me.

"I will," he said.

Neither of us was quick enough to keep our pledge. Six months later, on April 5, 1997, Allen died at the age of seventy-one, the day my father turned ninety-three.

— ∞ —

Seeing the poets together in the same place, as groups of them had so often been in Hanover and in Maine, I realized they'd known me since I was born. I'd been friends with their children when I was a kid, and several of them had loved me like a father would. I wondered if the next phase of my search would come not from the dusty pages of Dad's archives but from conversations in real time with the poets who knew him best.

I took Allen as a great elder ally, a sustainer of my morale, an early salvo in kicking down the doors of my paternal establishment. That night at the inn, he had laid down the first step on a journey I would take through a dozen visits with my father's famous friends. Allen had been able to say directly to Dad what he thought and felt—and did it without anger or meanness. It was a model I would carry forward to a time when I would do the same.

Chapter 25:

No Longer Willing

On June 7, 2005, Michael and I had opened every window in our house to attract a breeze. My home office on the second floor was hot, and my morning calls with clients had built up beads of sweat across my forehead. I joined Michael outside in the shade for lunch and lingered long enough to cut a bunch of Siberian iris stems, whose blossoms stood like soft sentries in the heat, shimmering against our stone garden wall. I'd transplanted the irises from my mother's garden in Hanover, and every June they heralded the sweet arrival of summer, their mild blue and yellow masses reminding me of her. I placed a vase of them on our dining room table. Turning back toward the kitchen, I saw the blinking red light of our answering machine.

"Gretchen, this is Brenda," the voice on the machine said. "It's about your father. Call Chris or me as soon as you can."

We had received many calls from my father's caregivers. He'd fallen a few times without breaking anything. He'd needed new pajamas. A friend of his had stopped by and had dinner; they just wanted me to know, since the bill would show on the next invoice. We'd celebrated Dad's one hundredth birthday with nearly a hundred people in the function room, and he had already passed 101.

I picked up the phone and got through to my father's physician, who told me, "He fell this morning. He may have broken his hip."

"I see."

"The possible break isn't what's worrying us," Chris said. "It's that we think his fall was precipitated by confusion related to his third pneumonia, this one likely viral."

Chris and I quickly determined the next steps, which I would relay to Dikkon. We wouldn't send him to the medical center, a trip we concluded would be traumatizing for Dad. He'd had two previous pneumonias that spring, both bacterial, but had come through them, though three data points was starting to look like a trend.

"Your father's old," Chris said, pausing. "He could die."

I thought that unlikely. My father's life just kept spooling out in front of us beyond any expectations we'd ever had. Dikkon and I thought he might go on forever, though we'd agreed we wouldn't go to extraordinary means if the tide turned. Since my mother had died, I'd managed my father's financial matters, shopped for his clothes, coordinated with his care, and responded to the press when poets in his literary circle died and reporters needed a sound bite. I often felt burdened by the tasks and then guilty for feeling so. How had he gone from being fine two days earlier, when I'd last seen him, to this? I filled in my brother by phone, and Dikkon didn't think Dad would die, either.

On my first of many thirty-minute drives to Hanover over the next four days, the hot midday air was as startling and oppressive as the cool dryness of my father's room. Neither environment felt right, the weather, both controlled and not, resurfacing my conflicting relationship with Dad. His room, his nurses, the mild smell of fresh paint on the walls in the community room—all those were familiar, but every moment inside his room felt unfamiliar. I was on my own that first day and stole five-minute phone breaks outside, sweating in the shade of a small maple tree, updating Michael and my kids, calling my cousins Kate and Susan, Eloise and Lil, my closest friends, and letting clients know I'd need to ignore them for a few days. By the end of that afternoon, the medical dominoes seemed to be falling out in front of us and I didn't see how my father could live.

Michael joined me after work and stayed until midnight, encouraging me to come home with him.

"You'll sleep better, and they'll call if something happens."

"If he dies, you mean?"

I didn't want to leave. Something was pinning me there. At 1:00 a.m., I took Dad's *Collected Poems* and thumbed through its well-worn pages, held together by stringy remnants of its spine. Landing on his best-known poems, I read each one aloud, trying to carry my father's voice as he listened. Dad didn't respond much, but when he did, he seemed still present, still my dad.

Nurses came and went frequently, and the clock next to his bed began to count down the final hours. I squeezed my father's hand and read a final poem, one of my favorites, called "Opulence":

Nothing is so magnificent
As the sun descending
Copernicus-gold over the horizon
With birds singing in the pine trees
When it is rich summer, when June
Has on her iris finery
And peony-bright, hesitates good-bye.

Nothing is so magnificent
As the full mind, stored with summers
With age approaching
The sun standing over the horizon
Wonders yet unknown, love not refusing
The world all a visionary
Guess, unspent clarity.

I've long pondered his phrase *the world all a visionary guess*, but it resonated for me that night—all that he was and wasn't to me, the visionary guess of him. I wasn't ready to let him go, nor did it seem he was ready, either.

Around 3:00 a.m., I headed home. Tropical air spilled through my open car windows, heating up my thoughts. A keen alertness led me to spot things in the utter stillness of small New Hampshire towns that I'd never noticed before. There was an especially full lilac tree by the side of the road and a small rubber ball in a ditch. Tidbits of the day threaded through my mind, odd things, like the seemingly unnecessary arrival of his final package of clothes and the CD of water music his social worker had delivered, music my father never would have listened to. Every minute change in his condition at every hour had been recorded in his file, as if there might be a future in which to consider them. The questions I kept asking everyone—What does that mean? What will happen next? How long might this go on?—went unanswered. It was all a visionary guess.

The next day would blur, as Dikkon arrived and Dad rallied, sank, then rallied again. Untethered to my real life, a world outside that kept spinning forward without me, I was suspended in private turmoil and clung, without knowing why, to every minute I could have within his four walls. A concentrated stew of emotions made me raw and vulnerable, which I'd thought I was over years before.

Dikkon and I talked some, each of us wrapped in our own experience of Dad, neither of us fully able to console the other.

By the fourth day, it was clear what was happening, and we invited family and friends, students and professors and staff, to say their goodbyes. Martha Hennessey retold her story of confusing the Pulitzer with the Poet's Surprise. Jay Parini thanked Dad for his gifts of friendship and mentorship. An LNA reminisced about his nightly hot-fudge sundaes and the full-size flashlights he carried in each pocket of his robe in case a power failure hit this high-tech facility.

By midafternoon, I was spent from listening. Dikkon and I were in the room on our own together and knew we were nearing the end. Moved in a different way by this event than I, my brother launched into a passionate soliloquy about the virtues of our father, focusing on Dad's single-minded attention to his art, which Dikkon concluded had ensured his lucky longevity. I'd been holding in my feelings for three days, none clearly named, a mash-up of contradictions, confusion, in the muddy middle of something I didn't comprehend. My brother's speech landed in the pit of my stomach with a thud. It was just that single-minded self-focus, I wanted to scream, that had robbed me of a father I could have still loved.

"I can't hear this," I said, exiting the room. I stumbled down the hall and found the meditation room I'd never been in during the twelve years my father had lived in his retirement community. I closed the door, lay facedown on the carpet, and wept. Everyone else's words were like a web of projections they held about my father, but none of them had spoken for me, and I'd not yet spoken for myself.

— ∽ —

At five o'clock that afternoon, Dikkon went outside to call my sister-in-law, and Brenda came in and sat next to me. Her soft face and warm smile were immediately comforting. It had been her answering machine message that had started the medical dice rolling on Thursday, but I'd yet to see her that week. The shades in my father's room were fully drawn, and blankets covered him.

"Why isn't he taking food or water?" I asked.

"We don't think he feels we have anything useful left to offer him."

Such honest yet delicate words. I appreciated them.

"How are you doing?" she asked.

"I'm okay. It's challenging."

I pulled Brenda away from Dad's bed, and we stood at the edge of his room, our voices barely louder than a whisper. "I need to tell you something," I said. "When I was six, he didn't protect me from the abuse of our summer caretaker. When I was seventeen, he molested me in my bed. You and Chris are in charge. I really don't even know if I should be here."

Tears welled in Brenda's eyes. "My father molested my sisters, Gretchen. I know exactly what you're going through. Your father's dying will raise all the issues you thought were settled. *You* are not dying here. Chris and I will take care of your father. Your job is to take care of yourself."

I shifted in my seat. *But how?* I wondered.

"You know," she said, "several times over the years, I've thought your father's comments were off. There was nothing very specific. He just said things that made me wonder if something might have happened."

I stared at her, again surprised that others had seen and heard things I hadn't been able to.

"There's been no space in my family for this side of him," I said. "He was our center. If I'd confided in my mother, it would have destroyed her, and if she'd known he did it, that would have destroyed me. If I'd confronted Dad, he would have shrugged it off and walked away. It took thirty-five years to refuse his kisses. For the last five, I've taken to shaking his hand. Do you know what it feels like to shake your father's hand?"

Brenda and I stood in silence. She was telling me I could go, but something else was telling me to stay.

"Can he hear me?" I whispered.

"We think hearing is the last thing to go, so most likely he can, but we don't really know for sure."

"He seems even more different now," I said, glancing over at Dad.

"Yes, his breath is very shallow."

Brenda smoothed the blanket over my father's legs, squeezed his toes, and embraced me, before walking out of the room and closing the door behind her. There was an essence in that concentrated darkness that stays with me—the spill of light from under his door mimicking my bedroom in Hanover, a slip of air between us, this time not mocked by alcohol or betrayal, just the two of us, daughter and father, victim and abuser. A final moment. My body had carried the depth of our history, and it took over that night, while I let go and got out of my own way. As soft water sounds tumbled over imaginary rock ledges in the background, I found my truth to tell.

I looked at my father, his breath wispy.

"Dad," I said, spreading the fingers of my right hand gently on his chest, my face eighteen inches from his. "I don't know if you can hear me, but if you can, it's okay— you can let go."

His eyes opened like a jack-in-the-box, shocking me, and words surfaced from that complicated four-day vigil and thirty-eight years of silence.

"I forgive you, Dad," I said quietly and firmly. "It was not right what you did. I was seventeen, and you were my father. You weren't supposed to do that. But I forgive you. You can let go now. I will be okay."

My father stared at me for a second and closed his eyes while I counted his next five, slow, even breaths. I don't know why I counted them, but every nerve ending in my body was on high alert, every muscle taut as piano wire, every sense trained on each detail, as if the rest of my life might depend on them.

The five thinnest wisps of air I've ever known.

"It's okay, Dad. Let this next breath be your last," I said.

And it was.

—— ∞ ——

Death is so unequivocally final. To which, were I reading this aloud to my father, he might charmingly profess, "The word *final means* final. It isn't made more final by qualifying it." True enough. And I couldn't have understood what *final* really meant had I not been with him in those last minutes.

I called for Chris, who came in to confirm the time of death and sat next to me.

"He's gone," I said.

"He is."

"What's next?"

"We've called the funeral home. You can stay as long as you want."

"Okay."

"Does Dikkon know?"

"Not yet. He's outside."

Chris looked at Dad and then at me. "It's a privilege for us to be here with someone when he dies," he said. "It's our privilege to help him make his final passage as best he can."

"Yes, and I'm so grateful to all of you."

"But we don't really know the whole story," Chris said, waving off my compliment. "We have only this one small slice. We see the photographs on the walls, we spend each day with them, we think we know them. We make assumptions about who they are and how they've lived their lives."

"Brenda told you?" I asked.

"She did."

Chris reached for my hand and I spoke.

"I don't think I need anyone else to change their experience of my father anymore. I'm just no longer willing to change mine."

— ∞ —

Two weeks after my father died, Michael and I drove to Hanover for his memorial service. It was a bright, blue-sky Saturday. Puffy white clouds hung over the New Hampshire hills like happy cherubs. Every corner of town was filled with blossoming pink and white crab apple, creamy verbena, late purple lilac, and sprawling masses of magenta rhododendron. Each blade of grass on my father's favorite college quad was a stunning green. *When June has on her iris finery and peony-bright hesitates goodbye*, I quoted to myself. I hadn't planned to forgive my father. It had risen of its own accord. For me, I'm sure, as much as for him.

Staring through the windshield, I said to Michael, "Dad would have been pleased with this beautiful day." A positive change in mood from that morning, when, in rising panic at the prospect of attending his memorial, I'd threatened not to go, certain I couldn't abide one more day of lauding my humanly flawed father. With little sleep over the two weeks since he'd died, and with no time to deal with my own scattered emotions, I'd reverted to being my father's full-time surrogate, focused entirely on his public persona: coordinating with the college for its press release; providing sound bites to TV and radio hosts in Minnesota and New Hampshire; fielding interviews with reporters from the *New York Times*, the *Boston Globe*, and the *LA Times*. In death, my father had again taken over my life. I was angry and overwhelmed.

"Believe me," I had said to Michael as we dressed that morning, "if I could, I'd leave town."

—⚬—

Inside the dark wooden chapel on the Dartmouth campus, Michael and I found Molly and Ben, who'd arrived on their own from their summer jobs. Whatever disappointments they had about me, they'd never hesitated to tell me in real time, and, if not perfectly, I'd listened and tried to understand. I was just happy to see them, to be with them.

We spotted John Hennessey in the front row and sat next to him.

"I feel guilty that I don't feel sad," I whispered to John, leaning against his tweed shoulder.

"You shouldn't," he said. "You've been saying goodbye to your father for more than thirty years."

"Really," I said, breathing in slowly and exhaling, "for the first time in my life, I feel free."

John squeezed my hand. How well he knew me. And how little time my father had ever taken to do the same. I thought of all the privileges I'd been given: a perfect summer cottage in Maine, introductions as a kid to a hundred fabulous writers, support from Gram and Mom to live in Lausanne, the sheer weight of books that filled my parents' homes and mine—all those things didn't equal the emotional privilege John had given me as my chosen father.

Eulogies were delivered with generosity and grace, including one by Don Hall, with whom I'd recently become friends. But I was only half listening, my mind retracing the prior weeks, remembering email snippets that had fallen from cyberspace, including one of my favorites, from summer friend Sarah: *The Barbie dolls are holding a wake in the woods behind Undercliff—dressed in their finest, of course!*

John tapped me on the arm, and I knew I was next. From the podium, I noticed the bright sun pouring through the high stained-glass windows of this simple wooden chapel on the Dartmouth campus, and guests sat up straight in their wooden chairs. John gave me a nod. Having been in front of hundreds of client gatherings, with the privilege of supporting not just the work they were doing, but the feelings they carried about that work and themselves, into conference rooms and auditoriums, I'd learned how to read the emotion in a room, how to time my interventions. I realized, standing before the audience, that I'd learned my timing, in part, from years of listening to poetic phrases. I knew a few beats of quiet were necessary that afternoon. My brother had just proffered a powerful, sobbing string of "I love yous" to his father, so passionately breathtaking I'd felt nearly pushed back against my chair. The cavernous chapel hushed, and, after embracing Dikkon as he descended from the podium, I let the silence linger. I wouldn't bash my father, or embarrass him or myself, but my words had to be truthful. If Dad's voice and power had once betrayed me, I'd reclaimed them and made them both my own. Anything less than honest would be a violation of all I'd come to believe. I thanked his legion of poet friends, some there in the chapel; I evoked our summers at Undercliff; and I brought my mother into the room. I wanted her there, too. As Don had told me not long before the

memorial, "You know I loved your father, Gretchen, but I abso-
lutely adored your mother." Everyone did.

My eulogy came in four narrative stanzas late the prior night,
fueled by a forty-mile bike ride with three friends. Rain fell through
much of the ride and we talked about everything but Dad: the
musty smell of wet pavement; the fresh green of new grass; how to
take a sharp turn at the bottom of a long, fast hill without pitching
over our bikes; Lance Armstrong's affair with Sheryl Crow; the
beauty of blue and yellow iris, brilliant pink peonies, orange day-
lilies, and purple delphinium—every mile a rolling testament to
nature's opulence and a gardener's green thumb. Just me and my
bike and these women on wheels. Each turning point in my recovery, it seemed, had been ignited by physical exertion that inspired
answers to the pining in my heart. I finished off with the last stanza:

It took three years for the irises I transplanted from my
mother's garden in Hanover to establish themselves into a thick
bunch in mine. Now, every June, they show off their blue and
yellow finery and make me think of her. In the end, the iris blossoms I cut on Tuesday and put on our dining room table lasted
about four days, the same time it took my father to let go.

Chapter 26:

My Family of Poets

In March 2017, twelve years after my father died, I shared my story at a celebration of International Women's Day in Hanover. Scheduled as the #MeToo movement was building steam, it was to be a public reading by abuse survivors, focused on the community of advocates who'd helped us heal. I had plenty of people to thank. At a venue just off the Dartmouth campus, where Dad had taught for forty years, I would tell my story in public for the first time.

The sharp stage lights blinded me. Standing at the microphone, I squinted to see if I recognized anyone in the audience. I'd prepared myself for a couple dozen people, but the place had swelled to 150. Michael and friends, along with my writing group, were taking up the rear, so as not to make me nervous. As I waited in the wings, my legs were shaking long before I was announced onstage. Now, I thought they might buckle. For decades, I'd believed the world would collapse if anyone knew my story—first that my original family would implode, then that I'd ruin my father's prodigious reputation—but not speaking up had come at a personal cost. Still, my palms were covered in sweat and my heart was pounding so loudly I thought it might push through my chest. I forced my shoulders back and lowered the microphone to my height. *Just breathe*, I said to myself. *Just breathe.*

There was a trick I'd learned decades earlier when I'd first had to stand up in front of large client meetings. It was to imagine myself as a confident speaker who enjoyed being there and to viscerally cement that image on my wrist, a place I could touch at any time if I was nervous. The trick had always worked. I touched my forefinger to my wrist, and, for the first time, it failed me.

I looked out at the crowd. In my father's time—and when I was growing up in this town—Hanover was nearly all white and Dartmouth was all male. Now, I saw a mix of ages, nationalities, races, gender expressions and orientations, high school and college students, professors, and community people, all coming together to celebrate women standing up to be heard. I thought of family structures and how they've changed—from the once paternal model to one of partnership, from the stay-at-home wife to two wives or two husbands contributing equally, from marriage condoned by the church and state to marriages condoned by those who chose to tie their own knots.

"The short story is this," I began. "My father molested me at seventeen while I was asleep in my bed. It's taken fifty years to say those words in public." I paused, taking in the sea of faces before me. "As Graham Greene once wrote, 'We live through our first twenty years and spend the rest of our life reflecting on them.' That has been true for me."

— ⬤ —

After Dartmouth's 1996 tribute to my father, I reached out to Dad's closest friends, mostly poets, both men and women, important members of his tribe, eager to understand their experiences and, if they were open, to share mine. Tentative at first, I didn't want to offend. I had no idea what their responses might be. The only surprise I got through each of those conversations was that not one of them was surprised by my revelation.

"He was so charming—and the most narcissistic person I've known," Cleopatra Mathis told me over coffee. "I loved your parents. Their parties were wonderful! Everyone was there. You wouldn't want to miss them. You couldn't miss them. I loved both your father and your mother, but Dick was so wrapped up in himself, he just expected you to be wrapped up in him, too."

"Your father was so tender with your mother, so devoted to her care," Maxine Kumin said as we sat in her living room, her husband, Victor, nodding in agreement. "She had a seizure at our house over dinner, and I'll never forget how he was with her. And, as you know, he was one of the best, really, to us early women poets. He supported us and promoted us, which other male poets didn't, and we gained from his mentoring and his associations."

In those first two meetings, I'd heard the breadth of my father. Both sides of who he was were equally true.

A month later, Dick and Charlee Wilbur welcomed me into their pastoral home in western Massachusetts. The Wilburs had enjoyed a remarkable friendship with my parents, each person equally drawn to the other three. "It was just a four-way friendship like none other we've ever had," Charlee noted. The relationship was cemented at 10 Hilliard Place, Charlee recalled. "We had so many good times there. We loved that house. Everyone did."

"Whatever Dick wrote was a delight to him," Dick Wilbur shared. "He cared less about the quality of the work than about the wonderful experience of it."

"That's true," I said.

"He's one of the few writers I can think of who really was inspired. It wasn't him. It was the muse, the divine fire. She would wake him in the middle of the night and offer him eight poems."

"But some weren't good," I offered. "Last year, a friend was visiting us at Undercliff, and wanted to hear some of my father's poetry, so I pulled a volume off the shelf and read them and a lot of them were bad poems!"

"It's true," Dick said. "He felt his poetry came from some deep well in his spirit, and who was he to guess about or mess with that?"

"He didn't see that as egotistical?" I asked.

"Of course, it was, but no, Dick really believed in his spirit so wholly that it was hard to argue with him."

The Wilburs and I talked long and late as the sun moved over the house, from one side to the other. Charlee pulled out leftovers for lunch as Dick searched for a pan of brownies in the pantry. I could see why my mother and father had loved them both so much, as had I as a child, each immediately engaging and generous, the two clearly a team. The Wilburs were as I remembered them—warm, candid, and real.

As I departed late in the afternoon, Dick offered a final thought. "Your father had an enormous hole. That was the source of his muse, but a hole that no one really could fill, though he likely attracted many to try."

—❦—

Of Dad's friends I got to know that year, it was Don Hall who took me under his wing. Between the end of 1996 and 2010, I visited him regularly at his farmhouse in Wilmot, New Hampshire. He made time and had empathy, even if he was particular about how we needed to communicate. He insisted we type out our letters and send them by mail, he simply didn't use email. If I needed to be in touch with him quickly, to re-schedule a visit, say, I could send a fax; don't bother calling, he added—"I won't answer voice mail." Don dictated his correspondence to an assistant, and I assume that's how he fashioned his letters to me.

On my first visit with Hall, late in 1996, he reminded me that he'd known my father for fifty years.

"And you followed him as New Hampshire's poet laureate," I added. "You also served as U.S. poet laureate, so you shared many of the same experiences."

Don and I were seated in his well-worn living room, piles of books stacked on every surface. His cat hopped back and forth from his lap to mine, during that visit. As our conversation widened and the light outside faded, I felt myself slump into the worn comfort of that chair and into our discussion, not sure I'd be able to get up. Don had facts and advice and was open about his own flaws; he was easy to trust.

"I can't say I'm surprised," Don said after I told him my story, his cat back on his lap, purring gently. "He used to French-kiss my first wife."

"Did everyone know this side of him? That's what I'm hearing. Why couldn't I have seen what was coming and protected myself?"

"That's a hard question to answer. And how would you have, if you had?"

Don suggested that Dad's inability to self-edit—whether in writing or in his personal life—held him back from being an even better poet and a better person than he was. His naiveté had kept him from fully growing up. Driving home from our first visit, I thought of the executives with whom I was working, in part to be better themselves at what they did and who they were. I agreed with Don, poets and businesspeople don't improve without growing and they don't grow without fully understanding the impact of their words, and their actions, on others.

After that visit, Hall sent me a letter that read, *I really enjoyed our talking. One portion disturbed me. Your scones are wonderful. I am glad you told me about the incident. It disturbed me.* He closed with *You seem to be doing very well with it. I'm sorry you have to.*

— ⚬ —

On my next visit, in the spring of 1997, and two years after Jane Kenyon had died, Don and I sat on his porch, looking out on Mount Kearsarge and Jane's lovely, long row of peonies in full bloom; all white, as I remember. We were struck by the bright green of New Hampshire awakening from winter. We contemplated the sunlight on his barn, the shadows it cast, and the look of the mountain's border against the blue sky. I'd told him I was writing about Dad.

On the occasion of my forty-seventh birthday, in 1998, Don sent me a note. We hadn't been in touch for a while. *It has been so long since I have heard from you. Are you all right? What is happening with the book? I've been thinking of you while living at thirty thousand feet, going around the country signing copies of* Without.

I'd read *Without*, his memoir about his life with Jane Kenyon, and knew he'd been traveling to promote it. I hadn't wanted to bother him. The next time I saw Don, I asked if he'd had to deal with any fallout from his family over his memoir. He shared no details but said, "You just have to write your own truth."

"Funny"—I smiled— "that's exactly what Dad told me."

"Dick was right on that. I'm glad he said that to you."

We took in the sweet summer air, the movement of tall grass, the skittering of birds.

"You know, Gretchen, I've told you I loved your father for all he did for me and always will. But I love him less now. What he did was plain wrong."

How I'd yearned for someone in my family of origin to say those words, to apologize for my father since I knew he never would. I thanked Don for doing so on his friend's behalf.

Before I left that day, he offered to get me the letters that he'd received from my father through the half-century they'd known each other, then contained in Don's archives at the University of New Hampshire. Within a week, a thick package arrived at my door. *Here are the letters,* Don wrote, *more, and more substantial than I feared. I read through them with pleasure. What you see is what you get, and Dick is here.* He reminisced about their old times and how much my father had meant to him. *Dick was vastly kind to me when I was a kid. We met at Grolier's Bookstore when he was a salesman for Butcher's (I got the notion that he wasn't doing a whole lot as a salesman!). He was kind to me and the vainest and most narcissistic of poets I've ever known. And all poets, including me, are vain and narcissistic. Growing up, your father largely ignored you because he was so busy writing and doing things with bunches of famous poets.* Don ended his note with *I adored your cartwheels!*

Don offered to read what I was writing about my father and to provide feedback. I mailed off a few new chapters, early versions, and got a three-page letter of notes returned, along with large letters written across one of the chapters: *WRITE MORE FIERCELY.* Too many adjectives, he said. Don't protect Dick, he wrote. If others don't like what you have to say, he added, they can write their own book. I smiled at that and quickly sent him a note with the line I love from Anne Lamott's *Bird by Bird: You own what happened to you. . . . If people wanted you to describe them warmly, they should have behaved better.*

Don wasn't afraid of bringing up the abuse when we talked, nor in our correspondence, which felt like support, allowing it to sit between us in real time, not dwelling on it but not denying it. *Writing about it all will be hard,* he wrote. *Very, very hard, writing about your own father. You loved him vastly, I know, and there were the other things.*

We met for the last time in 2010, when he told me that on the morning my mother died, in 1994, he was awakened by a phone call from Dad at 6:00 a.m., informing Don of the news. He was the first person Dad had called, but Don was certain my father intended to contact half a dozen other poets.

"Interesting," I said, looking into Don's clear, old eyes. "He called the poets first. That pretty much sums it up, doesn't it? Then he had Mom's nurse call me, and I called Dikkon."

Don's final note to me came in May 2011. *The White House visit, and all the photographs, and all the people that were also getting medals—it was a happy time. I congratulate you on your youth, as you turn sixty.* I had watched him receive his Presidential Medal of Freedom on TV, delighting in his slightly bent-over posture and his long mane of crazy hair, embracing our clipped and precise President Obama.

My friendship with Don helped me identify how my father's

bigheartedness had had as much to do with his neediness as it did with his generosity. Together, we explored the bigger systems that had colluded in keeping those needs fed: my family, my father's friends, the English departments and institutions for which he worked. As my father had been a mentor and advisor for Don, so Don became one for me.

In 1996, I'd arranged for an early dinner with Jay Parini in Middlebury, Vermont. Three years older than I, and like a surrogate son to my father and mother, I was eager to get his view. Jay knew my father as well as any other writer, if not for as long.

"Dick was well known in the U.K. and Scotland where I'd been before arriving at Dartmouth," Jay told me. "He was ebullient and had a legendary greatness over there. So, I was keen on meeting him. I'd never had surrogate parents before, but Betty and Dick took me in."

I laughed. "I think you ate dinner with them a lot more than I did."

"That's true," Jay said.

"I don't know how Mom did it, feeding people every night."

"What modern marriage—yours or mine—would allow for it?"

"It helps me understand why in my own family we guard our time together."

"I spent so much time with both of them—at dinners, but also traveling with Dick alone to readings in Boston and New York, or to Holderness to watch a football game of Dikkon's. I went to keep him company. We were very, very close, but all he wanted to talk about was poetry and philosophy, forever and ever."

"I would have found that utterly boring back then!"

"He talked about you and Dikkon a lot, especially when you were rebelling. I heard a thousand times about you dropping out of college, marrying Alex. He was bewildered by anyone's rebelliousness, if not his own."

Jay asked who Dad's really close friends were. I was surprised by the question, since I assumed he'd been one of them.

"Dick was enthralled with a crowd but unable to connect deeply and emotionally with an individual," Jay said. "There was always something a bit remote about him, something a bit protected. You could get only so far, and then a protective shield didn't let you go below that. And he never talked about his marriage."

"Really? I would have expected he would have."

"I sensed a depression sometimes. Especially as he got older, he was terrified of seeing his reputation fade, that no one would care anymore. One anthology missed—it was terrifying for him."

I'd drained my beer and had filled up a side of tape, recording our conversation. Jay was putting words to the confusion and isolation I'd felt around my father, feeling he was disconnected from me personally and uninterested in who I was. Parini was building coherence in my experience. He spoke of his own felt awkwardness when it was only him and Mom and Dad at a meal; an experience I had had too. But they both lit up when others were around.

"They were constantly partying," Jay went on. "He needed a vast crowd for ballast."

In a tribute to my father, Jay had once written that Dad had a "hard-won innocence." I asked him what he'd meant about that and what he knew about my grandparents A.L. and Lena Eberhart.

"A.L.'s ruin and Dick's mother's death, as he turned from seventeen to eighteen, was a real childhood trauma. He was bereft and an isolated guy much of his younger adult life. He loved and revered his father who he described as huge, looming, 'forbidding.' He was a burden to Dick," Jay continued. "Your father never felt he measured up to his father's Victorian entrepreneurship."

"And Lena?" I asked.

"Lena was his warmth. After he lost her, he was terrified of losing someone like her again."

"That helps explain how terrified he was of losing Louise Hawkes."

"He saw relationships as dark and dangerous. But Betty was a great connector; she could handle emotion, and she loved the twenty-four-hour party. She was a good match for him."

"Until she got older, I think, and had to endure his affair with Joy."

"His affair with Joy was so open," Jay said. "So brash and indiscreet; he didn't hide it at all. He was dumb in that way, as if saying, *Look at me—aren't you thrilled by my virility?*"

"I can't stand that about him. I feel so sad for Mom."

"But Betty got something, too. She got access and connection to a never-ending bevvy of fascinating people who loved her enormously. Somehow she knew Dick and Joy weren't 'serious,' that Dick wouldn't leave her. Your father was a man of immense physical appetites—for food, life, sex. Life was an ongoing fiction, and here's a new chapter. It's true, as you say—he was a narcissist, but such a lovely one."

— ∞ —

It took months to comprehend all I'd learned from Phil and Margaret Booth, Dan and Liz Hoffman, Maxine Kumin, Cleopatra Mathis, the Wilburs, Don Hall, and Jay Parini. They'd named my father's old-fashioned maleness—his love of hobnobbing with famous people, smoking cigars, and drinking bourbon on his boat or in men's clubs in Boston. I could see in my mind the sweep of family—from my Butcher and Eberhart grandparents to Mom and Dad to me and on to my own children, each generation redefining what relationships and family can be.

And, I saw myself as just one of millions of girls around the world who'd been molested, objectified, abused, or disregarded by our fathers, uncles, brothers, priests, and lovers—a never-ending stream of us, robbed of what was rightfully ours alone to give, our intimate injustices often silenced. Tangled in the old family systems, the primacy of men, who chose—still choose—to use their power to silence the voices they most need to hear.

The myths of my father had shattered like balls of mercury rolling over the edge of my past. I, too, had colluded in the systemic conspiracy of silence, for the sake of my family of origin, for myself, and especially for my father. I'd long wished my original family could have heard my story—really heard—but I suddenly realized the poets had been part of my family all along—connected to my parents, consuming our food, filling our living rooms, inhabiting our space. In rejecting them for a career in consulting, I'd discarded part of my heritage. Sitting in their homes, they'd heard and seen me. As if zipped into my skin, they could feel the things I'd felt. Parched for a father's love I should rightfully have called my own, I turned to the poets and cupped my hands at their trough, finding in them the advocates I'd long needed. Speaking truth to power, they warned, would make me vulnerable, but the poets were there to help me find my public voice. They'd taken me in, as family should. They'd helped me interpret the world I'd lived in, as my father never could.

— ✈ —

Fifteen minutes into my reading in Hanover, I was still shaking at the mic. I looked out from the microphone and sensed that the audience was with me. Public admission was my final admission to myself of all that had happened in my father's orbit. As I closed, I told the audience of a story I'd heard from my consulting colleague and friend Julie, who'd recently introduced me to the Japanese art of *kintsugi*, known as "golden repair." According to legend, a Japanese warrior in the fourteenth century broke a beloved ceramic bowl while traveling and sent it home for repair. Craftsmen applied metal staples, but the staples were unsightly. They tried every fix they could imagine, until, after many attempts, an artisan experimented by using liquid gold lacquer to fill the cracks. The showy glue held together the pieces of the bowl, cementing its original integrity while beautifully highlighting its broken places. To make myself whole again, I'd had to do the same—identify each broken piece and find a way to fix it—physically, emotionally, and spiritually. Michael and my two children, friends and physicians, my sister-cousins, and each in my poet-family were tributaries merging into a wide river of gold, stitching me back together again, stronger and better for the mending.

All systems—familial, religious, corporate, governmental—prefer maintaining the status quo. But we will change them. Some of us will whisper. Some of us will roar. Some of us will take to a stage, while others take to the streets. Some will speak only in a hushed voice to one trusted friend. Too many of us—as many as thirty percent—will speak to no one at all. Each of us has her own trustworthy reason.

I finished my piece and looked up. The crowd was silent for what seemed too long before they stunned me with a standing ovation. In a space in Hanover my father might have commanded previously, I'd come to the end of my sixty-year journey, back—full circle—to the place where it had begun.

Epilogue

It's 2019, fourteen years since my father died, and twenty-six years since I lost my mom. At Undercliff, I'm reclaiming her overgrown flower garden while Michael is renovating the cottage as we steward it toward the next generation. Pulling plants from the earth, I trace my parents' history with mine in the tangled roots of day lilies and mixed-up blossoms that float on their stems in the soft ocean breeze. The soil is porous and black, thanks to the years-ago offerings from Scott and Helen Nearing's compost piles and the free seaweed that Mom made us carry up from the beach. Today I'm battling her rugosa roses, which have grown so well in the rich dirt and salt air that they've taken over our view from inside the cottage. She transplanted them from our favorite picnic island during my father's long love affair. It's time for them to go.

Covered in dirt and dripping with sweat, I'm trying hard, like Mom did, to tame this rugged coast. It's a losing battle. I pull up lily tubers, crammed together under the earth like armies of baby mice. I'm tired of her old-fashioned orange day lilies, so I'll give most of them away. Then I think, *No, I want to hold a few back; I like having her spirit nearby.* It was Mom who gave me the joy of gardening. Gulls squawk overhead, and our resident osprey perches on his nest in the tallest spruce tree. His *chip-chip-chip* pierces the air as he keeps an eye out for his dinner. I bend and pull out weeds and toss them into buckets as he keeps his eye on me, too.

If Mom were here, she'd delight in her grandchildren and their families and friends making daily plans for sailing trips and island picnics. The next generation sprawls on the grass and talks about the same things the poets did: loves and losses, career triumphs and misses, fears and longings. Less alcohol, but the same free-ranging summer-after-summer conversations. I know Mom would enjoy their banter and occasionally deflate their egos, as she did so skillfully the Pulitzer Prize winners. I have no grand plan for this garden—just enough color and texture to wave in the breeze on a summer day.

A white-throated sparrow startles me with its plaintive call. I summon the memory of my mother's full-bellied laugh as I see her round middle push against the elastic of her denim shorts. She chews on a gnarly apple from the tree at the edge of the lawn, tossing its core in the shrubbery to make a point. Then a squirrel grabs it and runs off, to be featured later in a poem by my father, pipe between his teeth, about the meaning of squirrels and apple cores and how life goes on, as he plucks perfect phrases from the foggy ether and strings them together like pearls.

I regret that Mom and I never got to know the adult friendship that I've come to know with Molly. Neither she nor I made that happen. This is one of many regrets I ponder in the garden while I miss her every day. I go long stretches without thinking of my father, until one of his verses sticks in my brain for an afternoon and I circle my thoughts around him, still.

— ∞ —

Michael and I take showers after our work and change our clothes. We're pleased to know this coast not just for its headline months of July and August but also for its cold rains in April, its foliage-trimmed hills in October, its magical snow-covered islands in December. After casting off in our kayaks from the beach, with stale bread for the seagulls, we round a rocky ledge and see dozens of fork-tailed terns, as my father described, *drawing swift esprits across the sky.* We train our binoculars and marvel at a bald eagle clasping a bloody mackerel in its talons. Thirty young seals bask in the late-day sun as we approach their island. They slither into the water, circling our kayaks, their dark puppy eyes reminding us we're merely visitors. Through the island apertures of Penobscot Bay, we look, as my cousin Kate once told me, due south all the way to Venezuela.

Percy's shack is gone; in its place is a stand of spruce and birch. One day I fear I'll ride my bike past Lib's store, and it will have caved in, too. Otherwise, this place is just about as it was in my childhood.

— ⌇ —

Turning back toward the cottage, Michael and I paddle against the outgoing tide. We'll make a fire in the living room even though it's August.

I thought I could believe what I was told so empathically by my parents, but really, I've learned, I can believe only what I feel. What I feel is true. I cling to this place on a rocky coast when assessing the complicated balance sheet that was my father.

We beach our kayaks and carry them up to the lawn while a school of mackerel plays in the cove. A loon dips and surfaces. The seagulls are squawking out on Spectacle Island. Sun diamonds dance on the bay. Tomorrow, the lobster boats will head out to sea again before 5:00 a.m.

To My River of Gold

Editor, mentor, coach, and inspiration Brooke Warner: you knew exactly what I needed to do with a messy manuscript and expected the best book I could deliver; thank you for believing.

The visionary, collaborative, industry-changing team at She Writes Press: you collectively raise the bar; Brooke Warner, publisher, one of the best leaders I know; Shannon Green, editorial project manager, your management was equal to your editorial wisdom, care, and steadfast desire to get things right; Julie Metz, your perfect cover design itself tells the story; Annie Tucker, your skill as copyeditor and our shared love of South Brooksville were unexpected pleasures; Krissa Lagos and Samantha Strom, you stepped into the breach when really needed; Elizabeth Kauffman and Shannon Green, thank you for proofing my book; Tabitha Lahr for your inspired inside design; the talented and generous SWP author sisters, you were there for me whenever needed—*Write On, Sisters!*

Publicity team at BookSparks: Crystal Patriarche, CEO; Keely Platt, Publicity Director; Paige Herbert, Publicist. Thank you for taking me places I never thought I could go.

Earlier editors and coaches: Maggie Lichtenberg, Cinny Green, Jane Rosenman, and especially Amy Gash at Algonquin, you graciously pushed me through earlier MS renditions.

Earliest believers: Catherine Razi, Penny McConnel, Dikkon Eberhart, Sally Brady, Jane Ackerman, and Barbara Raives.

The Writer's Center in White River Junction, VT, and its cofounders, Joni Cole and Sarah Stewart Taylor: your pinot and prompts, craft workshops, and community of writers helped me hone my story; I'm honored to have sat with so many men and women who write in that orange-painted room on the second floor—love you each and all.

Monday Night Writers (MNW): Marj Matthews, Laura Nagy, Jen Duby, Jess Eakin; we rarely met on Monday nights, but wherever and whenever we did, you steadfastly believed, and each of you impacted this book profoundly.

Final beta readers and proofers: Molly Cherington, Ben Cherington, Ellen Schecter, Sarah Martel, Pennie O'Grady, Samantha Haskell, Jody Schubert, Jessica Eakin, Nora Kells Gordon, Kathy Belle, and Bob Bowers. Your candor and insight made me a better writer; and soul-sister Ellen, you have read every version through twenty years—that's a sister!

Oldest friends from school days and summers: Sarah Williams and Lisa Chase on Cape Rosier; Martha Hennessey, Pam Sears, Barb Rosborg, and Prue Arndt in Hanover; Catherine and Ioana Razi in D.C.; Lucy Tabor and Sarah Moffat in Lausanne; Janet Motlong in Seattle. Thank you all for the memories made and recently recalled.

Street team: Peggy O'Neil, Jill Marshall, Sara Kobylenski and Kate Rohdenburg. We will move the messages into live conversations in our communities.

Professionals: Mark Nunlist, MD, Christine Barney, MD, and Laurie Reed, MD. You were there when I needed you.

Daughters of famous and complex fathers whose memoirs I emulated: Susan Cheever, Sue Erikson Bloland, Margaret Salinger, Alysia Abbott, Elizabeth Garber, Melissa Coleman, Aeronwy Thomas, Janna Malamud Smith, Jessica Hendra, Honor Moore, Suzannah Lessard, Jamie Bernstein, Alexandra Styron, and Lisa Brennan-Jobs. You made me aspire to be among you.

Hundreds of clients who trusted me with their truths, and tangentially helped me own mine; colleagues Peter Axelson, John

Kerrick, and Lois Snow, who took me on great adventures for work around the world; Martha Torrance and Mary Hulburt, my teammates at GC CONSULTING, who took over so I could finish this book.

Sister-cousins: Eloise Eberhart Chevrier, Lil Eberhart Moffat, and in loving memory of Suzanne Galligan, Kate Butcher, and Susan Butcher; thanks to each of you for sharing insight on family.

Remarkable and wise children: Ben Cherington and Molly Cherington, two great gifts in our world who always expected my best—you are ever and always my inspirations; and to your bio father, Alex, for his kind review of the chapters he's in.

Michael, my one true love, for everything: each thing we build—out of wood or words—we do together. This book would not exist without you.

About the Author

Gretchen Eberhart Cherington grew up in a household that was populated by many of the most revered poets and writers of the twentieth century, from Robert Frost to James Dickey. She has spent her adult life advising top executives and their teams in changing their companies and themselves, and, as a leader in her regional community, has served on twenty corporate and not-for-profit boards. Born in Boston, she has lived in New Hampshire, Washington, D.C., Lausanne, Seattle, and Maine, and she received her undergraduate and MBA degrees from the University of New Hampshire. Her writing has been published in *Crack the Spine, Bloodroot Literary Magazine*, and *Yankee Magazine*, among other journals and newspapers, and her essay "Maine Roustabout" was nominated for a 2012 Pushcart Prize. Passionate about wild places, she has traveled widely through the world, skied the three-hundred mile length of Vermont, summitted the forty-eight 4,000-plus-foot peaks of New Hampshire, and, as a kid, cruised much of Penobscot Bay with her dad. She and her husband split their time between New Hampshire and Maine and wherever they find their children and grandchildren. This is Cherington's debut book. She is at work on her second memoir. Learn more at www.gretchencherington.com.

Author photo © Chris Milliman

SELECTED TITLES FROM SHE WRITES PRESS

She Writes Press is an independent publishing company founded to serve women writers everywhere. Visit us at www.shewritespress.com.

Implosion: Memoir of an Architect's Daughter by Elizabeth W. Garber. $16.95, 978-1-63152-351-9. When Elizabeth Garber, her architect father, and the rest of their family move into Woodie's modern masterpiece, a glass house, in 1966, they have no idea that over the next few years their family's life will be shattered—both by Woodie's madness and the turbulent 1970s.

I'm the One Who Got Away: A Memoir by Andrea Jarrell. $16.95, 978-1-63152-260-4. When Andrea Jarrell was a girl, her mother often told her of their escape from Jarrell's dangerous, cunning father as if it was a bedtime story. Here, Jarrell reveals the complicated legacy she inherited from her mother—and shares a life-affirming story of having the courage to become both safe enough and vulnerable enough to love and be loved.

Secrets in Big Sky Country: A Memoir by Mandy Smith. $16.95, 978-1-63152-814-9. A bold and unvarnished memoir about the shattering consequences of familial sexual abuse—and the strength it takes to overcome them.

Fourteen: A Daughter's Memoir of Adventure, Sailing, and Survival by Leslie Johansen Nack. $16.95, 978-1-63152-941-2. A coming-of-age adventure story about a young girl who comes into her own power, fights back against abuse, becomes an accomplished sailor, and falls in love with the ocean and the natural world.

Scattering Ashes: A Memoir of Letting Go by Joan Rough. $16.95, 978-1-63152-095-2. A daughter's chronicle of what happens when she invites her alcoholic and emotionally abusive mother to move in with her in hopes of helping her through the final stages of life—and her dream of mending their tattered relationship fails miserably.

The Coconut Latitudes: Secrets, Storms, and Survival in the Caribbean by Rita Gardner. $16.95, 978-1-63152-901-6. A haunting, lyrical memoir about a dysfunctional family's experiences in a reality far from the envisioned Eden—and the terrible cost of keeping secrets.